green stuff for kids

This book belongs to:

green stuff for Kids

An A to Z Guide to
What's Up with the Planet

WITHDRAWN

Tanya Ha

MELBOURNE
UNIVERSITY
PRESS

MELBOURNE UNIVERSITY PRESS
An imprint of Melbourne University Publishing Limited
187 Grattan Street, Carlton, Victoria 3053, Australia
mup-info@unimelb.edu.au
www.mup.com.au

First published 2009

Designed and typeset by Mauhaus
Illustrated by Elizabeth Botté
Printed by Griffin Press, South Australia

National Library of Australia Cataloguing-in-Publication entry

Ha, Tanya, 1972–
Green stuff for kids: an A to Z guide to what's up with the planet / Tanya Ha.

9780522855395 (pbk.)

Includes index.
For children.
Environmental protection—Citizen participation—Juvenile literature.

363.7

Every effort has been made to ensure that all the information in this book is correct and up-to-date at the time of publication. Neither the author nor the publisher may be held responsible for any accident, injury or damage that results from using the ideas, tips, information or advice offered in this book. Health-related advice is not intended to replace the service of a medical professional.

All products come at a cost to the environment, so a portion of the proceeds from the sale of this book will be donated to Trees for Life to plant the equivalent number of trees that were required to produce the paper for this book. The seedlings are planted in native, biodiverse revegetation projects. For further information visit www.treesforlife.org.au.

FSC
Mixed Sources
Product group from well-managed
forests and other controlled sources
Cert no. SGS-COC-005088
www.fsc.org
© 1996 Forest Stewardship Council

For Jasmin, my crazy, lovable girl, who is my inspiration for caring about the future and whose personality, thoughts and ideas permeate the pages of this book.

Foreword by the Planet Patrollers

Making sense of the environment is a massive task; it's huge, it's tricky and involves mad words such as 'biodiversity', 'sustainability' and 'chlorofluorocarbonation'. So it's a good job that Tanya decided to write this book before anyone else's brain exploded or eyes glazed over from having to concentrate so hard on all the technical stuff out there. She's done all the hard work for us, getting rid of the gobbledegook, political rambling and green gunk to provide an easy-to-understand book that will soon have your eyes uncrossed and brain full of incredible knowledge about our wonderful planet.

Reading this book helps us understand that it all starts with us as individuals. It's really important that car manufacturers cut emissions and that the government puts laws in place to make sure they do, but it's taking personal responsibility for our own carbon footprint that makes us a true citizen and friend of the world.

We learnt so much from this book and especially enjoyed the whacky humour and bizarre examples from the insane world of environmental science. You don't have to be a science geek to enjoy it though, as it's so easy to read: you can just dip in and enjoy. The only hard bit is putting it down again!

We're about the same age as you and we know that it will soon be our generation's turn to be making decisions that affect our planet. We want to make sure we make the right decisions, and that means being educated, informed and prepared.

Tanya's writing is very positive, and she makes it clear that we can ensure the survival of our planet if we each act now. She tells us how and gives us the facts about climate change so we can protect ourselves against those who say global warming is a pile of rubbish. Don't listen to them; read this book and make your own decisions.

ALASTAIR, FREYA AND IMOGEN WADLOW
Founders of Planet Patrol
www.planetpatrol.info

Foreword by Rove McManus

You probably know that I've been lucky enough to meet people like Zac Efron and Kelly Clarkson. But you might not know that I've also hung out with lemurs, elephants and gorillas (and, no, I'm not talking about Hughesy or Peter Hellier).

A while ago I became Vice President of Fauna & Flora International, a conservation group that's been around for longer than your grandparents, working to conserve threatened species and ecosystems. I spent a few months travelling the world to see FFI conservation projects with my own eyes. I've also got my hands dirty locally—planting trees on Schools Tree Day here in Australia.

I've seen some of our planet's problems *and* I've seen some of the solutions. So I can tell you from my own firsthand experience that trying to save the planet is not all about being an earnest goody-goody; it's actually great fun.

In writing *Green Stuff for Kids*, Tanya's made it interesting and sometimes hilarious to learn about our planet and how it works. I just want to know if she measured the amount of elephant dung produced in Kruger National Park herself!

Tanya wants to make everyone smarter than a 5th grader when it comes to the environment and I want future generations to have a better future. So bury yourself in green stuff, read and act on *Green Stuff for Kids*, make your parents read it too and, while you're at it, say 'hi' to your Mum for me.

ROVE McMANUS
Vice President Fauna & Flora International
www.fauna-flora.org.au

Contents

Throughout the text in this book you'll sometimes see the occasional word printed in green or white. This means that the subject has its own section elsewhere in the book.

Earth: a great place to live

In Greek mythology, Antaeus is the son of Poseidon, the god of the sea, but he gets his considerable strength from his mother the earth, or 'Gaia'. He's also known as the giant of Libya and liked to pick fights with passing travellers. Antaeus was strong as long as he remained in contact with the earth. His unfortunate opponents found that knocking him to the ground would only allow Gaia to renew his strength. The hero Heracles (or Hercules) was only able to defeat Antaeus by lifting him off the ground and crushing him in a bear hug. Being disconnected from Mother Earth made Antaeus weak and was, ultimately, his downfall.

We can learn some helpful lessons from the story of Antaeus. For one thing, mothers can be quite useful, so don't take them for granted! And it's probably not a good idea to fight with strangers, particularly if they're muscly Greek heroes. But when you really think about it, we're a bit like Antaeus—we draw strength from the earth.

The earth provides us with the food that nourishes our bodies, the beaches where we have fun, the landscapes that inspire us, the materials from which we can build things, and clean water to drink. Time spent in the natural environment can also make us feel good. When we're connected to the earth, we're healthy in both mind and body.

But we're starting to become disconnected from the earth. We, the human race, are not looking after the earth as well as we should. Now that the majority of people in developed nations don't have to plough the earth themselves to grow food, we're spending less time outdoors. We're shutting ourselves in our houses, schools, office buildings and shopping malls. Farming has developed into agriculture, and agriculture has developed into 'agribusiness', where farms are judged by how much money they make rather than how much food or fibre they grow. We're in danger of harming the earth through ignorance or greed. But we can change all that, and change it for the better.

If you step outside your house, building or shopping centre

and escape the concrete jungle, you'll find that our planet is really interesting. The forces of nature make kite surfing possible. Seahorses are one of the few species in which it's the blokes who become 'pregnant' and have the babies. There are animals that eat plants, and plants that eat animals. Frog numbers can warn you about pollution levels. You can grow food in your own backyard, and you can keep hundreds of pet worms to give you some help. And dried whale spew can be made into perfume or jewellery (though it's not always legal)!

This book is all about reconnecting with our bizarre and beautiful planet, discovering its weird and wonderful creatures, finding out what makes it tick, how its systems work, what problems it is facing and how we can do our best to fix them. As well as eco-information, there are **eco-activity** projects for you to try, **eco-action** tips that show you how you can make a difference and **eco-bytes** that show the thoughts and ideas of other green kids.

We're part of this world, not separate from it. Love the planet and look after it—and it will love you back.

Air

In the lead up to the 2008 Beijing Olympics, some countries delayed sending their athletes to the Games until the last minute, wanting to limit the effects of Beijing's air pollution on athletes' health. Clean air is a performance-enhancing substance (and a legal one at that), and one that we sometimes take for granted in Australia. We become more aware of the importance of air quality when our car is sitting behind a smoky vehicle, on smoggy days or in the company of someone wearing too much perfume.

The air we breathe is part of the earth's atmosphere. We live in the innermost layer, called the 'troposphere'—a life-supporting blend of 78 per cent nitrogen, 21 per cent oxygen and a 1 per cent mixture of carbon dioxide, argon, methane and numerous other trace gases.

Air provides the gases that plants and animals exchange to produce and harness energy in their tissues. It is needed to sustain life on land. Gases in the air are also dissolved into water, where they are similarly used by aquatic life. Air also carries water vapour and is involved in the water cycle. The atmosphere also protects life on our planet, like sunscreen and a blanket around the earth. Without it, our planet would be subject to extremes of temperature, not to mention the harmful effects of the sun's ultraviolet radiation.

The major environmental problems with air all relate to how well air can do its job of protecting the planet, and of supporting and nurturing life.

The most threatening air-related problems are those of global warming and climate change, brought about by an increase in the amount of greenhouse gases in the atmosphere since industrialisation. Another side effect of industrialisation is an increase in

The lower atmosphere

50 km_

40 km_

30 km_

Highest ozone concentrations

20 km_

✈

10 km_

Stratosphere

Troposphere

air pollution. Some pollutants, particularly chlorofluorocarbons (CFCs), are damaging the ozone layer, which protects us from the sun's more harmful skin cancer–causing rays. In the layers of the atmosphere where weather occurs, air pollution combines with water to make poisonous acid rain. Closer to the surface, indoor and outdoor air pollution is having a bad effect on our health and the health of other animals and plants.

The scary thing about air pollution is that air knows no boundaries and does not recognise international borders. Just as you can smell the sausages from your neighbour's barbecue in your own backyard, air pollution and greenhouse gases move with the air currents. Global warming is exactly that: global! There are a small number of nations that are serious greenhouse polluters, but the entire planet will have to suffer the consequences of global warming.

Why air is important: gas exchange between plants and animals

Photosynthesis is the basis of all energy in the living world. Plants, including the tiny phytoplankton in the ocean, take carbon dioxide from the air and combine it with water using energy from the sun. Through the magic of photosynthesis, this builds bigger molecules called carbohydrates (such as glucose) and oxygen. The chemical bonds in carbohydrates or sugars store energy from the sun in plant tissues. Animals do not have this photosynthetic ability. In other words, even if we paint ourselves green or drink liquid chlorophyll bought from a health-food store, we can't harness the sun's energy directly for use in our bodies. Animals, including humans, get this energy second-hand when they eat plants or other animals.

Plants need the carbon dioxide that we exhale for photosynthesis, and we need the plants to produce oxygen and make food for us and other animals. Air is one of the elements that allow plants and animals to coexist in such a mutually beneficial relationship. In short, air is a vital ingredient in the energy systems of all living things.

Air pollution

Air is simply a mixture of gases and fine airborne particles. Ideally it contains the right amounts of certain gases to keep life on earth happy. Sometimes dangerous amounts of human-made chemicals, fine particles or natural (but potentially harmful) materials are released into the atmosphere, polluting the air. This air pollution can damage sensitive ecosystems, cause acid rain, harm living things, contribute to environmental problems and cause illness and even death in humans.

Types of air pollutants

Air pollution can come in many different forms and from a range of sources:
- **sulphur oxides** (SO_x), **nitrogen oxides** (NO_x) and **carbon monoxide** from burning fuels
- **greenhouse gases**, including carbon dioxide
- **hydrocarbons**, such as methane
- **ozone**, which is great in the upper atmosphere but a breathing irritant at ground level
- **chlorofluorocarbons** (CFCs), which destroy ozone in the ozone layer and also contribute to the greenhouse effect
- **lead**
- **chemical fumes** from factories or incinerating rubbish
- **particulates** (particles of soot, dirt, unburnt fossil fuels and dust).

Sources of air pollution

Imagine two loads of grain on their way to market, one on a horsedrawn cart in Africa and the other on a semitrailer in the USA. It's easy to guess which carries more grain and also which produces more air pollution. The world's developed and highly industrialised countries use much of the world's energy and produce most of the air pollution.

There are many sources of air pollution:
- **Cars, trucks, motorbikes, aeroplanes and other vehicles** burn hydrocarbon fuels, such as petrol or liquefied petroleum gas (LPG), in their engines. The combustion of these fuels produces varying amounts of pollutants such as nitrogen oxides, carbon dioxide, carbon monoxide, sulphur dioxide and smoke.
- **Fossil fuel–fired power stations** similarly combust fuels to produce electricity, also producing air-polluting emissions.
- **Additives to fuels**, such as lead added to petrol to prevent engine knock, also add to the nasty chemical cocktail of air pollution.

Some of these pollutants are greenhouse gases, making transport and energy-production major contributors to climate change. In busy cities, with high car use and factory-filled industrial areas, smog is also a major health problem.

- The **disposal and breakdown of rubbish** can also add to air pollution, particularly the incineration (burning) of waste.
- **Burning wood** in an open fireplace in the lounge room also adds to smog in winter.
- There are also **natural sources of air pollution**, such as bushfires, volcanic activity and dust storms.

Eco-lingo

> **smog**—*First used a little over a hundred years ago by a man called Dr Henry Antoine Des Voeux, this term is an abbreviation of 'smoky fog', seen in great cities but not in the country.*

Controlling air pollution

While it's easy to avoid drinking from bottles with 'poison' written on the label, it's very difficult to avoid breathing toxic fumes, particularly when they're colourless and odourless. For this reason, air quality is rated as a top environmental priority by governments, companies, environment groups and individual people.

The first step in controlling air pollution is to avoid creating it in the first place. A range of measures—such as making cars less gas-guzzling, or improving the quality of fuels so that they have less pollution-causing additives or impurities—can do this. The next step is to prevent the release of pollution into the environment. The physical nature of gases makes them hard to collect or contain once they've escaped into the atmosphere. Gas molecules repel each other, so the moment they're produced or leaked from a container, they will do their best to spread out as far as possible and to mix with the surrounding air.

Laws have been written and technology developed to limit or control air pollutants that threaten the environment or human health. For example, lead was banned as a petrol additive in Australia from 1 January 2002. Before that, devices called catalytic converters were developed to reduce the toxic emissions from internal-combustion engines. Scientists and governments can do their bit, but there's also a role for ordinary people to play. We can use our cars less, produce less waste and be more careful with what we burn.

Eco-action: clean up the wood fire

Does your family use wood heating?
The Australian government has information on cleaner wood heating at
<www.environment.gov.au/atmosphere/airquality/>.

Air: acid rain

Imagine if you drank a mouthful of white vinegar thinking it was water. Nasty! The sour taste is partly due to the small amount of acetic acid in vinegar, and it's no substitute for clean, fresh drinking water. Imagine, then, what plants and animals think of acid rain.

Sulphur and nitrogen oxides, two kinds of air pollutant, cause acid rain. Although there are some natural sources of these gases, such as volcanoes, most come from industrial smokestacks and the exhaust pipes of motor vehicles. Taller factory chimneys have helped to ease air pollution at the local ground level, but they have also enabled air pollution to spread over larger, previously unaffected areas, carried by the wind. As a result, the harmful effects of pollution are no longer limited to urban or industrial areas; they are now also a problem for farmlands and areas of natural vegetation.

In the presence of sunlight and catalysts (such as ozone), sulphur and nitrogen oxides react with water vapour to form sulphuric and nitric acids. These acids can travel great distances, dissolved in cloud droplets. They fall to the ground as acid rain, snow and fog.

How acid rain is produced

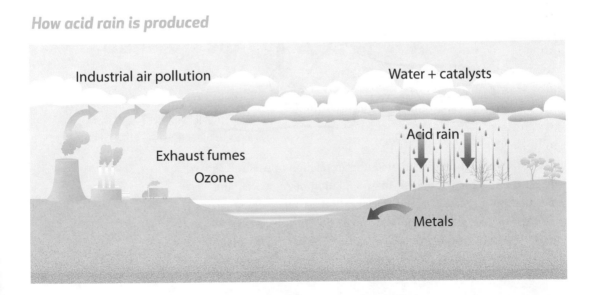

Acid rain poisons both aquatic and terrestrial (land-based) life, making plants and animals susceptible to disease, temperature extremes, pests and other stresses, which in turn can kill them. On land, acid rain causes the release of aluminium and heavy metals in soil. These metals damage plant roots and soil microbes, and are washed into waterways, where they also can kill fish and other marine life. The acidic rain also damages the leaves of plants, decimating forests, damaging crops and reducing soil fertility. In water ecosystems, acid rain is making lakes acidic and killing aquatic life, particularly in North America. Some countries are adding lime (the mineral, not the fruit), which is alkaline, to vulnerable lakes to neutralise the acidic water.

The effects of acid rain aren't confined to the natural world. Acid rain also corrodes bronze and other metals, dissolves paintwork and eats into stone buildings and statues. Several of the world's most famous monuments are under threat from acid-rain erosion, including the Sphinx in Egypt, the Taj Mahal in India, the Parthenon in Greece, and the Gettysburg monuments and the Statue of Liberty in the USA.

We don't hear much about acid rain in relation to Australia's environment. This is because the population of Australia, and consequently the scale of industrialisation, is relatively small when compared with Europe and North America. However, as Australia's population grows, we have to be careful to make sure that energy and product demands are met with minimal contribution to air pollution and the risk of acid rain.

Eco-activity: the effects of acid rain on plants

In this experiment, you'll see over several days and weeks the effects of acid rain on plants.

You will need

> *2 indoor pot plants of the same species and roughly the same size*

> *A measuring cup*

> *Tap water*

> *Lemons*

How to

Place two similar pot plants side by side where they will get the recommended amount of light without getting in the way. One will get normal watering and be the 'control' for this experiment, providing something for the other plant to be compared with. Label it as the 'control' and label the other as the 'experiment'. Water them periodically as instructed, always giving the same amount of water to each plant, but adding a squeeze of lemon juice from one half of a lemon to the water for the 'experiment' plant. Over time, this plant will start to look less healthy.

Air travel

Holidays are fantastic! A century ago, it took several weeks to travel from the United Kingdom to Australia by ship; nowadays it's several hours by plane. We now have far greater opportunity to see the world. This can help us to explore and learn about different natural landscapes, helping us to appreciate our beautiful planet. But there's such a thing as loving the planet to death!

We already know that cars are bad for the environment. Planes are a problem too. About 16 000 commercial aircraft carry people and goods around the planet. Together they pump out 600 million tonnes of carbon dioxide every year, consuming some 190 billion litres of jet fuel. Scientists estimate that aviation causes 3.5 per cent of human-made global warming. With flying cheaper and easier than ever before, this could rise to 15 per cent by 2050.

So can you take the trip without the guilt trip? One thing that can be done to reduce the environmental impact of flying is carbon offsetting. Overall, this neutralises the greenhouse impact of the travel. But don't forget there are also the concerns of local noise and air pollution. Try sleeping with a jet plane roaring over your house. Just as smog from car exhaust can cause illness in congested cities, the polluted air around airports and under busy flight paths can also be unhealthy, with higher levels of cancer-causing benzene, formaldehyde and other pollutants. The good news is that work is being done on making aviation fuels cleaner, and aeroplanes lighter and more fuel efficient, but flying will remain a more gas-guzzling way to travel than by road or rail. Carbon offsetting can deal with the climate impact of flying, but it can't purify the air around airports. For short trips, a coach or train may be a better way to go.

Airfreight

Not only are people travelling by plane, but products are too. Airfreight—the transportation of goods by plane instead of by rail, road or cargo ship—is increasing as we rush to get products and packages around the world in shorter periods of time. One small thing your family can do is to send Christmas and birthday presents to loved ones interstate and overseas in enough time to rely on 'snail mail', instead of leaving it to the last minute and sending parcels by airmail.

Animal welfare

Humans have many different relationships with animals. There are four-legged animals that get saddled up and ridden. Other animals are raised on farms to provide food for us to eat or fibre for making our clothes. Some animals we love; some we hate. There are some majestic animals—like whales—that we're content to admire from afar, while other small, creepy-crawly animals get sprayed with poison by people who don't want to share their homes with them. There are cute, furry creatures we feed and cuddle and keep as pets. Some assist with scientific experiments, though you couldn't call them 'volunteers'.

When it comes to the animal kingdom, humans are the top dogs. We are the planet's dominant species and have power to influence the wellbeing of other animals. Many people believe that it's the moral responsibility of those who have power and influence to protect and look after the welfare of those who don't. The difficulty with animals is that they don't have a voice to tell you in human language what they think, feel or want.

Animal welfare is sometimes defined as the idea that it is okay for humans to use non-human animals for food, in animal research, as clothing and in entertainment, so long as unnecessary suffering is avoided. But some people have stronger views, promoting **animal rights**—the idea that animals should not be used or considered as the property of humans. Here is an overview of some of the main animal welfare and rights issues.

Animals for food, fibre and materials

Some animals are hunted or fished from wild populations or raised on farms to provide meat. Others have been domesticated and kept to provide eggs or milk and milk-related products (such as cheese). The skins of animals killed for food can be made into leather products, such as shoes, clothing and furniture. However, some animals are killed mainly for their skins or pelts, which is why the fur industry has been criticised by animal lovers.

Farmed animals can be raised on free-range farms, where they are given room to move, or on factory farms, where they live out their lives in cramped cages. Battery hens, for example, which lay most of the eggs sold in supermarkets, often live in appalling conditions. Modern 'factory farms' can produce a lot of animal food products and make a lot of money, using a relatively small space and with lower running costs. They look nothing like Farmer Hoggett's farm in the movie *Babe*!

The five freedoms of animal welfare

The RSPCA, Australia's main animal welfare body, works with the idea and aim that animals should have five basic freedoms:

1   freedom from hunger and thirst

2   freedom from discomfort due to their environment

3   freedom from pain, injury or disease

4   freedom to express normal behaviour for their species

5   freedom from fear and distress.

Learn more

The web resource 'Animals in science', at <http://anzccart.rsnz.org/>, has been developed to provide information for young people on the pros and cons of using animals in science.

Animals in science

In some branches of science, animals are used for research, teaching and testing. This can help us to learn more about the animals themselves, to advance science and medicine, and to test the effects and safety of products and substances. Animal testing, in particular, has been a hot topic, sparking a lot of angry debate, especially in relation to the testing of cosmetics on animals. Activists question whether there are other testing alternatives that don't harm animals, and whether animals should be made to suffer for the sake of developing cosmetics, which are a luxury product, not a necessity of life.

Animals as entertainment

Animals can also be a source of entertainment. While many people enjoy watching or participating in rodeos, horseracing and greyhound racing, the animals involved can suffer. There are rules governing the operation of these sports that aim to reduce animal suffering (but they generally can't eliminate it). There are also sports that involve violence against animals, such as hunting and cockfighting. These sports are often called 'blood sports' and usually operate under tight government controls. Cockfighting is legal in some countries, including India and the Philippines, but banned in many others, such as Australia, the United Kingdom, the USA and France. Dancing bears and other circus animals can also have pain inflicted on them to make them 'perform'.

There's also a danger that we might love certain animals to death! Poorly managed animal-themed holiday tours can threaten the very creatures they rely on for their business. Though dolphins are social animals and appear to enjoy contact with people, for example, there is growing concern that pushy tour operators may be harassing wild dolphin pods and that their boat propellers may accidentally injure dolphins.

Learn more

See the entry on endangered and extinct species (page 46) for more on how human behaviour is threatening the survival of some species..

Other human threats to animals

Ultimately, damage to the natural environment harms the home that humans share with other animals. Human activity is changing habitat areas and threatening the welfare of the animals that live in these habitats.

Eco-action: act for animals

- Don't buy products or holiday souvenirs made from protected species, such as ivory products, tortoiseshell accessories, crocodile-skin boots and bags, animal fur, or perfumes made from natural musk.

- Make sure your holiday and weekend activities respect habitat and don't harm or frighten wildlife.

- Choose cruelty-free products and toiletries, from companies that don't use animal testing.

- Use forest-friendly wood and paper products.

- Don't take animals from the wild to keep as pets. Buy pets from reputable pet stores and breeders. Those offered for sale in newspaper advertisements or on the Internet may have been captured illegally from the wild.

Animals by numbers

Criminals steal an estimated **38 MILLION** animals from Brazil's forests each year. They earn around US$1 billion per year from their exploits.

A cow can drink up to **90** litres of water a day, while only producing **12** litres of milk!

The last Tasmanian tiger in captivity died in **1936**.

The giant Gippsland earthworm is about **2** centimetres thick and grows to **2–3** metres long.

The Siberian tiger is critically endangered. There are only **400–500** individuals left in the wild.

The rare red-tailed black cockatoo had a starring role as the mascot for the 2006 Commonwealth Games in Melbourne. There are about **1000** individuals left in the wild. Overseas collectors will pay up to **A$50 000** on the black market for a breeding pair.

With seahorses, it's the males that have the babies—up to **2000** at a time.

Kruger National Park in South Africa has about **12 500** elephants. Together they produce about **1875** tonnes of dung per day.

The heaviest bird is also the fastest on land. North African ostriches can run up to **72** kilometres per hour and weigh around **156** kilograms.

Vinegar flies go from egg to adulthood in one week, live for **20–30** days and during their lives lay **700–800** eggs.

The blue whale is the largest animal, weighing around **181** tonnes and growing to about **33** metres in length.

Sharks are lucky! They continually grow replacement teeth. Some species of sharks shed up to **30 000** teeth in a lifetime.

Illegal trade in animals

There are laws that ban the trade in endangered species or that set certain standards and conditions in which animals can legally be harvested from the wild or raised on farms for trade. These laws are designed with animal welfare in mind. However, there are criminals who willingly break these laws to make more money.

Sometimes the 'black market' is actually the black-and-white-striped zebra-skin market, or the tortoiseshell market, or the live-lizard market. Unfortunately, some people with a poor sense of what is right and wrong choose to make money out of endangered animals, threatening the survival of some species. A number of environment groups, education programs and government initiatives are working to stop illegal (black market) animal trade, including the CITES (Convention on International Trade in Endangered Species of Wild Fauna and Flora) international agreement, which restricts the trade in threatened plant and animal species.

Unfortunately, bans and regulations tend to increase the black market price of many rare products, offering a fast buck for those willing to break the law. Sometimes, laws that ban certain items lead to the development of illegal trade in these things.

The shameful *shahtoosh*

A few of New York's society ladies found themselves in the embarrassing situation of being questioned by police over *shahtoosh* shawls made from the hair of the endangered Tibetan antelope. The *shahtoosh* (its name meaning 'pleasure of kings') is considered to be very beautiful, but it's also very illegal to sell or own one. The hair of the Tibetan antelope is one of the softest, finest wools in the world, but around three of these animals die for every shawl produced. *Shahtoosh* shawls sell for up to US$15 000 each. The women who buy them see them as a status symbol, while the people who traffic in them and hunt the animals see them as good cash.

We can help to stop the trade in endangered species simply by reducing the demand for them. That means not buying the products made from them. We can also find alternative supplies to make similar products to those that have traditionally used threatened species. Chemists are finding ways to produce synthetic (produced in the lab, not in the wild) versions of valuable natural substances. For example, synthetic musk scent is being used to make perfume instead of natural musk from the male musk deer, though the vulnerable Siberian musk deer is still hunted.

There's another market for endangered animals, but this one wants them live. Some people like to make a statement with exotic, rare or unusual pets. Pop star Michael Jackson kept a range of weird and wonderful pets, including llamas and a chimpanzee called 'Bubbles'. Exotic animals can be bred to sell as pets, but some can come from illegal sources. High-value, rare animals or their eggs are being taken from the wild and smuggled over long distances from their natural habitats, often in cramped containers. Many die along the way. For example, it's estimated that for every live blue and yellow macaw smuggled from South America and sold, four more have died before reaching their intended destination.

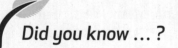

Did you know ... ?   Back in 1235, King Henry III of England received three leopards from Frederick II, Holy Roman Emperor, as a wedding present!

Popular but endangered pets include a wide range of exotic and colourful birds, small primates, butterflies, snakes, lizards and spiders. Exotic pets are fine as long as they come from approved sources and their owners know enough about the species to look after them properly. Instead of cutting their forests down, villagers in parts of Papua New Guinea, for example, are using their forests to breed birdwing butterflies for export.

The red-crowned Amazon (*Amazona viridigenalis*) is an endangered parrot native to the lush lowlands of north-eastern Mexico. There are also some feral populations in California and Florida, where they are an introduced species. Their affectionate, social personalities and their potential to be taught to 'talk' make them popular pets. They are bred in captivity for the legal pet market; however, the high price they fetch makes them a hot item in the illegal trade of animals caught in the wild. In the early 1990s, the wild population was estimated at 3000–6500 and is rapidly decreasing due to habitat loss and capture for the illegal pet trade. The good news is that the red-crowned Amazon is protected under the CITES international agreement. In recent years, there has also been a crackdown on illegal bird trade in an effort to control the spread of bird flu.

Online profile: Amanda Rose, the red-crowned Amazon

About me: I'm a bright, colourful chick from Mexico. I'm affectionate, playful and talkative, and I don't mind a bit of attention, though people say I'm a bit loud. I'm mostly green, but I'm also a redhead, and I look like I've got blue eye shadow on—which is cool because eighties style is back in fashion! Birds like me are so rare and beautiful that we're frequently kidnapped and sold for US$1500–2000 on the black market.

Interests: I'm a bit of an actress—I like mimicking sounds. I also like to have raucous parties with my friends.

Favourite foods: Seeds, fruits, berries, flowers and nectar

Favourite song: 'Turn Me Loose' by Young Divas

Favourite TV show: *The Bold and the Beautiful*

Favourite movie: any chick flick will do!

Biodegradability

Biodegradation is the breakdown of organic (living or once living) materials or the products made from them. It happens through the action of worms, insects and micro-organisms. Substances are said to be biodegradable if they decompose naturally into simpler materials, instead of hanging around in the environment. It's nature's recycling system of breaking down old materials into the simple substances and nutrients that are the building blocks for new living materials.

When people talk about biodegradability, they usually mean one of two sorts: the breakdown of harmful chemicals or the breakdown of solid materials, such as waste.

Biodegradability is important in products made from potentially harmful chemicals, such as cleaning products, toiletries, paints, solvents, poisons and pesticides. If these chemicals don't easily break down into harmless substances, they can build up in the environment and potentially be bad for your health, poison other living things or contribute to pollution.

The other sort of biodegradability is the breakdown of unwanted solid materials. This may be rubbish sent to landfill tips, or litter polluting urban areas or the natural environment. Materials made from plants or from animal ingredients, such as paper, leftover food or a wool jumper, are biodegradable. In contrast, the microbes that normally munch through most matter don't know what to do with plastics. As a result, plastics can sit in landfill for years and even centuries and not break down. This can be a huge problem in countries such as Japan, Italy and the United Kingdom, where there is a shortage of landfill space.

The level of heat, light, water and oxygen and other environmental conditions can speed up or slow down biodegradation and change the way the chemical process happens. For example, when organic materials break down after being buried in landfill, oxygen and sunlight are blocked out and more methane gas is produced. This is a problem because methane is a greenhouse gas, and it also doesn't smell too good! It's far better for plant materials to get recycled through organic waste collections (including garden waste or food waste), so long as your council provides them.

How degrading!

Conditions make a difference when it comes to biodegradation. Cigarette butts take:

- 1–2 months to break down in the presence of air
- 3–6 months to break down without air
- 12 months to break down in fresh water
- 36 months or more to break down in sea water.

Biodiversity

If it weren't for the magic and diversity of life, then air, water and land would be just a mixture of different chemicals. We share the world with a weird and wonderful collection of different life forms, from the tiniest microscopic amoeba to the gigantic blue whales of the sea.

Biologists have identified around one and a half million different species so far, and every year more are discovered. Who knows how many more there are yet to be discovered? Estimates of earth's total number of species range from ten million to a hundred million.

Eco-lingo

biodiversity   *This term is an abbreviation of 'biological diversity'. It refers to the number of different species in a particular habitat or area, and reflects the rich variety of life forms that live on our planet.*

No species can exist alone. Instead, groups of plant and animal species live together in harmonious ecosystems, providing each other with food, water, air and dissolved gases. Different species play different roles. In the sea, for example, predators such as sharks keep down the numbers of the fish on which they prey, green aquatic plants harness the energy of the sun, and crustaceans such as prawns are the vacuum cleaners of the sea, removing toxins to keep the marine environment healthy. Protecting biodiversity helps to keep an ecosystem healthy. After all, variety is the spice of life.

There are three aspects to biodiversity. First, there's the variety that occurs within a single species. We are a good example of this. Humans are a single species, but we come in different sizes, shapes, hair and skin colours, personalities and other features, as determined by our genes. Second, there's the variety of different species that exist in different environments. Finally, there's the variety of different ecosystems, such as grasslands, estuaries and alpine forests. These all combine to make up the biodiversity of our unique planet. Life on Planet Earth is made possible by a delicate balance between thousands of different species of living things. They coexist in ecosystems that ideally make up one big, happy, healthy biosphere.

Eco-action: enjoy biodiversity!

Go on bushwalks, visit a forest, investigate some pond slime with a microscope, or visit the zoo or aquarium and learn about animals.

Eco-bytes: what do you like about the environment?

Students from Altona North Primary School share their thoughts on what they like about nature and what the environment does for them.

'Without the environment we wouldn't survive. We should make a difference.' Zainab, 12

'The environment gives us shelter, food and homes.' Souraya, 12

'Trees provide oxygen to everybody.' Fred, 12

'The sun and rain do heaps for me. The sun warms us and rain gives us water to drink.' Brett, 12

'I like the sea because I can go jet-skiing with my uncles.' Youssef, 12

'The environment gives me a nice place to play at the park.' Christopher, 12

'The trees and plants provide shade for the world. If we take down too many for other uses, we'll be burnt to a crisp on hot days!' Brodie, 12

'The environment does a lot of things, but the most relevant to me is the rain. When it rains the evaporated water falls on the trees and grass, which allows me to get a cricket bat made from trees. It also allows the grass to grow so I can play cricket.' Wasim, 12

'The trees give you beautiful air to breathe—but it's too bad that it doesn't take people's bad breath away!' Chelsea, 12

'The environment is good for you. It helps you to relax and calm down.' Kaan, 11

'The wildlife that I see in the bush and the seas is so beautiful.' Monnie, 11

'The environment provides water for us to drink, to bathe in and to play in.' Kylie, 11

'Trees hold some of my favourite animals, like orang-utans and pandas.' Elizabeth, 11

'The environment is our world's food source. The environment gives us fruit and vegies to stay healthy. The environment is part of us because without the environment there is no fresh air and with no fresh air we cannot live. I am happy for what the environment gives us and we repay the environment with carbon dioxide and some dung!' Monnie, 11

'Trees give us shade on hot summer days. I like sitting outside under a tree on hot days and if we keep chopping our trees down we won't have a nice place to sit on hot days. Most of us will go inside and turn the aircon on and that will contribute to greenhouse gas.' Nikita, 12

'For me, the environment gives us shelter, food, peaceful places and great landscapes and clear water and fresh air and the sound of nature and animals.' Keegan, 10

'For me, the environment provides a lot of fun things— such as beaches, trees, drinking water and many more things. Without nature the world would be nothing. Everything would be dry, not green like you see. So let's act and make our environment as good as it looks.' Angie, 12

Carbon

It seems that everywhere you go, someone is talking about carbon. People are discussing carbon taxes, putting a price on carbon, carbon footprints and carbon dioxide. Some are even going on a carbon diet. To understand what all the fuss is about, we need to go back to basics.

The smallest simplest particles of matter are atoms. Atoms are a bit like people. Some like to hang around with a small group of friends; others like to pair up and spend most of their time with their partner, while others prefer to be alone. Similarly, some atoms bond easily, while others are 'inert' or non-reactive.

Carbon chemistry

Carbon is a chemical element that can exist on its own or combine with other elements to make a wide range of substances. As an element, it occurs naturally in three forms: graphite, coal and diamond. What makes carbon unique is that it can be the party animal of atoms. When carbon atoms bond with other atoms, the fun starts. Carbon atoms love to mix and hook up with other atoms. They can form small, simple molecules, like methane. One molecule of methane has one carbon atom and four hydrogen atoms. But unlike other elements, carbon also has the unique ability to form long chain-like molecules (like a long line of people holding hands or even a conga line). These range from simple to complex molecules, including simple sugars, the

hydrocarbons in petrol, amino acids, DNA and other complex molecules in living things. Carbon, put simply, is the stuff of life!

The carbon cycle

Carbon moves through the environment in its many forms. In fact, you could say that nature is constantly recycling carbon. At any given moment, some of the earth's carbon is present in the atmosphere in the form of carbon dioxide, methane and other gases. Some carbon is present in molecules that make up plant and animal tissues. Some carbon is in the soil as humus, the biological component

Eco-lingo

> **Carbon sequestration**—*This term refers to methods of taking up and storing (for the long term) carbon dioxide from the atmosphere and other forms of carbon. It is often talked about in relation to ways of reducing total greenhouse emissions and combating global warming.*

> **Carbon capture and storage**—*This is the method and technology (still in development) of capturing and storing carbon emissions from large single point sources, such as fossil-fuel power stations. It is envisaged that the captured carbon emissions could be stored deep in the earth's crust in suitable geological formations or deep in the ocean (although this presents the risk of making these parts of the ocean too acidic).*

of soil made from decomposing dead materials. And still more carbon is stored in the earth as fossil fuels.

The carbon cycle needs to maintain a delicate balance between the amounts of carbon in the atmosphere, in living tissues, in the earth and in the ocean. Over the last century, humans have burnt fossil fuels to produce energy, releasing huge amounts of carbon into the atmosphere. Scientists believe that the rising global temperatures we're experiencing are due to higher amounts of greenhouse gases, particularly carbon dioxide, in the atmosphere. They act like a blanket around the earth, keeping the heat in. In short, the carbon cycle is out of balance.

Carbon in trees

When a tree is growing, it takes carbon out of the atmosphere and uses it to build plant tissues. But when the tree dies, it decomposes, releasing carbon back into the atmosphere. So how can this process help fight climate change?

Ideally, the trees we're planting will become mature, 'steady-state forests'. In a steady-state forest, for every tree that dies a new one grows in its place. Commercial timber plantations can operate in this way. Climate change is reduced by increasing the total amount of forest, trees or vegetation, rather than decreasing it through land-clearing.

The carbon cycle

Carbon dioxide, methane and other carbon gases in the atmosphere.

Some carbon is stored in plant tissues. In a process called photosynthesis, plants use the sun's energy, carbon dioxide, water and soil nutrients to make sugars and carbohydrates.

Carbon dioxide is 'exhaled' into the atmosphere during respiration.

Animals eat plants. The carbohydrates provide energy and the building blocks for animal tissues.

Carbon is released into the atmosphere when fossil fuels and plants are burned.

Carbon dioxide and methane are released as dead plant and animal matter and waste decays.

The ocean also cycles and stores carbon through photosynthesis in aquatic plants and by dissolving some carbon dioxide.

Concentrated carbon is stored in the earth's crust as fossil fuels (coal and oil).

Climate and weather

You probably thought about the weather this morning when you were deciding what to wear. Your understanding of your local climate will have given you a general idea—that shorts are not a good idea in July because it's very cold or that you'll toast in an overcoat in summer. But a weather report can give you a more specific prediction, such as the chance of rain, so that you can finetune your choice of outfit.

In the past, an understanding of local climates has made the weather predictable. Meteorologists make a career out of this understanding, providing information to people who need to know what the weather will be. They produce the weather reports that help farmers to plan their work, surfers to find good swell, and all of us to decide what to wear. They can also warn of weather extremes that might threaten lives or cause severe damage, such as extreme bushfire conditions or storm and wind warnings.

Eco-lingo: weather and climate

Weather and *climate* are two words that people sometimes confuse.

weather *This is what we experience on a day-to-day basis. It's the current activity of temperature, air and water in the trophosphere, the lowest 10 kilometres of the atmosphere. We feel it as rain (and other types of precipitation, such as snow), wind, cloud cover, warmth, cold and humidity.*

climate *This is a more general term, describing the average weather of a particular region and its regular variations over time. So you might hear the climate of Las Vegas described as an arid desert climate, with very hot summers, mild winters and very little cloud cover and rainfall. Or you might hear that London has a temperate climate, with light rainfall and temperatures that are rarely extremely high or low.*

Thunderstorm asthma

Most people think rain is good for asthma sufferers, as it can 'wash' pollen, dust and other asthma triggers out of the air. For a long while, though, scientists and doctors were puzzled by a phenomenon called 'thunderstorm asthma'— a sudden increase in the number of asthma attack cases coming into hospital emergency rooms during or following thunderstorms. It turns out that some types of pollen grain burst when they come into contact with water, releasing smaller granules into the air. These tiny granules can move further into a person's lungs than the larger whole pollen grain. If the person is sensitive or allergic to pollen (or to the granules or bits of exploded pollen), then this deep penetration of the pollen bits into the lungs can cause a bad asthma attack. These people have an extra reason to keep an eye on the weather report.

Climate creators

The climate of any given location is determined by:

- **latitude** or how far north or south of the equator the location is. Equatorial latitudes are warmer, while the polar latitudes are colder and have longer days and nights (depending on the season)

- **the physical geography** or **terrain** of the region, such as nearby mountain ranges, lush rainforests or highly reflective sandy deserts

- **altitude** or how high above (or below) sea level the location is. As altitude gets higher, the temperature gets colder and atmospheric pressure decreases

- **persistent ice or snow** cover, which will keep a location chilly

- **nearby oceans,** which put moisture in the air. Warm and cold ocean currents can also warm or cool the air above them.

Australia's climate regions

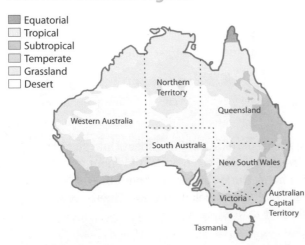

- Equatorial
- Tropical
- Subtropical
- Temperate
- Grassland
- Desert

Northern Territory

Queensland

Western Australia

South Australia

New South Wales

Victoria

Australian Capital Territory

Tasmania

- Warmer and more tropical towards the equator

- Colder towards the South Pole

- Cooler in the Eastern Highlands (Great Dividing Range), with higher rainfall than the lower regions to the west

- Central deserts, away from the moisture of coastal areas and covered with sand dunes

- Pacific Ocean and its El Niño weather cycles influence the east coast

Climate change

A few years ago, talking about the weather was considered polite but boring conversation. These days, the weather is talked about with great interest. In fact, it's sometimes front-page news. Why? Because the planet is getting warmer overall; the climate is changing, and we're seeing some really weird weather.

The earth's climate is constantly but gradually changing, with changes happening over tens of thousands and even millions of years. Part of this change is due to the greenhouse effect—the blanket of greenhouse gases in the atmosphere that keeps the earth liveable. Slight changes in the earth's orbit around the sun can affect the earth's climate by influencing how much of the sun's energy reaches the surface.

Earth's history includes varying climate periods, including cold glacial periods or 'ice ages' and warm interglacial periods. We're currently in an interglacial period known as the 'Holocene Warm Period'.

During the last ice age, which ended around 11 000 years ago, the average global temperature was about 6–10°C (11–18°F) colder than our present global average. Vast areas of land, including most of Canada and much of northern Europe, were covered in ice sheets. The changes in climate following the end of the ice age had a dramatic effect on wildlife. Some animals died out, while others thrived as a result of the gradual increase in temperature and its effect on the environment. The warmer climate was good for humans. Around 2000 years after the end of the ice age, humans started agriculture.

Recent changes

The fact that it took 10 000 years to warm a few degrees to the earth's current global average temperature shows that normal climate change happens very slowly. However, things seem to have sped up. The global average surface temperature increased by about 0.7°C over the last century. Scientists have also observed that, since the Industrial Revolution, the amounts of greenhouse gases in the atmosphere have increased as a result of human activities, such as burning fossil fuels (coal, natural gas and oil), clearing land and changing agricultural practices. These activities have upset the balance of nature's carbon cycle.

Did you know ... ? During glacial periods, polar ice sheets and glaciers grow. Ice ages in the past have lasted about 90 000 years or more. During interglacial periods glaciers gradually melt and shrink or 'retreat'. They have lasted about 10 000 years.

New York, New York!

New York, the 'city that never sleeps', has weather that varies through the year, from winter snow to hot summer days in the high thirties (Celsius). Its climate has also varied over tens of thousands of years, with a huge influence on the landscape and the life living there.

- **20 000 years ago**, during the ice age, New York was covered by a thick ice sheet.
- **15 000 years ago**, after the ice retreated from the area, the New York area was a treeless tundra with frozen soil.
- **7500 years ago**, the climate had warmed further, allowing forests to thrive.
- **Today**, New York's tall trees have been replaced by tall buildings. This has led to the 'urban heat island' effect, in which a city is warmer than surrounding rural areas. This is due to things like the tendency of concrete and asphalt to store heat, the extra heat produced by energy use in the city, and fewer plants, which cool the air as they release water vapour.

Climate scientists say this recent warming is unusual and that the changes in climate we've seen in the last century or so can't be explained by normal climate variation and natural causes alone.

As well as increasing temperatures, we've seen some strange weather and extreme weather events. Hurricane Katrina, strong El Niño events, hail storms in Sydney, unusually long drought periods in Australia and many other countries, snow in Baghdad for the first time in a century, melting ice sheets, early blooming flowers, and more storm activity and floods in the tropics are all symptoms of climate gone crazy!

Eco-lingo

The two terms are often used interchangeably, but what's the difference between global warming and climate change?

global warming   *This is the overall increase in the average temperature of the earth's lower atmosphere. This warming is caused by the extra heat trapped by higher levels of greenhouse gases in the atmosphere.*

climate change   *This term refers to the changes in climate characteristics and weather patterns that result from global warming.*

Climate change: the impacts

'So what's the big deal?' you may ask. How can a degree or two hurt the earth? Some people would argue that a few degrees more warmth would actually improve places like Melbourne, Seattle and most of the United Kingdom. But the consequences of climate change are much more complicated than warmer weather.

A few degrees can make a huge impact. The few degrees difference between the last ice age and modern times demonstrate this. Scientists predict that the global average temperature is likely to rise by 1.1–6.4°C by the year 2100. This would change the world as we know it.

What is a climate model?

No, it's not a supermodel showing the latest fashion for a hotter planet. A climate model is a scientific estimation of what the climate might be like in the future under various scenarios (sets of possible events or situations). A climate model is based on a complex series of mathematical equations. Entering information into these equations can help scientists simulate what climate systems will do. For example, climate modelling can give us a general idea of how a 2°C temperature increase might change rainfall patterns in farming regions.

As climate is a crucial part of the environment, climate change will have wide-ranging effects.

Temperature

The 1.1–6.4°C increase in global temperature is an estimate of the global average increase. But this average represents areas that will have more than the predicted warming and areas that will have less. Climate models show that the greatest warming will be in inland areas because of the greater land mass. Less warming will occur over oceans and near the coast. The Southern Ocean will have the least warming.

Rising sea levels

- Sea levels are predicted to rise as a result of increased water from melted glaciers and icecaps, and because materials (including water) expand slightly when warmed (this is called 'thermal expansion').
- Coastlines around the world could be submerged. Coastal cities, such as Sydney, Hong Kong, New York, Tokyo and Amsterdam will be under threat. Many low-lying Pacific islands will simply disappear.

Extreme weather and climate events

- Extremes in weather, such as drought, hurricanes and flooding, are predicted to become more common. For example, the

Atlantic hurricane season and the South-East Asian monsoon season are both expected to intensify.

- Heatwaves are also predicted.
- Drought and heatwaves can combine to increase the frequency and severity of bushfires. While bushfires are part of Australia's environment, they are happening more frequently than they used to, giving ecosystems less time to recover.

Water flows

- The amount and pattern of rainfall and other precipitation are predicted to change. This will reduce water supplies for people, agriculture and the environment in many areas. For example, the deserts in subtropical regions are expected to grow. Some areas may experience more rainfall and flooding.

- Some areas are predicted to have less frequent but more intense rainfall. This kind of rainfall tends to run off the surface of parched earth, rather than seeping in, resulting in less benefit to ecosystems and less water flowing into the water catchments that supply our cities with drinking water.

Human social and health impacts

- Flooding can cause increases in waterborne diseases such as dysentery.
- Changing rainfall patterns and the shift of tropical regions bring disease-carrying insects, such as mosquitos, with them. This can increase the range of insect-borne diseases such as malaria and Ross River fever.
- Desertification of farming lands, less water and more severe weather will hit the world's poorest people the hardest.

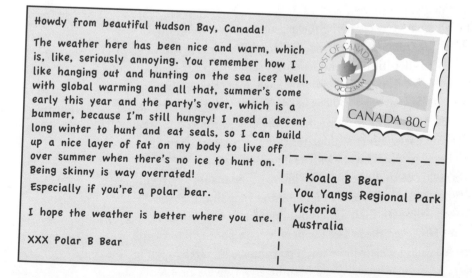

Howdy from beautiful Hudson Bay, Canada!

The weather here has been nice and warm, which is, like, seriously annoying. You remember how I like hanging out and hunting on the sea ice? Well, with global warming and all that, summer's come early this year and the party's over, which is a bummer, because I'm still hungry! I need a decent long winter to hunt and eat seals, so I can build up a nice layer of fat on my body to live off over summer when there's no ice to hunt on. Being skinny is way overrated!

Especially if you're a polar bear.

I hope the weather is better where you are.

XXX Polar B Bear

POST OF CANADA
QCC23MM
CANADA 80c

Koala B Bear
You Yangs Regional Park
Victoria
Australia

Biodiversity, ecosystems and agriculture

- Some plants and animals, such as frogs, are very sensitive to changes in climate. There are likely to be extinctions as a result of climate change.
- Alpine and polar species are at risk of losing their habitat.
- Oceans, soaking up more carbon dioxide, are likely to become more acidic, placing some marine species at risk.
- Ocean temperature changes affect marine ecosystems. Giant kelp forests, such as those around Tasmania, thrive in cooler waters. They're rich in biodiversity, providing shelter, nursery areas and food for fish, crustaceans, sea snails, seastars, seahorses and sea dragons. It's believed that they're declining due to the combined effects of climate change, pollution and the overfishing of rock lobsters.
- Coral is particularly sensitive to changes in temperature. A series of very hot days can cause coral bleaching, leading to the death of the coral, which is the centre of this diverse ecosystem. The Great Barrier Reef in Australia, a network of 2900 reefs teaming with tropical fish and other marine life, is under threat from climate change because of both the temperature increases and increased storm activity buffeting these delicate systems.
- Climate change is changing the seasons as they are known and felt by plants and animals. For example, shorter winters mean a shorter hunting and feeding season for polar bears. In the United Kingdom, biologists have noted that spring seems to be starting a few days earlier than it did decades ago, with birds laying eggs sooner. Gardeners have noticed flowers blooming early. There is a danger that the patterns of nature may become 'out of sync' with each other.
- Crop yields could be reduced in many of the planet's current food-producing nations. Cooler climates may find that the warmth improves their agricultural production to some extent. However, these areas generally have poor soil to begin with, so their yields will be low. Food shortages, already felt in many poorer countries, could become a worldwide problem.

Eco-action: get climate cooler

See if you can join the fight against climate change by doing the following:

- *Don't waste energy*—see the energy-saving tips on page 73.

- **Reduce your rubbish**—rotting waste in landfill produces greenhouse emissions.

- **Plant trees**—they take greenhouse gases out of the atmosphere and use them to build plant tissues.

- **Use pedal power**—if you live close enough, ride a bike to school instead of getting a lift in a car.

What can be done about climate change?

Though some climate change is natural, scientists believe that the climate change we've seen in the last century is largely a result of human activity. There are two things the human race can do to face this challenge.

The first thing we need to do is to change those activities that are producing the greenhouse emissions that are warming the planet. We need to produce less carbon emissions and, if possible, find ways of taking them out of the atmosphere. This will hopefully limit global warming to a manageable 1.1°C increase. The second thing we can do is to adapt our settlements, communities, agriculture and cities so that they can continue to function in a hotter planet.

Up, up and away?

The mountain nursery frog lives on mountains 1200 metres above sea level in cloud-shrouded rainforest in far north Queensland. These unusual frogs need damp leaf litter in which to lay eggs and breed, which is provided by the moist conditions of the cloud forest. This makes it vulnerable to climate change. With each degree of warming, the cloud layer moves up 150 metres. This is bad news for the mountain nursery frogs living on Mount Lewis, which is 1350 metres high. The 1.1°C increase that scientists say is now unavoidable could well push the frog up and off the top of the mountain, into extinction.

Compost

A plate of apple cores, brown, overripe bananas and the used grounds from a coffee plunger may not sound very appetising. But these are just some of the possible ingredients for making your own plant food by composting.

Composting is basically human-controlled biodegradation—the natural decaying of food, plant matter and other unwanted biodegradable materials, confined to a specific space or bin set aside for the purpose. Decomposition in nature is generally slow, but composting sets it on the fast track. Compost bins or heaps allow heat to build up inside the pile of rotting material; the heat speeds up the process. The resulting brown, crumbly stuff is called 'compost'.

There are two types of composting. **Home composting** can literally be done in your own backyard. Food scraps, lawn clippings, dry autumn leaves and other garden waste are put into a compost bin or on a compost heap. You can even throw in cow or chook manure for good measure—it makes the compost even more nutritious for the plants. Leave nature to do its thing for a few months and then you can use the mature compost to fertilise the garden.

Industrial composting works in the same way as home composting but on a much larger scale. It is often done with the materials collected through local council garden waste collections. Industrial composting can produce biofuels, soil conditioner for farming, and bags of compost sold at garden supplies stores.

Composting is an easy way to cut down the amount of waste your household sends to landfill, where it's no longer useful. Fifty per cent or more of the waste that people put into their rubbish bins could be composted.

Eco-byte

'After lunch every day at school I choose about three people to come with me and get the food scraps and take them to the compost tumbler and the worm farm. After about 2 weeks the food scraps in the compost tumbler crush down and we use it as fertiliser on the vegetables.' **William, 11**

Compost it!

Here are some of the more unusual items that you can put into your compost bin:

- tea bags
- coffee grounds
- vacuum dust
- egg shells
- hair clippings from a haircut, or hair removed from a hairbrush
- ash from wood fires
- shredded paper and cardboard
- dried flower arrangements

Conservation

Conservation is the practice of protecting, preserving, keeping and caring for something so that it doesn't change, get damaged, run out or disappear. It is the wise protection or use of natural resources so that we can enjoy them now, while ensuring their availability for future generations, all ideally in balance with the needs of the natural environment and other living species.

We human beings are a really high-maintenance species, using far more resources than other species. The Industrial Revolution (in the late eighteenth and early nineteenth centuries) saw incredible advances in the ability of humans to do work, make things and change nature. But it also saw sudden increases in air pollution from burning fuels, as well as water and land contamination, and the production of solid waste. Some people were worried about the environmental impacts they saw, and the environmental movement was born.

Since then the environmental movement has spread worldwide, with individual conservation efforts focusing on the needs of the local environment. From breeding programs in zoos to sand dune restoration, there are many and varied conservation initiatives spreading to the four corners of the earth.

Conservation initiatives around the world

Number plates for birds

More than twenty environmental groups in Victoria, Australia, are involved in protecting the red-tailed black cockatoo. Their activities range from planting trees and purchasing land with habitat through to population-monitoring and contributing to a National Recovery Plan. Loss of habitat is a major threat to these beautiful birds, with only about a thousand left in the wild. They nest in mature trees, so tree-planting alone can't give them homes quickly enough.

Some of these conservation activities need money to continue. In the lead-up to the 2006 Commonwealth Games in Melbourne, Australia, the Victorian state government sold 1000 special, limited-edition number plates featuring 'Karak', the red-tailed black cockatoo mascot of the games. The money raised was used to support red-tailed black cockatoo conservation efforts.

National Parks

National Parks are areas of land, sea and natural vegetation that are set aside for conservation and recreation, and protected from pollution and development. They are generally owned and managed by the government. There are over 6500 national parks around the world, including:

- Yellowstone National Park in the USA. This is an important habitat for large mammals, including the endangered gray wolf, which has been established there as part of a wolf reintroduction program
- Sagarmatha National Park in Nepal. This includes the southern half of Mount Everest
- The Great Barrier Reef, which is a marine national park off the east coast of Australia
- Marii Chodra National Park in Russia, which was created to protect rare plants.

Clean Up the World

In 1989, a yachtsman named Ian Kiernan organised a litter-collecting event called 'Clean Up Sydney Harbour' in Sydney, Australia. The event was a huge success, with 40 000 volunteers lending a hand. This became a national event—Clean Up Australia Day. Since then, it has evolved into one of the world's largest conservation volunteering events. Clean Up the World is now held in September, with an estimated thirty-five million people in 120 countries participating each year. It's a brilliant effort—but don't you just wish that people didn't litter in the first place?

War on Weeds in South Africa

Some 9000 non-native plants have been introduced to South Africa, and some are causing environmental trouble. One hundred and ninety-eight of these are currently classified as invasive, including the prickly pear. In recent years, South Africa has stepped up the battle to remove these water-sucking weeds from the Kruger National Park. Teams from South Africa's Working for Water project faced the invading South American cactus armed with herbicide spray and machetes.

The Working for Water project combines conservation with employment for the country's rural poor. The prickly pear drinks more than its fair share of water. In this dry area, where every drop of water counts, removing these weeds will ultimately save water and reduce poverty. Since the program began, more than a million hectares of invasive alien plants have been cleared, providing jobs and training to approximately 20 000 people.

'Never doubt that a small group of thoughtful, committed citizens can change the world. Indeed, it is the only thing that ever has.'

Margaret Mead (1901–1978), US anthropologist

The seed saver's safety stash

Halfway between the coast of Norway and the North Pole is a group of icy, inhospitable islands called Svalbard. One island, Spitsbergen Island, is the location of the Global Seed Vault—also known as the 'Doomsday Vault'. This vault has been tunnelled deep into the permafrost rock of a sandstone mountain. Deep inside, the temperature is a steady −18°C. In this giant freezer, a vast collection of seeds is stored in suspended animation. This collection aims to store and protect plant biodiversity, keeping a living record of the genetic information of a wide variety of species and protecting against the threat of these species disappearing. There are hundreds of crop seed banks around the world, all aimed at keeping our agricultural options open. There are also seed banks that aim to save biodiversity in general. Australia's network of botanic gardens has created a national seed bank plan to preserve plants in peril.

Butterfly gardening

The Richmond Birdwing Conservation Project involves households and school children in the effort to save the Richmond birdwing butterfly. This large and magnificent tropical butterfly was once common in northern New South Wales and Queensland, Australia, but is now extinct in two-thirds of its original range. The community is helping to save the butterfly by gardening in a way that helps to sustain its caterpillar. Residents and school children are being encouraged to remove the introduced Dutchman's pipe vine, which poisons the caterpillars, and are instead planting its food plant, the Richmond birdwing vine.

Eco-action: volunteer for conservation

There are a number of community conservation initiatives to which you, your family or school might like to lend a hand:

* Get dirty on Planet Ark's National Tree Day or Schools Tree Day (go to <treeday.planetark.org> to find out more).

* Pick up litter on Clean Up Australia Day (see <www.cleanup.org.au>)

* Find out about opportunities to be a Conservation Volunteer on any week of the year at <www.conservationvolunteers.com.au>.

* Join with your community to make your town or neighbourhood a cleaner, greener place, and Keep Australia Beautiful (see <www.kab.org.au>).

Answer the call

Gorillas in Central Africa are endangered partly because mining for coltan, a mineral needed to make mobile phones, is destroying some of their habitat. Australia Zoo and Fauna & Flora International have developed 'Answer the Call'—a program that helps gorillas by recycling mobile phones. More info: <www.fauna-flora.org.au>.

Consumption

Consuming stuff is part of life. Eating, for example, is the simplest type of consumption, and one that keeps us alive and healthy. But too much consumption of food can make us obese and unhealthy.

Beyond food, there are other things we buy and consume—things like clothing, magazines, energy, gadgets, sporting goods, CDs, shampoo and other toiletries and beauty products. All of these things come at an environmental cost and have an impact, though it's usually not something we see. What happens that we don't see? How much energy was needed to make that product? Did

its manufacture cause pollution? Was it made from a resource that's not sustainable? Was your Auntie Beryl's bracelet made from endangered tortoiseshell? For that species, is it a case of good buy or goodbye?

Every product has a life cycle, and we own and use the product for only part of that life cycle. But it's worth thinking about the stages of a product's life cycle that we don't see. Take a music CD, for example, as pictured below.

As the life story of a CD shows, every product represents the use of energy, water and material resources, and it has other environmental impacts over the course of its life, right through to the disposal stage. The question you have to ask yourself is: 'Are the

The life cycle of a CD

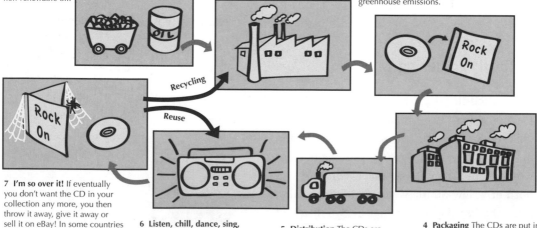

1 Get the materials CDs are made from a range of materials, including aluminium, plastics, gold and dyes. These plastics are made from non-renewable oil.

2 Process the materials Mined materials need to be processed to improve their quality. This requires water and energy, and produces wastes, pollution and greenhouse gases.

3 Manufacturing The materials are melted, moulded and put together. The music information is 'written' into a thin reflective metal layer, which is then coated with a protective layer of lacquer. Again, this process requires energy and produces greenhouse emissions.

7 I'm so over it! If eventually you don't want the CD in your collection any more, you then throw it away, give it away or sell it on eBay! In some countries there are CD recycling programs.

6 Listen, chill, dance, sing, shake that groove thing Once you've bought the CD, you get to use it. Your CD player uses electricity.

5 Distribution The CDs are transported to shops, where you can buy them, using fuel and producing polluting emissions.

4 Packaging The CDs are put in plastic cases with printed paper sleeves, requiring more material and energy use and generating more emissions.

Think about it

Are the good things about this product worth the resources needed to make it?

good things about this product worth the resources needed to make it?' Sometimes the answer will be a big, loud 'yes', and sometimes it will be a reluctant 'no'. Music, for example, is a wonderful part of life, and our tastes in music are part of our character. Music can make you feel good; it can motivate you and get you on your feet exercising, and it can sooth you when you're feeling down or angry. So there's a reasonable case for buying the CD.

The good news is that we're finding better ways to make and deliver goods and services, with fewer environmental costs. You can buy music online and download it as digital files, completely bypassing the impacts of the manufacture and distribution of CDs. Still, you can make a huge difference to the environment by avoiding buying and consuming too much stuff! Buy things you know you will get good use of, and know when enough is enough.

Eco-action: e-entertainment and music

Buy music tracks online as downloadable digital files, instead of CDs. But e-entertainment doesn't end with music. You can also get audio books, a paper-free alternative to reading (which is great to have in the background when you're cleaning your bedroom!). Even some TV shows and movies are available as downloadable video files, using fewer material resources than store-bought DVDs.

Consumerism by numbers

CDs were first introduced in the USA in 1983, and that year 800 000 discs were sold. By 1990, the number had grown to nearly 1 BILLION.

An estimated 45 BILLION pairs of disposable chopsticks are used in China every year.

Australians spent an estimated A$123.5 MILLION on chewing gum, A$282.4 MILLION on deodorant, A$74.2 MILLION on mouthwash, A$141.8 MILLION on air freshener and A$18.3 MILLION on disposable cleaning gloves in supermarkets alone in 2007.

More than 1 BILLION mobile phones were sold worldwide in 2007, 160 MILLION more than the previous year.

If laid end to end, enough of the famous 'mouse ear' hats are sold each year at Walt Disney World to stretch 282 kilometres.

The gold needed for a single 0.33 ounce, 18 karat gold ring results in more than 18 tonnes of mine waste.

The total annual volume of junk mail, including glossy catalogues, sent in the USA consumes 100 MILLION trees. Much of this is wasted—the US Environmental Protection Agency reports that 44% of the unsolicited (not asked for) mail received by Americans heads to landfill or recycling without being read.

The world's largest catalogue is a German Bon Prix fashion catalogue, with 212 pages, each measuring 1.2 x 1.5 metres.

Michael Zarnock of Deerfield, New York, holds the Guinness World Record for the largest collection of model cars. He has 8128 different Hot Wheels cars.

Disposable products

In the section on consumption, we looked at how all products come at a cost to the environment and are an investment of the energy, water and material resources needed to make them. Financial gurus will tell you that it is good to get a return on your investment or 'a bigger bang for your buck'.

The more you use a given product, the better the return on your investment in the product. If you use it a lot, then it gives you good value for the money you spent on it. In much the same way, when a product can be reused repeatedly, you get good value or a good return on the resources needed to make it.

Reusable versus disposable

If reusable products are so good and green, then why are we buying disposable products? Convenience is the answer. If we can use something once only, then chuck it out, we don't have to wash it or bother to look after it. We don't have to carry it with us. Instead we can put it in the nearest bin when we're finished with it. However, remember that this rubbish doesn't disappear; it heads to landfill.

Choosing reusable products instead of disposable alternatives is an easy way to cut waste. Reusable products are also often better quality than disposable products because they are expected to last a lot longer. There is a time and a place for single-use products, such as hospitals and doctors' surgeries, when reusing tools or materials may spread illness. But otherwise, choose reusable produces as part of your efforts to reduce, reuse and recycle.

Reusable and disposable options

Reusable	Disposable
Cloth, string and green bags	Plastic checkout bags
Refillable drink bottle	Bottled water
Handkerchief	Tissues
Lunch box	Cling wrap and paper bag
Cloth hand towel or air dryer	Paper towel
Rechargeable batteries	Single-use batteries

Ecological footprint

Not since Cinderella and her stepsisters slugged it out for the glass slipper (and Prince Charming's hand in marriage) has the size of your footprint been so important! The ecological footprint is not a fairytale though; it's a lesson in the cold, hard reality that our comfortable lifestyle comes at a cost.

The ecological footprint is a way of measuring the environmental impact of a person's lifestyle. It's nothing to do with the size of your ballet shoes, or even something smelly you've stepped in. It estimates the amount of productive land or sea needed to provide the resources to support a particular way of living. For example, a certain amount of land would be needed to produce food, with more needed to graze sheep to produce wool for clothes or to farm cotton for T-shirts, more to provide mined materials (mineral resources), and so on. An ecological footprint compares our consumption of natural resources with the earth's ability to keep providing them.

Things like the size of your house, the amount of energy you use and where it comes from, the kinds of food you eat and the transport you use all affect the size of your ecological footprint. It's measured in 'global hectares', where one global hectare (gha) is equivalent to one hectare of biologically productive space that has the world-average ability to produce the stuff we need. If you take the world's total global hectares of productive land and sea and divide them by the total population, there are 2.1 global hectares per person, but they're under threat from overpopulation, land degradation and pollution. In total, our world's footprint is 2.7 global hectares per person, so we're basically consuming natural resources faster than the earth can replace them.

Rich nations have a higher standard of living, with bigger homes, more food and plenty of stuff bought at shopping malls, resulting in generally large footprints ranging from 3 to nearly 10 global hectares per person. By contrast, people in developing nations have footprints of less than 1 global hectare per person. The average Australian ecological footprint is 7.8 global hectares. This means that we would need an extra three planet earths to allow for all of the world's population to have the same standard of living as that enjoyed in Australia.

Big foot versus little foot

Signs of a bigger footprint

Signs of a smaller footprint

Food

- I eat lots of red meat, white meat and dairy products.
- I eat lots of fast food and takeaway meals.
- I have lots of packaged snacks and drinks.
- The food I eat at home is mostly packaged and processed, such as canned pasta stew and 2-minute noodles.
- I eat what I want, when I want it—even cherries in the middle of winter!

Food

- I limit my meat, fish and chicken intake.
- I get some protein from plant sources, such as peas and other legumes.
- Most of my meals are prepared at home and eaten there.
- My meals are prepared from fresh ingredients, with little or no packaging and processing.
- I try to grow some food at home or get food that's locally grown.
- I'm happy to eat the food that is in season—it usually tastes better that way!

Home

- I live in a big house, with only a few people.
- Our house has huge energy bills.
- In winter, we usually have a heater on. If the heater isn't on, that means it's summer and the airconditioner is on.
- We've got lots of electrical appliances, and the bigger the better.

Home

- Our house is a reasonable size for the number of people living there—not too big.
- Our house is pretty draught-proof and energy efficient. It doesn't get too hot in summer or too cold in winter because it's well shaded and insulated.
- We chose energy-efficient appliances. We have a couple of home-entertainment gadgets, but they're running on GreenPower or, more likely, turned off.

Transport

- Our car is a four-wheel drive, V6 or V8.
- We go everywhere in the car.

Transport

- Our car is smaller than the average, and very fuel efficient.
- We don't use the car all the time. Bikes and public transport get us around, too.

Goods and services

- Our rubbish bin is usually overflowing.
- I always buy the latest fashion.
- I love retail therapy.
- I've got all the latest gadgets.

Goods and services

- We recycle what we can and avoid packaged goods, and there's always extra room in our rubbish bin.
- I'd rather get a good-quality piece of clothing I really love than three throw-away pieces.
- Retail therapy? No way! After all, the best things in life aren't things.
- I make my own fun and save up for the gadgets I really want. That way you really appreciate them.

World: 2.7

North America: 9.2
- Canada: 7.1
- United States of America: 9.4

Around the world: ecological footprint*

Ecological footprint is measured in average global hectares per person for each country and region.

Source: average ecological footprint estimates from WWF, *Living Planet Report 2008*, WWF, .Gland, Switzerland, 2008.

Latin America and the Caribbean: 2.4
- Argentina: 2.5
- Colombia: 1.8
- Haiti: 0.5
- Trinidad and Tobago: 2.1

Europe (European Union members): 4.7
- Denmark: 8.0
- France: 4.9
- Germany: 4.2
- Greece: 5.9
- Italy: 4.8
- United Kingdom: 5.3

Europe (non-EU): 3.5
- Albania: 2.2
- Russian Federation: 3.7

Middle East and Central Asia: 2.3
- Afghanistan: 0.5
- Kazakhstan: 3.4
- Lebanon: 3.1
- United Arab Emirates: 9.5

Asia-Pacific: 1.6
- Australia: 7.8
- Bangladesh: 0.6
- China: 2.1
- India: 0.9
- Indonesia: 0.9
- Japan: 4.9
- New Zealand: 7.7

Africa: 1.4
- Cameroon: 1.3
- Egypt: 1.7
- Somalia: 1.4
- South Africa: 2.1

Australia: 7.8

Ecology and ecosystems

The complexity of ecology starts with an **individual** life form, such as a single tree or one fish. Groups of individuals make up a **population** of that animal, such as a pride of lions, a forest of oaks or a school of fish. Different populations of species live together in a **community**, and several different communities can combine to make an **ecosystem**. Different ecosystems within the same geographical or climate zone make up a **biome**, such as the African savannah or the North American tundra. These biomes together make up the ultimate **biosphere** of Planet Earth.

Plants are the primary producers of the environment. In other words, they do all the groundwork of getting energy from the sun and converting it into stored energy as sugars, starches and cellulose in their tissues. This energy is transferred to other species through the food chain. The animals that eat plants are called primary consumers. These animals store the energy that they don't immediately need in their flesh. Predatory animals that eat the primary consumer animals are called secondary consumers, and so on to the top predators, such as lions and humans. When all plants and animals die, they decompose, providing nourishment for the soil and food for the plants. As Mufasa said in *The Lion King*, it's 'all part of the circle of life'.

You would think that the best place to be is at the top of the food chain, but in a way top predators are at the mercy of their prey. When the numbers of their prey are high, predators thrive. But their numbers can only increase while there's food to support them. The moment the available prey decreases, the predator populations start to decline. In the future, the lack of food will slow the growth of the human population.

Levels of the biosphere

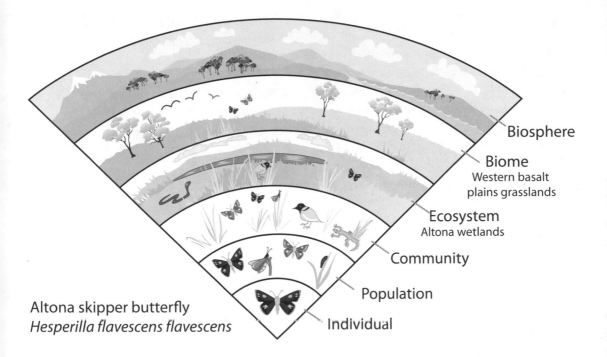

Biosphere

Biome
Western basalt
plains grasslands

Ecosystem
Altona wetlands

Community

Population

Individual

Altona skipper butterfly
Hesperilla flavescens flavescens

Eco-lingo

ecosystem   *This is quite literally an ecological system, where plants and animals live in give-and-take relationships.*

ecology   *This is the study of the relationships between living things and their natural environment.*

Eco-activity: make a terrarium

A terrarium is like an enclosed, miniature ecosystem. It has living plants and animals that are able to live in balance with each other in the right conditions, despite being closed off from the outside environment.

You will need

- A washed plastic bottle with the top cut off
- A plastic ice-cream container
- Soil, small rocks, gravel and mulch
- Activated charcoal
- Small plants
- A few worms

How to

1 Put a 2-centimetre layer of gravel in the bottom of the ice-cream container.

2 Over this, put in a 1.5-centimetre layer of activated charcoal. The charcoal will help filter the air inside the enclosed terrarium.

3 Half fill the ice-cream container with soil and pack it down loosely.

4 Plant your plants in the centre of the container and water them a little.

5 Add a few worms.

6 Put mulch and small rocks around the plants, keeping it all within the area that will be covered by the plastic bottle.

7 Turn the plastic bottle upside down and push the cut edge into the soil so that the clear plastic bottle now houses the plants, rocks and mulch.

8 Keep the terrarium in a sunny (but not too sunny) place. Occasionally water it. Occasionally put a little carrot peel in the soil to provide extra food for the worms.

9 If you like, keep a record of how the system changes over the coming weeks and months.

Do you want something a little more sophisticated? You can make a terrarium inside a more decorative glass container, such as a cookie jar, a large apothecary jar (these are the old fashioned medicine jars) or even an old fish tank. Just make sure the jar is thoroughly cleaned first.

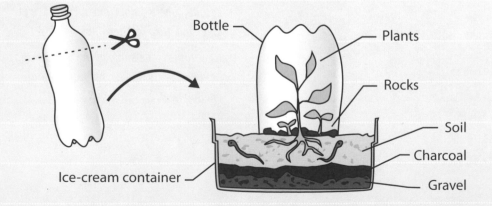

El Niño and La Niña

You've probably heard of El Niño. It seems to get the blame when we get bad weather. El Niño, which means 'boy child' in Spanish, is a change in the normal temperature, wind and weather patterns in the Pacific Ocean. Trade winds normally drag warm weather along the equator from east to west, bringing rain to Australia and pushing up cool, nutrient-rich water along the South American coastline. (This 'upwelling' of food-laden water means feast time for South American fish!) In an El Niño event, this climatic pattern is reversed, but this is part of the normal variation of the earth's climate.

The result is less upwelling of nutrient-rich cold water, and higher rainfall along the South American coastline. The lower nutrient levels in upper sea water leads to declines in marine life and spells disaster for local fishermen. On the other side of the Pacific, dry cold air builds up over Australia's eastern coastline during the normally wet season. El Niño causes floods in the south-west of the USA and in western Latin America, and drought in eastern Australia, South-East Asia and southern Africa. It also increases the frequency of bushfires in Australia.

Recent years have seen dramatic El Niño events. In Australia, we seem to be experiencing drought conditions more frequently and severely, with higher incidences of bushfires. The last few years have seen the worst drought and bushfire seasons for decades, both in Australia and in many other parts of the world. Australia, Canada and Spain, in particular, have had dramatic wildfire seasons in recent summers. Many, but not all, scientists believe that global warming is altering El Niño patterns, possibly leading to more frequent or more intense El Niño events.

As well as a 'boy child', there's also a 'girl child'. Unusually cold ocean temperatures in the eastern Pacific near the equator characterise La Niña (while El Niño is known for unusually warm ocean temperatures). La Niña events give rise to tropical cyclone activity in the Atlantic Ocean.

Endangered and extinct species

'There are plenty more fish in the sea' is an expression that is often trotted out to cheer up someone whose boyfriend or girlfriend has dumped them. While it may be true for broken hearts, the situation for real scaly, slimy fish is quite different. Around the world, the populations of a number of fish species (also called 'fish stocks') are declining because of overfishing, the destruction or pollution of aquatic (water) ecosystems and the impact of exotic species. The number of known threatened fish species in 2008 was estimated at 1275.

Why species become endangered

There are a variety of reasons why species fall in numbers, becoming endangered and potentially extinct.

Loss or degradation of habitat

Habitat is the natural conditions and environment that a particular plant or animal species normally lives in. You could say that 'habitat' is biology's word for 'home'. Pollution, land-clearing and human activity (such as reckless off-road driving on sand dunes or the use of power boats in marine sanctuaries) can all destroy habitat. Natural habitat areas can also be part of the 'collateral damage' (the damage that's not intended) of war.

Eco-lingo

endangered species   *These are those species that are threatened with extinction—those in danger of dying out completely, unable to survive in a changing world with increasing pressures.*

Natural disasters

Drought, bushfires, floods, hurricanes and other extreme weather events all take a heavy toll on wildlife.

Introduced plants and animals

Plants and animals in their natural habitat exist in a delicate balance. But outside their natural habitat they can become pests. Introduced animals can kill native wildlife and compete for food and habitat. Introduced plants can compete with or smother native plants, poison native animals or livestock, and upset the balance of an ecosystem.

Hunting and harvesting

Wild plants and animals are hunted and harvested from the land, sky, fresh-water bodies and sea. They may be wanted to provide food or other materials and products, such as fur, medicines, materials, skins (for leather) and tusks. If the rate of natural breeding of these species in the wild can't replace those taken, the numbers start to decline. Animals hunted to extinction include the Bali tiger, passenger pigeon and various species of moa (a native bird of New Zealand).

Extinct (abbreviated EX)

Extinct in the wild (EW): species for which the only known living examples are in captivity (such as zoos) or as naturalised populations outside of their original natural habitat.

These three groups are referred to as 'threatened' and are all considered vulnerable to extinction in the near future

Critically endangered (CR)

Endangered (EN)

Vulnerable (VU)

Near threatened (NT): species that may be threatened with extinction in the near future

Least concern (LC): species that have been evaluated and aren't considered threatened or endangered

Data deficient (DD): species for which there is not enough information available to do a proper assessment of conservation status

Not evaluated (NE)

Classifying endangered species

Understanding a problem is the first step towards solving it, making official studies and the classification of endangered species vitally important in our efforts to conserve and protect the world's rich biodiversity. Formal assessments of the numbers of plants and animals, and their threats, give us a clearer picture of the issue. Classifying species according to how threatened they are also provides the basis for governments to make new laws or develop programs that will protect vulnerable species.

The International Union for Conservation of Nature (IUCN), which used to have the shorter name of the World Conservation Union, is an international organisation of both governments and non-government organisations that together want to protect and conserve the diversity of nature. It has over a thousand member organisations and input from nearly 11 000 voluntary scientists and experts, from over 160 different countries. It is recognised around the world as the leading authority on the 'conservation statuses' of species, a measure of how much a given species is at risk of extinction.

The IUCN *Red List of Threatened Species* is a comprehensive list of the conservation status of many of the world's known plant and animal species. A given species is evaluated every few years and given a conservation status category that reflects how serious its current situation is.

The *Red List* conservation status categories (from most to least serious) are set out in the diagram at left.

Back from the brink

While it's sad to think of all of the plants and animals we've lost, there is some good news. We've been able to intervene and curb some of the human activities that are threatening wildlife in time to save certain species from extinction.

Conservation programs are also replanting vegetation to provide suitable habitat for animals on the critical list. Breeding programs in national parks and zoos around the world are doing their best to preserve endangered species, re-establish their numbers and introduce them back into the wild. The danger with these programs is that the animals become too dependent on the captive lifestyle and lose the ability to survive in the wild.

Amazonian and American alligators were once hunted to make boots and handbags from their skins. Both are now back from the brink of extinction through controls on endangered species and through conservation programs. The American alligator is even off the endangered list.

Some animals just need to be left alone, particularly those that are being overhunted. International bans on whaling have allowed whale numbers to recover after being nearly hunted to extinction. Similarly, grey wolves are making a comeback, helped by hunting laws as well as habitat-protection and breeding programs. Sea otters survived hunting by being hidden. These otters were once abundant on North Pacific coastlines but were hunted for their fur. In California, populations were once between 16 000 and 20 000, but were decimated by hunting. It was thought that they were extinct in California, but around fifty remained in a small colony. The people who knew about the otters kept it secret to protect them. By the time the public found out about the colony, it had grown to several hundred otters.

Extinction

If you could jump in a time machine and go back anywhere between 65 million and 230 million years into the past, you might find yourself face to face with a real, live dinosaur. These days, the nearest you can get to this experience is seeing a dinosaur skeleton in a museum or a computer-generated image in a movie or video game.

Extinction is the death of all members of a species of organism. Endangered species are those at risk of becoming extinct. The extinction of plants and animals results in a loss of biodiversity. Extinction can be caused by a range of factors, including changes in climate, loss of habitat, competition from other species or the overhunting or overharvesting of a species by humans. Gradual extinction is part of how our dynamic planet works and is connected to the ever-changing climate. The range of species alive today is just a small fraction of the total number of species that have ever lived.

Lonesome George is literally 'one of a kind'. He is the last known living Pinta Island tortoise, a subspecies of the Galapagos tortoise species. Experts say that it's not possible to tell the age of adult giant tortoises, but George is in good health, and from a breeding point of view, he's in his prime. However, efforts to encourage him to breed with females from another Galapagos tortoise subspecies have so far been unsuccessful. It seems George really wants a wife from his own subspecies; researchers hold the slim hope of finding one. A search for a female Pinta Island tortoise has been ongoing for over thirty years, even going so far as offering a US$10 000 reward for finding one. Since giant tortoises are believed to live for 150–200 years, George may have many more lonely nights ahead. When he dies, the Pinta Island tortoise will become classed as extinct.

Online profile: Lonesome George

About me: I'm a unique guy who is looking for love. I'm about 1 metre long and weigh 90 kilograms. I'm somewhere between sixty and ninety years old, but I'm just coming out of my shell. I'm the only known example of my species, so I'm confident in saying I'm the hottest looking. I live at the Charles Darwin Research Station in Santa Cruz, where I have all the creature comforts.

Interests: My hobbies include eating, hanging out in my enclosure and sunbaking.

Relationship status: I'm single, but looking for the right lady.

Favourite song: 'Leave me alone (I'm lonely)' by Pink

Favourite TV show: *Survivor*

Favourite movie: *Teenage Mutant Ninja Turtles*

Favourite book: my biography naturally—*Lonesome George* by Henry Nicholls—though I also like Aesop's fable 'The Tortoise and the Hare'.

In earth's history, before the increase in the numbers and spread of humans, extinction was mostly gradual, but there were also occasional periods of mass extinction, called 'extinction events'. There is much debate among scientists over the causes of past extinction events. Suggested causes include periods of high volcanic activity and widespread lava flows, sea-level falls and asteroid impacts. For example, it's believed that the mass extinction that occurred 65 million years ago (called the 'end cretaceous extinction event'), which saw dinosaurs and many other species wiped out, was caused by the impact of a gigantic meteorite, which sent huge dust clouds into the atmosphere, blocking out the sunlight needed for warmth and photosynthesis.

Over the past 500 million years, there have been five mass extinctions. It took between 20 million and 100 million years for biodiversity to recover after each one. Some scientists believe we're entering earth's sixth period of mass extinction, and this time it's our fault!

There are still so many species to be discovered. There are great hopes that the tropical rainforests of the world will give us new species and substances that will cure diseases and ease suffering. If we continue to chew through our planet's natural assets, we'll lose them long before we ever get a chance to discover their full value.

Many people hope that cloning will enable the human race to bring animals, such as the Tasmanian tiger and even dinosaurs, back from extinction. For some, this idea reduces the sense of urgency in relation to protecting the endangered species on the verge of extinction. Do we know enough about cloning to rely on it to bring back biodiversity? Experts say that there may not be enough samples of Tasmanian tiger DNA to provide the genetic variation needed to re-establish the species without the problems of inbreeding. Dolly, the famous sheep who was the world's first cloned mammal, died at the relatively young age of six years old (the life expectancy of her species is 12–15 years), reigniting concerns that cloning may cause genetic defects.

Lazarus species

Sometimes a species previously thought to be extinct makes a surprise reappearance. Such species are called 'Lazarus species', after the Bible character Lazarus, who was miraculously raised from the dead by Jesus. For example, coelacanths (an order of fish species) are well represented among fossil records, but appeared to become extinct over 65 million years ago. Then in 1938, a *Latimeria* specimen of the coelacanth order was found off the coast of South Africa. Further sightings have occurred in the waters around southern Africa since. In 1999, a second species of the coelacanth order was documented in Indonesian waters.

Lazarus species aren't confined to the animal kingdom. In 1994, David Noble, a parks and wildlife officer walking in Wollemi National Park in the Blue Mountains in New South Wales, stumbled across an unusual looking tree and took some specimens. On asking scientists to identify it, they found that they had discovered a species new to science. It was named *Wollemia nobilis* in its discoverer's honour and is the only living member of its genus. Fossils from the genus had been previously found and studied, but the discovery of living specimens took both the science world and the broader public by storm. With so many people curious about the 'dinosaur tree', the location of the few known living trees in the wild is protected and a closely guarded secret. Both coelacanths and the Wollemi pine are classified as critically endangered.

Palaeontologists use a term that's a bit more specific. A 'Lazarus taxon' is a species that disappears from fossil record only to reappear again later. But sometimes a species suspected to be a Lazarus taxon turns out to be a look-alike. Palaeontologists have a name for this too: an 'Elvis taxon'.

North America and northern Eurasia (including Siberia):
woolly mammoth (EX since about 1700 BCE)

Spain and Portugal:
Iberian lynx (CR, the world's most
threatened species of cat)

Costa Rica:
golden toad (EX since 1989, as a
result, it is believed, of climate
change)

Hawaii:
Hawaiian crow (EW since 2002)

Galapagos Islands:
Pinta Island tortoise (EW)

Colombia:
painted frog (CR, a Lazarus species,
believed to be extinct in the 1990s,
but spotted in 2006)

Around the world: extinctions and endangered species

For more information, see <www.redlist.org>.

Falkland Islands:
Falkland Islands wolf (EX since 1876)

China:
baiji—the Yangtze River freshwater dolphin (CR according to the 2007 Red List, which notes that it may already be extinct)

Caspian and Black seas and occasionally the Adriatic Sea: Beluga sturgeon (EN)

North Africa:
Barbary lion (also called Atlas lion and Nubian lion) (EW)

Guam:
Guam rail (EW since 1980)

Indonesian island of Sumatra:
Sumatran tiger (CR) and Sumatran orang-utan (CR)

Mauritius:
dodo bird (EX since the mid–late seventeenth century)

Australia:
greater bilby (VU) and lesser bilby (EX since the 1950s

New Zealand:
New Zealand flax snail (VU)

Energy

When you sit by a sunny window on a cold winter's day, you're enjoying the heat energy from the sun (just be careful of the ultraviolet rays that come with it). When you toast a marshmallow over an open fire, you're using heat energy converted from the stored energy in the wood. The energy in the food you eat is stored energy too, originally produced by plants using the energy of the sun. Energy is constantly changing in form and is being used all around us, every day, with or without the flicking of switches.

What is energy?

Scientists describe energy as the ability of a body or system to do work. Unfortunately, this is demonstrated all too well by our lack of 'energy' (as in 'the ability to do work') at precisely 9 a.m. on Monday mornings.

Energy comes in a variety of different forms, which can be divided into two types, **potential** and **kinetic**.

Potential energy

Potential energy is stored energy, such as the 'plant power' energy stored in fossil fuels. The different forms of potential energy are:

- **chemical energy**
  This is the energy stored in the bonds between atoms and molecules. When these bonds are broken, energy is released. Natural gas and other fossil fuels are examples of stored chemical energy, as

is the 'spare tyre' of fat around your Uncle Bob's waist.

- **nuclear energy**
  This is the energy that holds the nucleus of an atom together. Energy is released both when nuclei are split apart (nuclear fission) and when they are combined together (nuclear fusion).
- **stored mechanical energy**
  When you compress a spring, you are storing mechanical energy. Stored mechanical energy is produced when you apply a force or pressure to certain objects or materials.
- **gravitational energy**
  What goes up must come down—we have gravity to thank for that. Any object that has a weight (in other words, pretty much everything) can gain gravitational potential energy when it's moved to a higher place. The law of gravity means that the object can potentially do work on its way back down. Hydroelectric power plants harness gravitational energy by halting the flow of water downhill with a dam.

Kinetic energy

Kinetic energy is the energy of motion (or movement), including the motion of huge waves down to the motion of atoms and electrons. The different forms of kinetic energy are:

- **electrical energy**
  This is the energy produced by the movement of electrons. Electrons are tiny charged particles that, together with protons and neutrons, make up atoms.

Some electrons can move when a force is applied.
The flow of electrons through a wire is called electricity.
Another example of electrical energy is lightning.

- **motion energy**
  This is the energy from the movement of objects or
  substances from one place to another. Wind energy
  is one example.

- **radiant energy**
  Radiant energy is the energy from electromagnetic
  radiation, such as visible light, X-rays, radio waves and
  gamma rays (yes, they're the rays that turned David Banner
  into the *Incredible Hulk*—but remember, it's fiction!).
  Radiant energy moves in *transverse* waves (think of
  transverse and longitudinal waves as differently shaped
  waves, and therefore able to move in different ways).
  Solar energy is a form of radiant energy.

- **heat energy**
  Do you get hot when you're dancing or doing exercise?
  It turns out that atoms and molecule also produce heat
  when they jiggle. Also known as thermal energy, heat
  energy is the internal energy (or inside energy) of
  substances, produced by the movement or vibration
  of the atoms and molecules within. It's felt as heat.

- **sound energy**
  Sound is the movement of energy through substances in
  longitudinal waves. The vibration of an object produces
  sound.

Energy rules

Even energy has to obey the laws of the universe. The law of conservation of
energy says that the universe always has the same amount of energy. None is
lost, but it can change from one form to another. One object can lose energy, but
this lost energy is gained by another object or system. For example, a light bulb
converts electrical energy to heat energy. Some of the heat is converted to light
energy, while some is lost to the surrounding air and objects.

Energy and the environment

Energy is one of the greatest global green issues. Why? Because energy is so useful: we use it to make our lives easier, to keep our cities thriving and to make food and products. It's also part of how businesses make money. Some of our energy comes from things such as oil and coal, of which the planet doesn't have endless supplies. Some countries even fight wars over the ownership of energy resources such as oil reserves. Plus, many kinds of energy can harm the environment through the way we extract and use them. The planet has uneven supplies of energy resources, just as it has uneven supplies of water. Some countries have many rivers, making hydroelectricity a possibility, while others have large reserves of fossil fuels that offer the temptation of cheap power, despite its environmental problems. It is not surprising that energy is a hot topic.

Where does our energy come from?

Think about the energy you use in your life. You use electricity in your home and school to power lights, computers, TVs, washing machines, fridges and other devices. Your household might also use natural gas, liquid petroleum gas (LPG) or wood in a wood heater to provide heat. The bus or car that takes you to school, the shops, friends' houses and other places needs energy too, which comes from fuels such as petrol, LPG, diesel fuel and occasionally natural gas. With greener products and technologies starting to take off, you might even get electricity for use in the home or energy to heat your household hot water from the sun, using solar systems.

Have you ever stopped to wonder where this energy comes from?

- **Petrol, diesel** and **LPG** are made from oil, which is basically concentrated, stored chemical energy. Oil comes from plants and animals that lived in the oceans millions of years ago, even before dinosaurs. This organic matter lay buried under layers of mud. Heat and pressure turned it into liquid crude oil. Oil wells are drilled into the earth to extract this.

- **Natural gas** is a mixture of gases (mostly methane) that, like oil, comes from organic matter that has been compressed and heated over hundreds of millions of years. It is also tapped from the earth via wells.

- **Wood** used in wood heaters generally comes from trees through forestry operations. Sometimes these trees were grown in plantations specifically for the purpose; sometimes the wood is logged from areas of natural vegetation.

- **Coal**, a solid fossil fuel, can also be used in solid-fuel heaters and barbecues. It is mined from the earth's crust.

- **Electricity** comes from a range of sources. It can come from the flow of a river in hydroelectric schemes, from burning fossil fuels extracted from the earth, from wind turbines, from solar power stations or rooftop solar cells, or even from nuclear reactors powered by uranium mined from the earth.

You could say that our energy, in simple terms, comes from the environment. And it also has an impact on the environment.

Energy now: the current global situation

There are now around 6.7 billion of us on earth, all wanting energy for cooking, for providing light and heating, and, in more developed countries, to power our fabulous lifestyles. Fossil fuels provide over 80 per cent of the world's energy. However, fossil fuel supplies are not limitless. The extraction of fossil fuels from the earth's crust has an environmental impact, harming habitats and contributing to erosion and pollution. Burning fossil fuels also produces air pollution, causing breathing problems in

humans, harming wildlife and causing acid rain. The biggest problem is that the fossil fuels we currently use produce greenhouse gases, which are contributing to global warming and changing the climate.

After the Industrial Revolution, cities such as London became dark and hazy from the smog and soot of burning fuel. We're now producing more pollution and greenhouse gases than in these early industrial years, even though we're now using fossil fuels more efficiently and cleanly. This is because the sheer size of the global population and the scale of industry have increased so dramatically over the past century, and with it the demand for energy has increased. In the future, this demand will continue to increase; former developing nations will become more developed and the global population will continue to climb. There is now an undeniable need for long-term, cleaner, renewable sources of energy.

Where the world's energy comes from

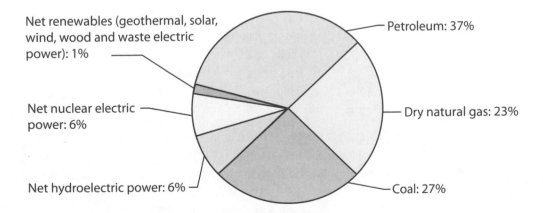

Source: Energy Information Administration, *International Energy Annual 2005*, US Department of Energy, Washington, 2005.

Energy: electricity

What is electricity?

Electricity is the energy created by the movement of charged particles, such as electrons. It's the flow of electric charge through materials called conductors. Many metals are good electrical conductors, which is why our electricity comes through metal wires.

The ability of electricity to flow through wires and other conductors makes it a very flexible and useful form of energy—much easier and more convenient than lugging kerosene for lamps or coal for heating from house to house.

How does electricity get around?

Most Australian homes get their electricity through the national grid network—a network of powerlines that carries electricity from where it is produced and distributes it to the users. Electricity from both coal-fired power stations and from greener, renewable sources supplies local areas, with the remainder fed into the grid system. Once fed into the grid, electricity from greener sources is indistinguishable from that produced by more polluting methods.

Zap!

Have you ever given yourself an electric shock by rubbing your feet on the carpet, then touching a metal door handle? When two surfaces rub together, they build up a separation of positive and negative charge. Electric charge doesn't like to build up, so it looks for a conductor to provide a pathway for it to discharge. The metal door handle provides the means for the charge to escape from your body, so you feel the discharge as a small electric shock.

Lightning is a huge bolt of electricity produced by a thunderstorm. Tiny droplets of ice within a cloud bump together, collectively producing a huge build up of charge. The lightning you see flash across the sky is a huge amount of electricity discharging from a cloud to the earth or to another cloud. Lightning can be quite useful—it produces ozone in the atmosphere to protect us from ultraviolet rays. Lightning can have up to a billion volts, and contains billions of watts. Unfortunately, it is too unpredictable and produces too much power at once for us to capture it and turn it into power for our homes.

Energy to electricity: lost in translation

One of the problems with Australia's electricity is that a lot of it comes from coal-fired power stations, delivered by the grid over great distances to our homes. Some of the processes in using coal to make electricity need energy, which reduces the overall amount produced. Plus, some energy is lost along the way, for example, dissipated as heat. Of the original amount of energy stored in the coal, about a third gets through to our homes.

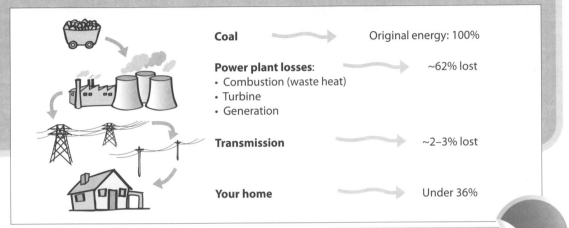

Coal	→	Original energy: 100%
Power plant losses: • Combustion (waste heat) • Turbine • Generation	→	~62% lost
Transmission	→	~2–3% lost
Your home	→	Under 36%

From sunlight to lamp light

Imagine a ray of sunshine sending energy from the sun to the earth millions of years ago. The energy was absorbed by a green plant and, through photosynthesis, was turned into stored plant energy. The plant died and was buried with other organic matter. With time, heat and pressure, it became coal. More recently, it was dug up by a mining company and transported to a power station, where the coal was burned, turning the stored energy into heat energy and releasing greenhouse gases. The heat turned water into steam, which, rising up in the air, pushed a turbine. The turning of this turbine transformed the energy into flowing electrons, or electricity. This electrical energy flowed through powerlines, eventually into a home, where it turned into light energy inside a lamp.

Imagine another ray of sunshine, but not so long ago. The heat energy of the sunshine fell on the ocean, evaporating some water, which rose up into the atmosphere as vapour. At a certain height it became part of a cloud, drifting over the ocean and eventually over land. On reaching the Snowy Mountains in Australia, the cloud lifted and produced some rain, so that our bit of water returned to the earth by falling on the mountains and flowing into the Snowy River. With the help of gravity, it flowed downhill through the Snowy Mountains Hydro-electric Scheme, where it helped push a turbine. This turbine also produced electricity, which flowed through powerlines to light a lamp in another home.

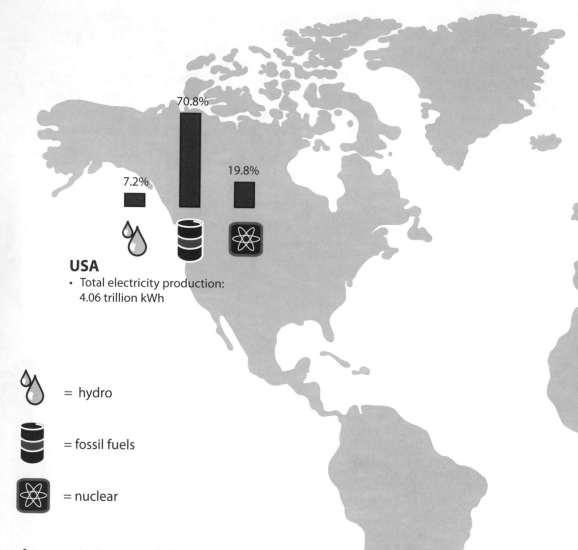

70.8%

7.2%

19.8%

USA
- Total electricity production:
  4.06 trillion kWh

= hydro

= fossil fuels

= nuclear

Around the world: electricity sources

Electricity is an important and convenient source of power in homes, businesses, factories and buildings all around the world. It can come from a variety of sources, such as flowing water (hydroelectricity), nuclear power plants, burning fossil fuels (such as natural gas, coal and oil), burning rubbish, and even the sun (using photovoltaic cells). Here is a look at a number of different countries and their main sources of electricity.

Note: the remaining percentages are other sources too small to note.

Source: based on records for the year 2005.

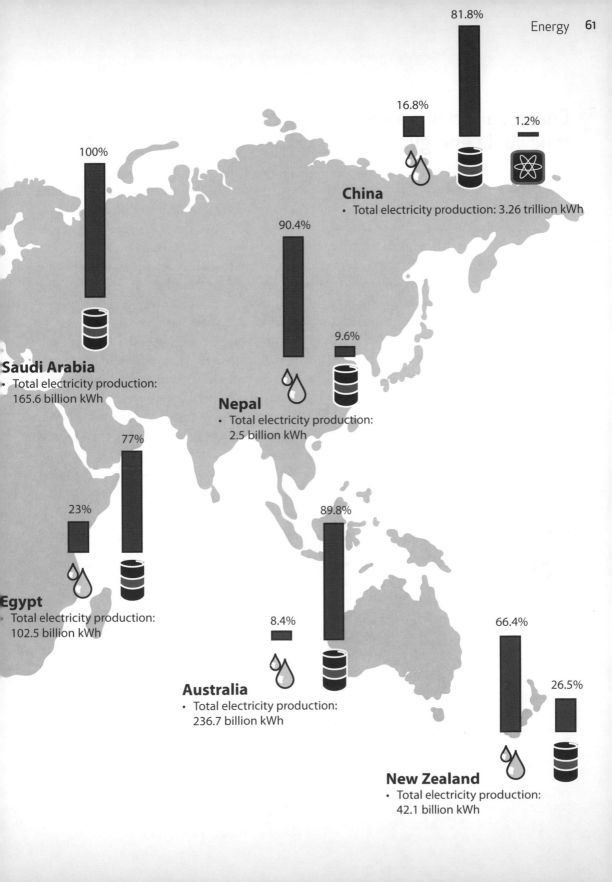

81.8%

16.8%

1.2%

China
- Total electricity production: 3.26 trillion kWh

100%

90.4%

Saudi Arabia
- Total electricity production:
  165.6 billion kWh

9.6%

Nepal
- Total electricity production:
  2.5 billion kWh

77%

23%

Egypt
- Total electricity production:
  102.5 billion kWh

89.8%

8.4%

Australia
- Total electricity production:
  236.7 billion kWh

66.4%

26.5%

New Zealand
- Total electricity production:
  42.1 billion kWh

Energy: alternative and renewable energy

Around the world, governments, corporations and consumers are dipping their toes into renewable energy. In the past, the domination of fossil fuels meant that many countries have had to buy the fuel for their power supplies from other countries. Few countries have been able to be self-reliant. Renewable energy brings a whole range of other options. For example, countries with large, powerful river systems are already harnessing the power of a river's current in hydroelectric plants. Similarly, windy coastlines are becoming dotted with wind farms, and countries that lie on geothermal belts, such as New Zealand, are experimenting with geothermal energy. Countries can look at their natural landscape and choose the option that best suits their natural conditions and economy. For the first time in decades, some are able to imagine a future where they have energy security and independence.

It's important to remember that renewable energy sources, while better than fossil fuels for the health of the planet, are not without their own environmental impacts. It's important that alternative energy sources are chosen well and carefully developed, so that the solution to our energy problem doesn't become a problem itself.

In basic terms, our homes, factories and buildings generally need energy in two forms. We need electricity to power equipment and lighting. We need heat to make our homes warm, to cook with and to provide hot water. Renewable energy options can provide heat directly, use heat to produce electricity or produce electricity directly. Here is a look at the major renewable energy options.

Did you know ... ?

- The *Vanguard 1* was launched into space in 1958, becoming the first satellite to produce its own electricity from the sun using solar cells.
- Homebush Bay, the site of the athletes' village of the Sydney 2000 Olympic Games, is one of the world's largest solar-powered suburbs.
- The roof of Melbourne's Queen Victoria Market is covered with green, electricity-producing solar photovoltaic panels.

Did you know ... ?

- Leading wind-power nations include Germany, the USA, Denmark, Spain and India.
- The latitudes 40–50° South of the equator are among the world's windiest places. There is lots of ocean for wind to blow over and very little land to slow it down. These latitudes are called the roaring forties. Tasmania is one of the few land masses within the roaring forties, giving it great potential for producing wind energy.

Solar

Solar energy can be captured and used to provide heating and to generate power. The main types of solar energy technology are:

- **solar thermal collectors**, which collect heat (like a solar hot water system on a roof)
- **photovoltaic (PV) cells**, which produce electricity directly from sunlight. These are often small systems, producing enough electricity for the needs of a single product, a home, a building or a community
- **solar thermal power stations**, which use huge mirrors to reflect the sun's energy and concentrate it on a single point. The heat generated at this point is used to produce steam or convection currents to drive turbines for electricity generation.

Wind

Anyone who has been caught outdoors on a windy day knows the power of wind. As well as driving windmills and wind turbines, wind has the power to fill sails and move huge ships. Windmills have been used for centuries to pump water and grind grain. Modern wind turbines harness wind power and turn it into electricity.

Hydro

The movement of water can also be used to drive turbines and produce electricity in hydroelectric power plants. There are two main types of hydroelectric scheme:

- **Impoundment** hydroelectric schemes use dams to limit the water flow and store the water, releasing it according to the demand for electricity.
- '**Run-of-river**' hydroelectric schemes are smaller installations that don't require large dams and so have less impact on the local environment.

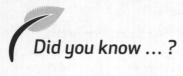

Did you know ... ?   Inland rivers aren't the only water bodies that can produce power. Scientists and engineers are developing ways of harnessing the power of ocean waves and tides. For example, wave-power projects are under way near Port Kembla, New South Wales, and in Portland, Victoria.

Biomass

Biomass is the name given to all living and dead plant and animal matter. Biomass energy, like fossil fuels, is energy from living things, which capture and store solar energy. While fossil fuels provide stored solar energy from hundreds of millions of years ago, biomass fuels provide more recently stored solar energy. Energy from biomass includes electricity produced from biomass-fuelled power stations, liquid fuels from plant oils and alcohols, and even gas from decomposing organic matter, such as methane gas extracted from landfills. The main types of biofuel are wood, alcohol fermented from plants, plant oils (biodiesel) and biogas.

Geothermal

Geothermal energy is heat energy from deep inside the earth. The source of this heat is the earth's core itself, where the natural radioactive decay of the core materials causes temperatures to reach up to 6000°C (10 800°F). Molten rock and steam from beneath the earth's crust can escape through the cracks where the continental plates meet. Water can seep into these cracks, where it is heated. Heat, steam and molten rock escape to the surface as volcanic eruptions, geysers, hot springs and fumaroles. This activity is known as geothermal activity, and the areas with high surface temperature or 'high-grade' geothermal activity are often referred to as geothermal belts. The heat can be piped directly to homes and buildings, or it can be used in power stations to produce electricity.

Hydrogen

Hydrogen combines with oxygen in a fuel cell to make water and energy. Imagine that: a carbon-free energy source that only produces water or steam as a by-product!

Energy: go with the flow

Renewable energy sources are those that can be renewed by the cycles of nature, such as solar energy, hydro and biomass. Non-renewable energy sources are those that are lost once used: we can't get them back again, so they will eventually run out. Fossil fuels and nuclear energy are non-renewable.

Some experts have defined a special category within renewable energy resources. They are 'flow resources'. These are the energy sources that flow freely and quickly through the environment and that can be immediately tapped into. These are tidal and wave energy, ocean currents, wind, flowing water (rivers) and solar energy. These are distinct from other types of renewable energy, such as biomass, that require growth, harvesting, processing and extraction in varying degrees.

Renewable energy: pros and cons

Energy option	Pros	Cons
Solar	• It is limitless. • Solar power is available all around the world (the polar regions get their supplies in bulk). • It is a useful source of power for remote areas. • Solar power produces no greenhouse gases. • Once the initial cost of equipment is covered, ongoing power is free. • Passive solar energy can be used to heat homes, without the cost of photovoltaic cells. • Australia particularly has a lot of sunshine.	• High-tech solar systems using solar panels and photovoltaic cells are expensive to produce and set up. • Cloudy and overcast days can limit the amount of energy they produce. • Solar generators require a lot of space, which can sometimes be a problem.
Wind	• Once the initial cost of equipment is covered, ongoing power is free. • Wind, like sunshine, won't run out. • It is a useful source of power for remote areas. • Wind produces no greenhouse gases. • The land used for wind farms can be used for other purposes as well. In fact, leasing sites to wind energy companies can provide farmers with extra income, which may help them through tough times, such as drought.	• Wind speed can frequently change, and on some days there is no wind at all. • Windy areas tend to be on coastlines, where land value is often high. • Wind farms can be noisy. • It's believed that wind turbines can harm wildlife (particularly birds) and so can't be built near particular bird habitats. • Some people think that they're an eyesore, so local tourism operators may oppose them. Mind you, coal-fired power stations are bigger, uglier and more polluting!
Plant fuels	• Because fuel crops can be harvested and replenished, they are renewable. • Plant alcohols can be made from the waste parts of some crops and so make better use of our resources.	• Plant fuels are still polluting, though less so than fossil fuels. • Land used for growing fuel crops may one day be needed for producing food for our planet's growing population.

Energy option	Pros	Cons
Landfill gas (energy from rotting rubbish)	• Landfill can be considered a renewable resource (since we haven't yet stopped producing waste). • Landfill gas power plants capture and use the greenhouse gases produced by landfills, which would otherwise contribute to the greenhouse effect. • Collection and use of the gas reduces the odours in the area of the landfill. • Landfill gas power plants are very expensive to build.	• Landfill volumes will change as we change our waste-producing habits. • Much larger amounts of landfill gases are needed to produce electricity (compared with fossil fuels).
Hydro	• Once the initial cost of the hydroelectric power station is covered, ongoing power is relatively inexpensive. • Water can be stored, so it can be a more reliable power source. • Hydro produces less greenhouse gas and waste product. • Small-scale projects can be used instead of large-scale projects to reduce the environmental impacts.	• Large dams take up a lot of land, and they flood previously 'dry' areas, requiring fish, animals and sometimes people to relocate. • Hydroelectric schemes can greatly upset and disturb aquatic ecosystems. In particular, they can stop the migration of fish. • They reduce the flows in these river systems, causing environmental problems downstream.
Geothermal	• Once the initial cost of equipment and installation is covered, ongoing power is free. • Geothermal energy is renewable (since the molten core of the earth isn't going to cool down in the near future). • The capture of geothermal energy doesn't require a lot of land.	• Geothermal energy is restricted to areas with geothermal activity. • There is a limit to how much steam or water can be drawn from one geothermal site.
Hydrogen	• Hydrogen is a source of non-polluting carbon-free energy. The only by-product is water. • It is one of the most common elements in the universe.	• Hydrogen is difficult to concentrate and store. Storage tanks for liquid hydrogen are both costly and bulky.

Energy: fossil fuels

Renewable energy is hot, but fossil fuels are so last century! Fossil fuels are on their way out, both from an environmental and a long-term economic point of view. Business and industry know that supplies will eventually run out, so they're looking at the alternatives now. However, environmentally, we need to dramatically curb our use of fossil fuels, long before supplies dwindle. While we can see the 'bottom of the oil barrel' approaching, there's still enough oil left in the barrel, and enough gas and coal left in the ground, to seriously affect our planet's climate through the greenhouse effect.

Where do fossil fuels come from?

Fossil fuels are basically 'stored sunshine' from around 300 million years ago. Prehistoric plants and tiny phytoplankton captured this radiant solar energy with their chlorophyll and converted it into stored chemical energy in the compounds that made their tissues, exactly the same way that plants do today. The sea was full of a host of animals that fed on these tiny plants. As they died, the dead organic matter would fall to the sea floor, where they would slowly decompose through the action of bacteria. Clays and silts were deposited on top. Little by little, more layers were added, and old layers became compacted into rock. Over time, the pressure of the many layers of earth above and the occasional dinosaur stampede, along with a build-up of heat and further decomposition, caused the organic matter to be converted into a range of compounds called 'hydrocarbons'. They are called hydrocarbons because they are mostly, if not entirely, made up of just hydrogen and carbon and take the form of oil and natural gas. Coal is formed in a similar way. Although fossil fuels come from organic matter, they are referred to as 'mineral' resources because they come from the earth's crust.

How coal was formed

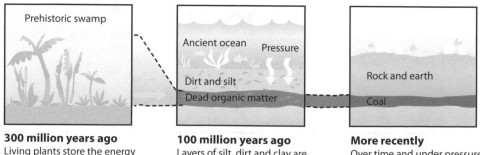

300 million years ago
Living plants store the energy of prehistoric sunshine. When they die, they form a layer of rotting dead plant matter at the bottom of the swamp.

100 million years ago
Layers of silt, dirt and clay are deposited over the layer of dead organic matter. The weight of these layers and earth movement puts pressure on the layer of organic matter.

More recently
Over time and under pressure, the compressed organic matter becomes coal.

How oil and natural gas were formed

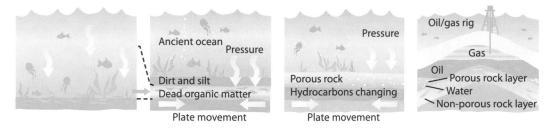

300–400 million years ago
Marine plants and animals die and float to the ocean floor.

50–100 million years ago
Layers of silt, dirt and clay are deposited over the layer of dead organic matter. Over time and under pressure, these layers compress. The hydrocarbons in the organic matter change. Movement in the earth's crust adds pressure and changes the shape of the layers.

More recently
Oil and gas have formed, trapped in layers of porous rock, sealed between layers of non-porous rock. Oil, being lighter than water, floats above it, and gas rises to the top.

What is wrong with fossil fuels?

Although there are large fossil fuel reserves remaining, pollution and the potential contribution to the greenhouse effect should limit how much we use. Mining also causes major damage to ecosystems. There is also the competing need for coal to make steel. Similarly, plastics and a host of other materials are made from oil. Natural gas is the cleanest of the fossil fuels, but there is less of it, and it is still a non-renewable resource and a fuel that contributes to the greenhouse effect.

Politically, many countries don't want to rely on oil from the Middle East, where there are often wars and conflict. In the late 1960s and early 1970s, many of the oil-producing nations, such as Kuwait, Iraq, Venezuela and Saudi Arabia, joined together to form OPEC (the Organization of the Petroleum Exporting Countries). Together, the OPEC nations controlled oil production, and in 1973, pushed the price of oil from US$3 a barrel to US$11. Since then, war in the oil-rich Middle East has lead to a series of oil crises, resulting in oil-supply shortages and price increases. So the move towards renewable energy in some countries is politically motivated. Also, there is rapidly growing demand for fuel from countries such as India and China, which are quickly shifting from reliance on agriculture to money from manufacturing and industry.

We need to see a major increase in the use of alternative energy sources to secure the future of our planet and the life on it. Environmentally and politically, when it comes to power, green is definitely the new black.

Energy: nuclear

Nuclear energy is one hugely contentious option. It is not considered a renewable energy source because it relies on limited resources for fuel, such as uranium. The main benefit of nuclear fuels is that they are not fossil fuels and do not contribute to air pollution and the greenhouse effect. Some people venture to call nuclear energy a 'clean' source of energy. I'd bet any money that these people don't live near Chernobyl.

What is nuclear energy?

Atoms are made up of tiny particles. In the centre of the atom is the nucleus, made up of particles called proton and neutrons. Electrons circle around the nucleus. When the nuclei of atoms are changed, huge amounts of heat energy are produced. This heat is used to produce steam, which in turn is used to make electricity.

And now for the bad news …

Nuclear power plants use uranium as the fuel. Uranium mining produces large amounts of 'tailings', the excavated rock left over once the valued ore is removed. These tailings contain over 80 per cent of the radioactivity of the original unmined ore. While the public and media focus on the problems of disposing of radioactive waste from spent reactor fuel, there are millions of tonnes of exposed radioactive tailings left at uranium mines. The wind disperses them and rainfall leaches them into the groundwater.

Many naturally occurring substances are radioactive. Even without human interference, there is always a small, generally safe amount of 'background' radioactivity in nature. However, the advent of nuclear power has produced radioactivity in dangerous quantities. The radioactivity of both the mining waste and the spent reactor waste is a huge risk to environmental health. There are complicated procedures and protection measures that need to be undertaken in order to minimise this risk. The waste must first be sealed in aluminium foil to block alpha and beta radiation, then sealed in lead to block X-ray radiation from escaping; finally, it must be sealed in a thick layer of concrete to block the gamma radiation.

Exposure to uranium and other sources of radioactivity have been linked with cancer and other major health problems. Nuclear energy is only truly a viable option if:

- adequate solutions can be found to clean up uranium mining sites
- we find better ways to take care of radioactive waste
- we find ways to make reactors accident-proof and human-proof. Nuclear accidents can and have happened, with serious results.

Even meeting these needs, nuclear energy is at best a 'bridging technology': there is a limited amount of nuclear fuel in the ground. This could buy humans more time, but renewable energy sources are still the best option for our long-term future.

Think about it

What happens when a nuclear reactor or any other power station reaches its use-by date? It is 'decommissioned', a process in which it is dismantled and any remaining health risks are removed or contained. The presence of radioactive material makes the decommissioning of nuclear power stations more difficult and expensive.

Chernobyl

On 26 April 1986, there was a major accident at the Chernobyl nuclear reactor in northern Ukraine. Operational errors and inadequate safety precautions resulted in a sudden increase in heat generation, rupturing part of the nuclear fuel. The reactor was not encased in a concrete containment vessel. The ruptured fuel particles caused two steam explosions, which destroyed the Unit 4 reactor core and blew off the roof of the building. Firefighters extinguished the original fires, but another fire began and was not extinguished for ten days.

The reactor meltdown, the explosions and the fire sent a huge, poisonous, highly radioactive cloud over Belarus, Ukraine and parts of Russia. Traces of radiation were found as far away as the Antarctic.

It was the worst nuclear accident in history, causing thousands of deaths (though the exact numbers are hotly debated) and making vast areas of farmland useless. The US Department of Energy estimates that 4.9 million people were exposed to radiation. Chernobyl and its nearby towns are now virtually deserted.

Energy use in the home

Most of the energy we use in our homes comes directly from burning fuel such as firewood or natural gas, or indirectly in the form of electricity. In Australia, over 90 per cent of electricity is generated by burning coal, another fossil fuel. By comparison, two-thirds of New Zealand's electricity is generated by hydroelectric schemes. Why save energy? Because we need to cut our greenhouse gas emissions. Plus your parents won't mind having smaller energy bills.

With recent talk of climate change and rising energy prices, we've become more aware of how much energy we use and the need to use less. There are many things that you can do to save energy. The bonus is that saving energy will save your family money. Start by thinking about where you use energy in your home:

Energy use in the home

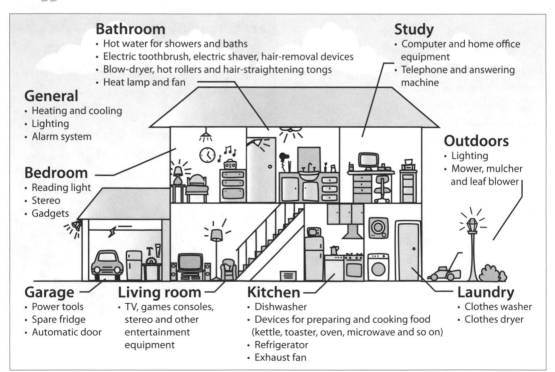

Bathroom
- Hot water for showers and baths
- Electric toothbrush, electric shaver, hair-removal devices
- Blow-dryer, hot rollers and hair-straightening tongs
- Heat lamp and fan

Study
- Computer and home office equipment
- Telephone and answering machine

General
- Heating and cooling
- Lighting
- Alarm system

Outdoors
- Lighting
- Mower, mulcher and leaf blower

Bedroom
- Reading light
- Stereo
- Gadgets

Garage
- Power tools
- Spare fridge
- Automatic door

Living room
- TV, games consoles, stereo and other entertainment equipment

Kitchen
- Dishwasher
- Devices for preparing and cooking food (kettle, toaster, oven, microwave and so on)
- Refrigerator
- Exhaust fan

Laundry
- Clothes washer
- Clothes dryer

Eco-action: what *you* can do to save energy

- Take shorter showers, even if you've got a solar hot water system, as they usually use gas or electricity as a back-up energy supply.

- Limit your screen time. Electronic games and TV all need electricity.

- To reduce standby power use, turn the TV and other entertainment equipment off at the wall instead of using the remote control.

- Turn the light off when you leave a room.

- Let your hair dry naturally instead of blow-drying it.

- Don't spend ages browsing the fridge with the door open, letting all the cold air out.

- Wear a jumper instead of turning the heating up.

- Get a rooster instead of an electric alarm clock to wake you up (just kidding).

- On your computer, use the screen sleep and other energy-saving features, instead of using a screen saver.

Learn more

To find out what standby power use is, turn to page 96.

High energy and low energy options

High energy	Low energy
Desktop computers	Laptop computers
Incandescent lights	Compact fluorescent lights
Airconditioners	Fan/evaporative cooling
Clothes dryer	Clothes line
Hair dryer	Towel-drying hair
Vacuum cleaner	Broom, dustpan and hand brush
Leaf blower	Rake

Eco-activity: do an energy audit quiz

Are you an energy guzzler, or are you lean and green with your energy use? Take the quiz and find out.

1 *What happens when you're not using your computer?*

   a *You turn it off.*

   b *It will go to sleep—you've set it up to do so.*

   c *It sits there with the screen lit, perhaps with a screen saver going.*

2 *How do you dry your hair?*

   a *I get most of the water off with a towel, then I forget about it.*

   b *I blow-dry it if it's cold or if I'm about to go out.*

   c *I blow dry it every day, then tong it.*

3 *Do you have a second fridge?*

   a *No.*

   b *Yes, but we only turn it on when we have a party or extra people staying.*

   c *Yes, it's in the garage and on all the time.*

4 *What do you do when you have spare time?*

   a *I read or play sport.*

   b *I do a range of things, some indoors and some outdoors, with a bit of TV.*

   c *I play my PlayStation or watch TV.*

5 *How do you get yourself clean?*

   a *I take a short daily shower.*

   b *I take a bath or a long shower.*

   c *I have a shower in the morning to wake myself up and one at night to wash off the day's sweat.*

6 *How to you get to school?*

   a *I walk or ride my bike.*

   b *I catch the bus.*

   c *I go by car.*

7 *What's your secret for a snugly, warm bed?*

   a *I use blankets, plus a hot water bottle or heated wheat bag when it's really cold.*

   b *I turn an electric blanket on for a few minutes before getting into bed.*

   c *I use an electric blanket, and I turn the heater on in my room.*

8 *What do you do on a hot day?*

   a *I close the blinds to block out the heat and head for the beach or the local pool. Yay! Or I cool down with a cold drink in the shade.*

   b *I turn on a fan or evaporative cooler.*

   c *I crank up the airconditioning to full arctic blast!*

How did you score?

- *Mostly a's: You're **eco-cool**! You deserve a hug from a panda bear.*

- *Mostly b's—You're **green around the edges**. You're making an effort but there's room for improvement.*

- *Mostly c's—You're **eco-challenged**. But don't worry—being green is easier than you think. Try the eco-action ideas throughout this book.*

Household energy and the greenhouse effect

Different sorts of energy produce differing amounts of greenhouse gas emissions. The following graph shows where energy is used in the average Australian home and how this is related to household greenhouse emissions. You'll see that heating and cooling use a lot of energy but seem to produce fewer greenhouse emissions than you would expect. This is because a lot of heating is done using natural gas, which is less 'greenhouse intensive' than electricity on average in Australia. Similarly, appliances and lighting represent about a third of the energy use but half the emissions resulting from it. This is because most appliances run on greenhouse-intensive electricity.

Energy use and emissions

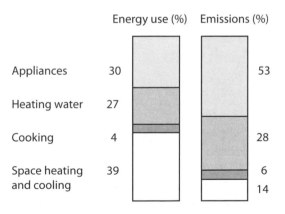

	Energy use (%)	Emissions (%)
Appliances	30	53
Heating water	27	
Cooking	4	28
Space heating and cooling	39	6
		14

Instead of electricity from polluting fossil fuels, people can choose electricity from government-accredited GreenPower sources. An amount equivalent to your household's electricity use is sourced from cleaner, renewable sources, such as wind and solar power, and put into the grid.

Home energy systems

Another option for household electricity is to make your own using solar photovoltaic systems, a mini wind turbine or a mini hydro system (if your property has a river or large creek running through or past it). These electricity systems can be connected to the grid or completely separate from it.

- **Off-the-grid power systems** store excess electricity in a battery so that it can be used in times of low output. They are sometimes used on caravans and mobile homes.
- **Grid-connected systems** allow the electricity grid to provide back-up electricity supplies when your home's system isn't supplying enough to meet the needs of the moment. Conversely, any electricity produced that isn't immediately needed in the house is fed into the grid. If you use more electricity than your system produces, you pay your retailer only for the net difference. However, if you use less electricity than your system produces, you might be able to send a bill to your electricity provider for it!

Energy efficiency

Efficiency is defined as the ability to do something well without wasting effort or energy. Take your parents, for example. One may take ages to wash the dishes, while the other seems to do them more quickly. One is more time efficient than the other. (Or maybe someone is trying to get out of doing them!)

Energy efficiency relates to how much energy is needed to do a task and to whether it can be done as well with less energy. Lighting is a good example. Old-fashioned incandescent light bulbs use electricity to produce light. They pass electricity through a filament, heating it until it gets so hot that it produces visible light. However, much of the energy is wasted as dissipated heat. In contrast, compact fluorescent lights use electricity to get the atoms in mercury vapour to get so excited that they produce invisible short-wave ultraviolet light, which then makes phosphorescent materials in the lamp produce visible light. In both cases the outcome is the same—light is produced—but the compact fluorescent lamp has done the job using 80 per cent less electricity than the filament light bulb.

There are two sides to energy efficiency: the technology and the way you use it.

Efficient technology: Energy Rating labels

Like the lighting example, there is a range of technologies that can do similar jobs using varying amounts of energy. But how do you tell a guzzler from a green machine? There is an Energy Rating label program in Australia and New Zealand that tests and identifies the efficiency of appliances, such as dishwashers, airconditioners, washing machines, dryers and fridges.

Eco-activity: find the greenest and meanest machines

The government Energy Rating labelling program for appliances has a website that allows you to see the tested energy efficiency of various appliances, see how much energy they typically use, and estimate how much money they will add to power bills over their lifetime. Visit <www.energyrating.gov.au/appsearch/> and see if you can find out the difference between the best and worst in a product category.

Efficient habits

Efficient electrical goods are only part of the answer. How efficient they are in practice depends on how you use them. For example, if you use a heater while the window is open, it will need to use more power to replace the heat lost out of the window. Use common sense when using electricity, and look after your gadgets and keep them clean so that they can run more efficiently.

Energy in products

When you have a piece of cake, you're actually consuming energy. Some of that energy was used to bake the cake. But it needed more energy than that to come into existence. In fact, that piece of cake has 'embodied energy' as well as calories and lots of sugar.

Embodied energy is the total energy needed to produce a product. It is also known as 'embedded energy' or 'virtual energy'. It includes the energy needed to mine or grow its raw materials, refine them and manufacture them into a finished product, as well the energy used in any transportation needed along the way. This might include the fuel powering machinery that extracts iron ore, or electricity used to power sewing machines in a clothing factory. By adding in the greenhouse emissions of these different uses of energy, experts can also measure the embodied greenhouse emissions of a product or its 'total carbon footprint'. To get an idea of a product's true greenhouse impact, you have to count all of the greenhouse emissions from basic raw materials to finished product.

Embodied energy is becoming an important consideration as we start to tackle climate change. With many countries now considering carbon trading and carbon taxes, materials with a high embodied energy will become more expensive to discourage people from using them.

Embodied energy in building materials

Think about your house. It's a huge product made of a lot of different materials, and of all the things your family has, it probably has the greatest total embodied energy. Builders and architects are starting to think about embodied energy when choosing materials. Here is a quick look at the embodied energy of some building materials.

Material	Embodied energy
(megajoules per kilogram)	
Sawn hardwood dried in a kiln	2.0
Air-dried sawn hardwood	0.5
Particleboard	8.0
Plastics (general)	90.0
Synthetic rubber	110.0
Imported dimension granite	13.9
Local dimension granite	5.9
Glass	12.7
Aluminium	170.0
Copper	100.0

Eco-action: cut embodied energy

You don't have to be an energy expert to cut your embodied energy. All products need energy, water and material resources to be made. You can make a difference by simply buying and consuming less stuff! Also, recycling things such as glass, aluminium and steel greatly reduces the embodied energy of the products made from them, so keep recycling.

Environmentalism

Environmentalism is the active involvement of people in efforts to solve environmental problems. The environmental movement is the collective efforts of people at a community level to bring about the protection of the environment. People who are leaders or are particularly active in eco-efforts are often called 'environmentalists'. Environmentalism also aims to give a voice to the natural world in the arena of human affairs.

In the past, people have thought of environmentalism as being all about protests, boycotts, fights between activists and companies or governments, and conflict. This confrontational type of environmentalism was important because it brought public attention to environmental issues of which many people were unaware. For example, many people wouldn't know about the practices of Japanese 'scientific' whaling programs if not for the loud and controversial protesting of anti-whaling groups.

But this aggressive approach to environmentalism is just one of many. Just as there are many shades of the colour green, there are many different types of greenie. More recently we've seen 'mainstream' environmentalism, in which ordinary people, who probably wouldn't describe themselves as 'greenies', are actively trying to reduce their impact and getting involved in conservation efforts. There are also 'free-market' environmentalists, who believe that money, property rights and the free market are tools that can solve environmental problems. Some other types of environmentalist disagree.

Learn more

See the section at the end of this book (pages 214–15) for a list of environment groups and their web addresses.

Environment groups

Environment groups are an important feature of environmentalism. They are generally non-profit organisations (as opposed to money-making businesses) made up of people who want to make a difference and have a common environmental focus. For example, The Wilderness Society is particularly concerned with the conservation of native forests, while the Surfrider Foundation focuses on protecting the world's oceans, beaches and waves. People can get information and advice from environmental groups, become members or volunteer to join in with their activities.

Celebrity greenies: who did what?

Match the celebrity to his or her environmental efforts.

1 Cate Blanchett

2 Hayden Panettiere

3 Ian Thorpe

4 Leonardo DiCaprio

5 John Butler

6 HRH Prince Charles

7 Brad Pitt

8 Olivia Newton-John

a made a documentary about water issues

b planted 10 000 trees on his or her property

c is renovating his or her Sydney mansion to make it greener

d has an organic farm that produces a range of organic products, with proceeds going to charity

e was arrested for protesting against Japanese whaling operations

f likes his or her Prius hybrid car so much that he or she bought one for his or her mother

g got involved in an initiative to build affordable eco-housing as part of the rebuilding of New Orleans after it was hit by Hurricane Katrina

h joined a tree-sit to protest against old-growth logging in Tasmania

Answers: 1c, 2e, 3a, 4f, 5h, 6d, 7g, 8b

Australian environment groups

- Australian Conservation Foundation
- Australian Marine Conservation Society
- Clean Up Australia
- Keep Australia Beautiful
- Landcare Australia
- Planet Ark
- The Wilderness Society
- Trees for Life
- Wildlife Warriors

International environment groups

- Fauna & Flora International
- Forest Stewardship Council
- Friends of the Earth
- Greenpeace
- Sierra Club
- World Conservation Union
- Worldwatch Institute
- WWF

E-waste

Over 70 per cent of all Australian households now have a computer, and nearly two-thirds use the Internet at home. In Australia, we've seen rapid uptake of new technology, from VCRs to iPods to DVD players. In fact, Australia is one of the top countries in the world in terms of spending on communication and information technology as a percentage of income. In short, we love spending money on gadgets. It's 'out with the old and in with the new'.

The problem is that the more electronic goods we consume, the more electronic waste we send to landfill. 'E-waste' (short for 'electronic waste') consists of our old or unwanted electronic goods and is one of the fastest growing waste types. New electronic equipment technology is constantly being developed; it quickly goes to market and is quickly bought, and we are keeping such products for shorter and shorter periods of time.

So just what do you do with a computer that you no longer need? Give it away? Trash it? Recycle it?

In Australia, we're good at recycling through council collections. The materials collected through these programs are largely simple materials—such as glass, aluminium and mixed paper—that can be easily sorted and reused. The problem with electronic waste and many other products is that they are

Eco-action: recycle your e-waste

Find out if you can recycle computers, mobile phones and printer cartridges in your area. Visit <www.recyclingnearyou.com.au> and type in your suburb or postcode.

made from a huge range of component materials that can't be used until the product is pulled apart and the component materials separated—usually a very difficult and expensive process.

Computers and other electronic equipment are made from hundreds of different materials. Many of these materials are valuable, such as gold and platinum, and many are non-renewable. If they can be extracted they can be recycled. It's difficult, but it can be done.

There are also some nasties in e-waste. Heavy metals including lead, cadmium, mercury and arsenic are used in electronic equipment. Brominated flame retardants used in computer equipment are also an environmental health threat. Printer inks and toners often contain toxic materials such as carbon black and cadmium. It is these environmental health implications that have put e-waste under the spotlight of international governments and environmentalists alike.

Did you know ... ?   Australians produce an estimated 140 000 tonnes of e-waste each year, but only about 4 per cent is recycled.

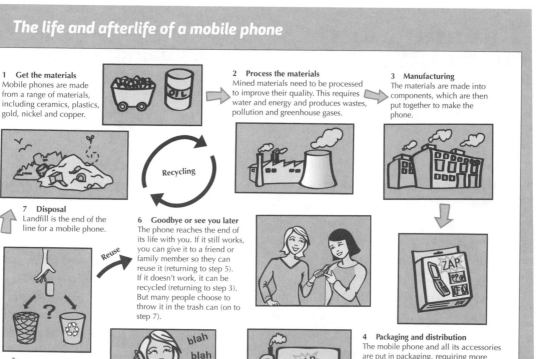

The life and afterlife of a mobile phone

1 Get the materials
Mobile phones are made from a range of materials, including ceramics, plastics, gold, nickel and copper.

2 Process the materials
Mined materials need to be processed to improve their quality. This requires water and energy and produces wastes, pollution and greenhouse gases.

3 Manufacturing
The materials are made into components, which are then put together to make the phone.

Recycling

7 Disposal
Landfill is the end of the line for a mobile phone.

6 Goodbye or see you later
The phone reaches the end of its life with you. If it still works, you can give it to a friend or family member so they can reuse it (returning to step 5). If it doesn't work, it can be recycled (returning to step 3). But many people choose to throw it in the trash can (on to step 7).

Reuse

4 Packaging and distribution
The mobile phone and all its accessories are put in packaging, requiring more material and energy use and generating more emissions. The package is then transported to stores. This requires fuel and produces polluting emissions.

5 Ring, ring, SMS
The mobile phone is used.

blah blah blah

ZAP

E-waste: what you might be sending to landfill

Mobile phones
- plastics
- ceramics
- copper and copper compounds
- iron
- nickel and nickel compounds
- zinc and zinc compounds
- silver
- flame retardants
- others (under 1 per cent by weight): tin, lead, tantalum, cobalt, aluminium, tungsten, gold, palladium, antimony, manganese, lithium compounds, ceramic oxides, liquid crystal, beryllium, phosphorus, molybdenum

Desktop computers
- silica
- plastics
- aluminium
- copper
- iron
- lead
- zinc
- others (under 1 per cent by weight): tin silver, tantalum cobalt, arsenic, barium, tungsten, gold, palladium, antimony, bismuth, manganese, cadmium, chromium, europium, gallium, germanium, gold, indium, mercury, nickel, niobium, platinum, ruthenium, titanium, beryllium, vanadium, yttrium

Farming and agriculture

Early humans were hunters and gatherers. They got the food and useful materials they needed by hunting wild animals or gathering what they needed from natural vegetation. Around the end of the ice age, about ten thousand years ago, groups of people were able to settle in one place, keep certain kinds of useful animals, and plant and harvest crops, ensuring a reliable supply of food. Agriculture was born. Since then, it has literally changed the face of the earth and allowed the human race to thrive. In the quest to create new farmlands, humans have cleared forests and woodlands, irrigated savannah grasslands and drained wetlands, converting them into agricultural areas. The rate of land-clearing has climbed dramatically with the increase in the world's human population. Plus, the invention of farm machinery, such as tractors and combine harvesters, has made it faster and easier to farm the land.

Globally, around 850 million hectares of land (an area larger than the whole of Australia) were brought under cultivation from 1860 to 1980, mainly to provide food for the world's growing population. The conversion of natural ecosystems into agricultural land comes at the expense of habitat for wildlife.

Environmental problems of farming and agriculture

Farming and agriculture have been a fantastic and useful development. Thanks to farmers, we have delicious food to eat, clothes to wear, warm woolly blankets to sleep under, and many more practical and fun products to enjoy. However, these good things come at an environmental cost. Some of the environmental problems with farming are listed below:

- Millions of hectares of land are now devoted to grazing livestock or raising crops, limiting the land's ability to support native wildlife. This can push some native wildlife species to the brink of extinction.
- The use of artificial fertiliser and pesticides on crops can pollute the local environment and harm the health of farm workers.
- If too much water for crop irrigation is taken from rivers, lakes and other watercourses, it can leave these water bodies and the aquatic species that live there in very bad health. For example, the Coorong and the Lower Lakes at the end of the Murray River are drying out and dying, due to the combined effects of drought and the over-withdrawal of water.
- The clearing of land destroys habitats and causes erosion.
- Growing a single species in a crop can deplete the soil of its nutrients, reducing its fertility.
- Modern 'factory farms' aren't much like Farmer Hoggett's farm in the movie *Babe*.

Did you know ... ?

The world has doubled food production in the last thirty-five years. A third of the world's agricultural lands are used to grow crops, with the remaining two-thirds used as livestock pasture.

Animals may be raised in cramped and appalling conditions, raising animal health and welfare concerns. Intensive animal farms can also produce pollution, such as huge amounts of animal wastes (droppings and so on). Animal wastes must be managed very carefully to prevent the spread of bad odours and disease.

Organic farming

Organic farming offers an alternative to modern farming methods that works in harmony with nature, rather than against it. Organic farming produces food and fibre (for making textiles and clothing) without the use of artificial pesticides or fertilisers. A mix of crops is grown, instead of a single species or 'monoculture'. This crop diversity is a good thing as it prevents the pests of a single crop from being given a feast that would allow their numbers to multiply and dominate. The diversity also ensures that the soil is kept fertile and its nutrients aren't depleted by the demands of a single crop.

Many organic farmers keep livestock animals alongside their plant crops. The manure provides natural fertiliser to keep the soil healthy and productive. Food crops are rotated with soil-enriching plant crops such as legumes, which feed the soil. Workers on organic farms also experience less risk to their health from overexposure to crop chemicals, which is often a problem in poorer countries.

However, organic farming tends to produce less food per hectare than industrialised farming, raising the question of whether or not the world can feed its human population solely through organic farming without the need to clear more land for farming. The ultimate solution may be a compromise between the two, in which industrialised farming adopts some of the methods of organic farming.

Eco-action: go organic

Think about the land and the farmers when you buy food and clothing. See if you can get an organic cotton T-shirt, instead of one that isn't organic. Or have an organic apple as a snack.

Fashion

Everybody needs clothes. Clothes keep us warm and modest. And they help us look the way we want to look. In fact, clothes can be a lot of fun. But fabrics and clothing have a host of environmental implications. Growing fibres and dyeing them or making them from petrochemicals uses lots of energy, water and materials, and produces waste and pollution. Plus, the fashion industry itself thrives on trends that are so hot for a moment, before becoming 'so yesterday'. The result is out-of-fashion clothes that are thrown away long before they've worn out—something fundamentally *not* green!

The good news is that a new breed of fashion designer is emerging—one who considers the health of the planet as well as what looks good.

Eco-action: good green gear

- *Less is more! Get a few good quality pieces that will last, instead of heaps of cheap clothes that will fall apart or look daggy sooner.*

- *Avoid buying clothes that can only be dry-cleaned.*

- *See if you can buy clothes made from alternative fibres, such as hemp, bamboo and organic cotton. Surf-wear label Billabong even makes board shorts from fabric made from recycled soft-drink bottles.*

- *Go retro and look for cool second-hand clothes at op-shops, vintage clothing stores or online sites such as eBay.*

- *Swap clothes with friends. You can even get together and hold a swap party.*

- *Only wash your clothes when they need it.*

Fast fashion

Fashion is a big-bucks business! In 2000 alone, the world's consumers spent around US$1 trillion worldwide buying clothes. The greatest profits are often made in the volume markets, where manufacturers aim to sell large quantities of low-priced items. Experts call this fast fashion, the clothing equivalent of cheap but unhealthy fast food. These are clothes with a very limited life span—they live fast and die young!

Faster fashion

Imagine Emma Watson at the premier of the next Harry Potter movie. Photographs of her wearing a one-shouldered red dress appear in magazines and on websites across the globe. Suddenly, everyone wants one-shouldered red dresses, so clothing companies email designs to factories in China, which rapidly produce them and then airfreight them to stores around the world before the trend dies. This need for airfreight, instead of slower sea freight, consumes more fuel and creates more greenhouse emissions.

Life cycle of a T-shirt

1 Getting the materials

☹ Natural fibres may be grown with fertiliser and pesticides, and may use lots of energy and water. Synthetics largely come from non-renewable petroleum.

☺ Alternative fibres, such as organic cotton, hemp and bamboo fabric, can reduce these impacts.

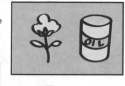

2 Processing the materials

☹ This may use energy, harsh cleaners (particularly in wool scouring) and polluting dyes.

☺ There are ways to manage the polluted waste water better, and vegetable dyes can be used.

Reuse

7 RIP, reuse or recycle

☹ Most unwanted T-shirts end up in the rubbish bin. But a T-shirt in good condition can be reused—given away or swapped with a friend, or donated to a charity to be sold through an

☺ op-shop. Alternatively, the materials may be recycled.

Recycling

6 Wash, wear and wardrobe

☹ Clothes are washed using energy, water and detergents. If they are tumble-dried and ironed, this uses more energy. Or they are dry-cleaned using potentially harmful chemicals.

☺ Clothes that are looked after last longer. They can be washed with greener detergents and dried on the line.

3 Manufacturing

☹ Manufacturing can use large amounts of energy, produce waste and expose workers to poor conditions.

☺ Cleaner production processes can reduce waste, and companies can make a commitment to fair labour practices.

4 Packaging

☹ Some clothes are over-packaged, using paper and plastics and creating waste.

☺ Some do without packaging (men's shirts on hangers instead of in packets, for instance), or have recycling programs (such as coathanger recycling).

5 Distribution

☹ Clothes, including T-shirts, are shipped around the world, using fuel and generating greenhouse gases and pollution. Worst are those that are airfreighted.

Fish

Humans live on land, but only a quarter or so of the earth's surface is land. The rest is covered with water, which is why the earth is known as 'the Blue Planet'. Though we generally don't dwell there, humans make good use of lakes, rivers and oceans. For many people, the creatures that live in water are an important source of food. There is a lot we don't know about our oceans in particular. Their vast depths are largely unexplored, so it's easy for people to think of oceans as limitless and to assume that they go on forever. But there is a limit to how much food the ocean can provide, just as there is a limit to the amount of food that a given patch of land can grow. Human exploitation of fish and other marine species is placing some at risk of extinction.

Overfishing and by-catch

Small-scale local fishing, such as that done by Pacific Islanders to feed themselves, has very little or no impact on the environment. But larger-scale fishing starts to create problems. If more fish are taken from water ecosystems than can be replaced by normal fish reproduction, their numbers (called 'fish stocks') start to decline. Overfishing happens when too many fish are caught, placing the fish species and their local ecosystems at risk.

Forests for fish

Coral reefs are particularly at risk from global warming. Coral reefs are the rainforests of the ocean. These living reefs are rich, thriving habitats for aquatic life. Just a few kilometres of reef can contain more than three thousand different species. They also provide food for a wide range of seabirds and bring in billions of dollars in revenue through the fishing and tourism industries. Coral lives in a symbiotic relationship with tiny photosynthetic plants called zooxanthellae, which give coral its colour. But coral reefs are fragile structures and sensitive to even slight changes in ocean temperature. When the surface ocean temperature rises by even a single degree, the coral loses its zooxanthellae and appears white. Hence the death of a coral reef is often called 'coral bleaching'. If the zooxanthellae don't return, the coral dies, and all the species that depend on it suffer and their numbers decline. Earth's hottest year on record was 1998—a year that also saw the world's worst episode of coral bleaching.

Large-scale fishing vessels, equipped with advanced technology, have aided overfishing. These ships are able to cast out and pull in huge nets, catching large quantities of the desired fish, along with millions of tonnes of unwanted marine life or 'by-catch'. This by-catch can include dolphins, turtles and sea birds, which are tossed back into the sea, usually killed by their ordeal.

Did you know ... ? The IUCN *Red List* in 2003 listed 750 fish species as threatened. The list for 2008 grew to 1275 threatened fish species. In the twenty-first century, instead of finding Nemo, we may need to think about saving Nemo!

Aquaculture

Globally, demand for fish is increasing. As well as catching fish from the wild, we can also raise fish for human consumption in 'fish farms', which may be specially built pools of water or floating 'net cages'. This kind of farming is known as aquaculture. Fish farms are becoming bigger and more common. Some are managed unsustainably, with serious effects on local aquatic ecosystems and native fish stocks. Many fish farms raise fish such as salmon in densely packed conditions for commercial sales and profit. Like all intensive farming, they produce huge amounts of wastes, including drug-laden faeces and excess food. Farmed salmon are given more antibiotics (drugs to fight certain diseases) by weight than any other livestock. This is contributing to the development of antibiotic-resistant strains of disease-causing bacteria, nicknamed 'superbugs'. Some farm fish escape from their net cages and compete with native fish for food and habitat. These fish farms can also pass parasites and disease to wild populations. Good management, however, can limit these problems.

Did you know ... ?

Fish can be milked! Fish eggs, known as caviar, are taken from live fish grown for the purpose at a fish farm. Clove oil is put in the water, which knocks them out for about five minutes. The fish are then 'milked'—gently massaged to bring the eggs out. Milking a fish (usually salmon or trout, instead of the endangered sturgeon) takes between thirty seconds and one minute.

Eco-action: sustainable seafood

- Look for canned fish that is 'dolphin friendly'. This means that the fisheries have taken measures to reduce or stop by-catch.

- Ask your local fish and chip shop to get their fish from sustainable sources that aren't overfished. Tell them to contact the Australian Marine Conservation Society (<www.amcs.org.au>) or the international Marine Stewardship Council (<www.msc.org>) for advice.

Fish food for thought

- One in every five people on earth depends on fish as the main source of protein.

- About 200 million people, largely in the developing world, depend on fishing for food and as a means to earn a living.

Whales on watch

Humans throughout history have found uses for local plants and animals, and whales are no exception. For thousands of years, whales have been hunted along their migration routes in the oceans near countries such as Japan, Canada, Norway and Greenland. Whales are largely hunted for whale oil and whale meat, but other parts of the whale have been and still are used. For example, whalebone has been sewn into women's corsetry and umbrellas to provide stiffening, and ambergris, a waxy substance from the digestive systems of whales, has been used in perfume-making (the ancient Chinese called it 'dragon's spittle fragrance'!)

Hunters once used small boats and hand-held spears or harpoons. More recently, fast boats and harpoons made it easier to catch whales, supporting a whaling industry that caught huge numbers in the period between 1850 and 1950. During this time, whale numbers became dangerously decimated. Then, in 1946, the United Nations set up the International Whaling Commission to regulate whaling, protect threatened whale species and make sure that humans and marine mammals can coexist. Since then, whale numbers have gradually returned to healthier levels.

Today there is fierce argument about whether or not whaling should continue. Here is a look at the arguments for and against whaling:

Did you know ... ? Whales are marine mammals. All whales belong to the animal order Cetacea. Other cetaceans include dolphins, porpoises and dugongs. Cetaceans eat things such as fish, squid and even krill (tiny marine crustaceans that look like shrimp).

For	Against
• Some whale species eat large amounts of fish, competing with fisheries that may want to catch the same fish.	• Scientists and anti-whaling campaigners argue that whales mostly eat species that humans don't eat (such as krill and deep sea squid) and therefore aren't a serious threat to fisheries.
• Whaling is part of the history, culture and survival of some groups, such as the Inuit people in Canada, Alaska, Russia and Greenland.	• Whales are now killed with explosive harpoons, which anti-whaling campaigners say is cruel, particularly since whales can take several minutes to die.
	• Whales eat a wide range of marine species and large quantities, so changes in their numbers can have a huge impact on ocean ecosystems.

Eco-action:
save the whales

- *If you want to save the whales and dolphins, you also have to save the ecosystems and species on which they rely, even odd-looking krill. Sometimes, to save the magnificent and beautiful animals, you have to save some 'ugly' ones too!*

- *Plastic bags and other litter items have been found in the stomachs of dead whales and other marine mammals. Make sure you don't add to the problem by littering.*

Food

Food is our most basic item of consumption. With most Australians (87 per cent) and Kiwis (84 per cent) now living in urban areas, and being relatively wealthy compared with those in developing nations, food can be taken for granted, and its production is often poorly understood. City-dwellers are less likely than their country cousins to appreciate that the consumption of food entails the consumption of the water needed to grow it, the loss of topsoil and the use of crop inputs, such as fertilisers and pesticides. For example, it takes 13 litres of water to produce a tomato, and every tonne of wheat harvested represents approximately 3 kilograms of phosphorous removed from the soil. Water and topsoil are two resources Australia has in limited supply.

Some of the by-products of producing and consuming food are packaging waste (in the case of packaged food) and food waste from uneaten portions. Plus, we often eat food that has travelled great distances.

Take, for example, a packet of flavoured rice crackers. Most people looking at the crackers would say that the only environmental problem with them is the packaging itself,

Food production, consumption and disposal

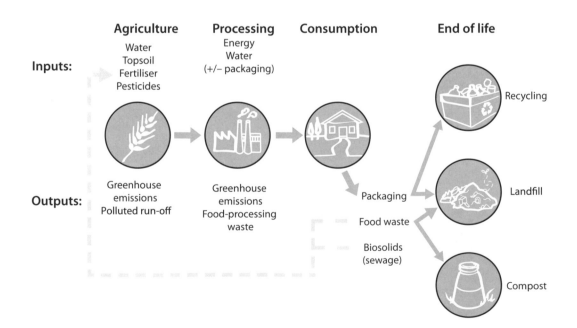

because it's not biodegradable and is even more of a problem if it's littered. In fact, that packet of crackers represents an investment of many resources. It took topsoil and water to grow the rice, energy to grind the rice into flour, more energy and water to make it into crackers, energy and materials to package them, and fuel to deliver the final product.

Similarly, land, water and energy are used to produce all the food in your local shops. Fresh produce—such as eggs, fruit and vegetables, meat, fish and poultry—uses fewer resources than the aisles and aisles of processed food in the average supermarket.

Food choices

There are a number of things you may wish to think about when choosing what to eat:
- Organic food has been grown without pesticides and synthetic fertilisers, making it healthier for you and the farmer who grew it.
- Red meat has the highest environmental costs, because it needs a lot of land and water to be produced. Plus, livestock are a major source of greenhouse emissions. Limit the amount of red meat you eat. Poultry (white meat, such as chicken) has the next highest eco-costs, followed by seafood. Vegetarian alternatives are the greenest foods. A given patch of land will also feed more people if it is used to grow grain to make bread than if it is used to grow grain to feed livestock.
- You may wish to avoid meat, poultry and fish products for animal rights reasons,

Eco-trivia question

You might have heard that cows contribute to the greenhouse effect because their farts contain a lot of methane gas.

Question: *What is a greater greenhouse problem: the gases that come out of the front or back of a cow?*

Answer: *The front! Cows burp more greenhouse gases than they fart!*

depending on how you feel about such issues. It's your choice. If you're particularly concerned about animal rights, you might also wish to cut out eggs and dairy products, which come from animals.
- It is better environmentally to eat fruit and vegetables that are in season. For example, raspberries and strawberries are summer fruits. If you're eating them in winter, they've probably been shipped using refrigerated transport from the other side of the world, where it's warmer. Refrigerated transport uses a lot of energy and generates extra greenhouse gas emissions. And foods that are in season also taste better.
- Processing and packaging food adds to the environmental cost of food and can also make it less healthy.

Food miles

Food miles is a term that describes the great distances that some foods travel from farm to fork. It is one aspect of the environmental impact of food. Food miles are sometimes measured to work out the greenhouse impact of a food, but many experts believe that this measure is too narrow to show the true sustainability of a particular food. While there is a benefit to eating food that is grown locally, reducing transport fuel use, people would have to limit their diets to foods that can be grown locally.

Sometimes foods are greener when they come from further afield, having been grown in a climate and soil that better suit the needs

Eco-byte

'At the beginning of the year, we started a vegetable patch. We do not use fertiliser or any sprays as the vegetables are all organic. We have a potato competition. We got into groups and made stacks of tyres and planted some potatoes into the tyres. By growing our own food and not using sprays we can protect the environment and keep healthy at the same time.' **Stephanie, 11**

Eco-action: give food waste the chop

Here are some tips for avoiding food waste:

• *Only put on a plate what you will definitely eat. You can always go back for seconds. Freeze or refrigerate the leftovers and reheat them for tomorrow's lunch.*

• *Resist the temptation to 'supersize' fast food meals. They are not good value if you don't eat them.*

• *Put fruit and vegetable scraps, peelings and any food that has gone 'off' into a compost bin or worm farm, instead of sending it to landfill.*

of the food, thereby reducing the need for extra fertiliser and other crop chemicals. Plus, food production may provide employment in developing nations and a path out of poverty.

Food waste

It's estimated that Australian households throw away a whopping A$5.3 billion worth of unused food each year. This includes leftovers from large serving sizes, uneaten takeaway food, unfinished drinks, and fresh food that went off in the fridge before it could be eaten. We're not alone in our wasteful behaviour. It's estimated that along the path from fields to forks, more than a quarter of the USA's food, or 43.5 million tonnes of food a year goes to waste. This wastes the resources—particularly topsoil and water—that have gone into producing the food.

Eco-activity: grow your own food in a no-dig garden

So you're a lazy gardener—you want to start a small garden but can't be bothered doing the hard preparation and groundwork? Or perhaps the earth in your garden is more like clay or is too compacted or just poor quality. No problem! You can build a no-dig garden. They're great for growing vegetables, herbs, strawberries and other yummy things.

No-dig gardens are raised, boxed garden beds built directly on top of the surface of the ground. With the help of an adult, it's easy to build a raised garden bed, and they are well suited to vegetable gardens. Because they're built on top of the soil with new organic matter, they can provide a fertile garden bed in a garden (or school yard) with otherwise poor soil.

First, you need to build the walls of the garden bed. The walls can be bricks or rocks or timber. Many people use old timber railway sleepers. Spread out a thick layer (around 1.5 centimetres) of overlapping sheets of newspaper. Soak it with water. Then put down a 5–7-centimetre layer of lucerne hay or pea straw. If you have some, put down an additional layer of old leaves, twigs and/or pieces of seaweed. Soak with a hose. Spread a thin layer of animal manure (chicken, horse, cow or sheep) over the lucerne and twig layer. Next add a 5-centimetre layer of straw. Finally add a 3–4-centimetre layer of compost.

Plant seedlings directly into the compost layer and water them in well. Water regularly while the seedlings establish themselves. Over time, the hay, straw, manure, paper and compost will break down into a dark, rich and well-aerated soil.

No-dig garden layers

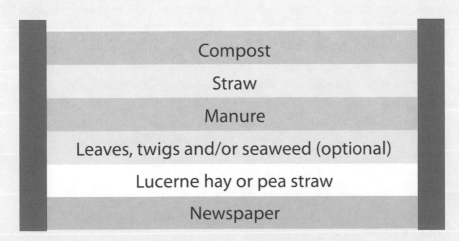

Compost
Straw
Manure
Leaves, twigs and/or seaweed (optional)
Lucerne hay or pea straw
Newspaper

Forests and forestry

Forests are a vital resource, both for people and for the planet. There are many forest products that people use—ranging from timber to maple syrup. But there are also things that forests do for the environment. Forests have both economic and environmental value, and sometimes these two values can work against each other.

What forests do for people

- They provide us with timber and materials for paper- and cardboard-making. As well as wood products, logs can be turned into woodchips, which are used to make cardboard, paper, tissues and toilet paper.
- They provide a beautiful place to visit, and many forests are ecotourism destinations.
- Forests give people jobs, in both the forestry and tourism industries.
- The many different species that live in forests provide the materials and ingredients to make medicines and other products.
- They provide us with clean drinking water by filtering rainwater and melted snow and enabling it to flow into water catchments.

What forests do for the planet

- They hold down soil.
- Leaf litter rots and boosts soil fertility.
- Forests provide homes for millions of different plant and animal species.
- Forests help regulate the climate and weather patterns.
- The evaporation of water from forest plants (called 'transpiration') is an important part of the water cycle. This water becomes clouds and later rain.

Forestry debates

Timber, in theory, is a renewable material in that harvested timber can be replaced by replanting a new seedling. One of the great things about timber is that it effectively stores carbon. As trees grow, they remove carbon dioxide from the atmosphere and use it to build wood. But it's important to remember that there is no greenhouse benefit in removing timber from existing natural forests instead of raising trees for the purpose of producing timber. In fact, logging and land-clearing to make room for plantations is often followed by a massive burn-off, which releases huge amounts of smoke and greenhouse gases into the atmosphere.

Did you know ... ? The World Bank estimates that deforestation accounts for 10–30 per cent of global carbon emissions, because of rotting and burning vegetation, largely in poorly managed forestry operations.

In addition, timber and other plant materials may be sourced from natural ecosystems that take centuries to establish. For example, some native animals nest in the hollows of very old trees in 'old growth' forests. Newly planted trees don't have these hollows. Unfortunately, some of our wood comes from old growth forests that provide habitat to threatened species, such as the spotted-tail quoll, the Tasmanian wedge-tailed eagle and the long-footed potoroo. As well as its effects on wildlife, logging in catchment areas reduces the flow of water into our drinking-water catchments.

The key to the survival of our forests and the industries that rely on them is good management; but this may be difficult to achieve. Many countries have laws that determine the areas that can be logged and how this is to be done, but in some countries these laws aren't policed well. Illegal logging is still a major environmental problem. It is estimated that illegal logging accounts for 73 per cent of log production in Indonesia, and 80 per cent in Brazil.

Forest facts

- Deforestation is the permanent destruction of natural forests.

- Over 45 per cent of the world's native forests have been destroyed.

- About 120 000 square kilometres of forests are cleared annually to provide space for agriculture, to provide wood for fuel for heating and cooking, and to provide wood for timber and paper production.

- Nearly 10 per cent of the world's rainforests are in Indonesia.

Eco-action: becoming forest friendly

- Use a handkerchief instead of tissues.

- Reduce your use of paper.

- When you do buy paper and tissue products, choose those that are made from recycled materials.

- Get your family to buy recycled-content toilet paper.

- When you're bushwalking in a forest, be careful not to disturb fallen hollow logs as these may be homes for animals. You should also take any rubbish with you instead of littering it.

Gadgets

The average Australian home is full of gadgets, gizmos and electronic devices that (theoretically) make our lives easier and entertain us. Most homes have a television set, video and sound system. Many also have DVD players, PlayStations, electric musical equipment, electric toys, and home computer systems. In the bathroom there may be hairdryers, hair-straightening tongs, electric toothbrushes and electric hair removers. All these appliances use electricity and so contribute to the greenhouse effect. Some even use a small amount of electricity when they're turned off. This is called 'standby power'. It all adds up.

Eco-action: gadgets off!

- *Limit how many gadgets and electronic games you buy and how much you use them.*

- *Allow your hair to dry naturally instead of blow-drying it.*

- *Use a manual toothbrush, instead of an electric one (unless your dentist insists upon it).*

- *When you have finished watching television, listening to music or using another electronic device, don't forget to turn it off.*

Entertainment without electricity

The ultimate way to cut down the energy use of electronic gadgets is to use them less. Instead of staying inside watching the TV or playing electronic games:

- go for a walk, bike ride or rollerblade around the neighbourhood

- join a sporting club or become a member at your local tennis courts or gym, and use the facilities

- use a little electricity to power a radio or MP3 player and dance around your lounge room (when no one is looking)

- play a board game, or do a crossword or Sudoku.

- read a book (or even write one).

Standby wattage = standby wastage

If you wander around your house in the middle of the night, you will see the lit numbers of digital displays or the tiny red or green lights of electronic devices silently waiting on standby. These lights and displays all represent a small but constant drain on electricity supplies. Even without obvious signs like lights or displays, some products nevertheless draw a small amount of current. This 'standby' electricity consumption can add up to over 10 per cent of the total electricity used in the home. The more gadgets you have plugged into the wall, the higher your standby energy use will be.

Like any other electricity used in the home, increased standby power means increased greenhouse gas emissions if your electricity comes from fossil fuel sources. The difference is that your family has to pay for this standby electricity, while getting nothing useful in return.

The main culprits are televisions, game consoles, DVDs and VCRs left in standby mode after being turned off using a remote control. The simple solution here is to turn them off using the button on the machine when they're not in use. Electronic game consoles, sound systems, computer equipment, printers and some other appliances can also use small amounts of electricity, even when switched off.

Eco-action: standby power—turn it off

To reduce standby power wastage, do the following:

- Switch TVs, DVD players and other appliances off properly (rather than leaving them on standby by turning them off using the remote control).

- Switch off the appliances you only use occasionally at the wall.

- Recharging plugs for mobile phones and iPods that are left plugged in but not charging a device can continue to use power, particularly older models. Unplug the charger when you've finished charging your phone.

Think about it

If the emissions were 'made in China', shouldn't they be the first to reduce their carbon footprint? China's emissions are very high and are rapidly rising partly because China produces a lot of the things bought in stores around the world. China is a developing country that has been poorer than many Western nations. Many Chinese workers have little choice but to work for far lower wages than those received by workers in North America, the United Kingdom or Australia, so many companies do their manufacturing in China to reduce their costs. That way, they can sell their products at a lower price than their competitors. Have a look at your calculator, MP3 player or favourite pair of jeans. Chances are they were made in China, using energy and producing emissions that add to China's total. Is this fair? Who is ultimately responsible for the emissions of a product: the producer or the person who created the demand for it, bought and used it? It is an important ethical question.

Think about the electricity use in your bedroom. Are you more like the lean and green teen or the technophile teen? What does your power use cost your parents? Compare the following two pictures, which also show the average annual greenhouse emissions resulting from the use of each gadget (based on the Australian average emissions from electricity use—about 1 kilogram of carbon dioxide per kilowatt hour).

Note: Carbon dioxide emissions and running costs are per annum. Running costs are based on electricity at 15 cents per kilowatt hour.

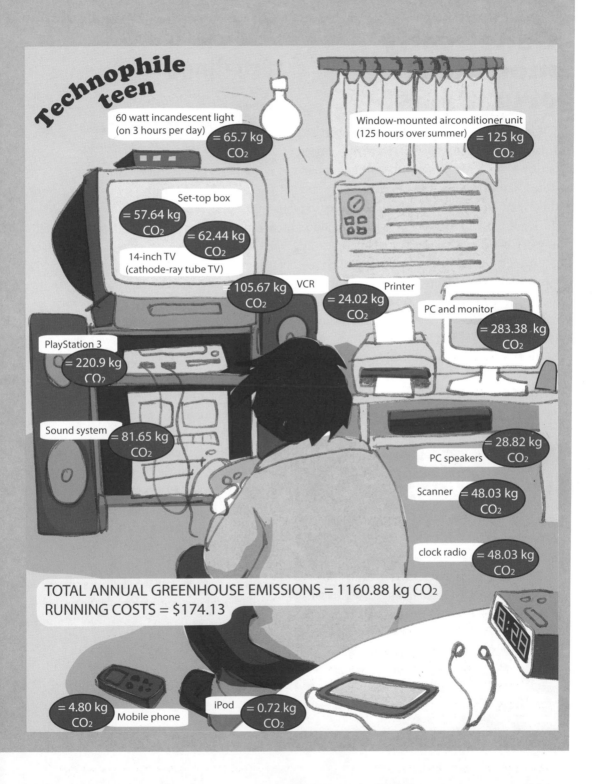

Technophile teen

60 watt incandescent light
(on 3 hours per day)
= 65.7 kg CO_2

Window-mounted airconditioner unit
(125 hours over summer)
= 125 kg CO_2

Set-top box
= 57.64 kg CO_2

= 62.44 kg CO_2

14-inch TV
(cathode-ray tube TV)
= 105.67 kg CO_2

VCR
= 24.02 kg CO_2

Printer

PC and monitor
= 283.38 kg CO_2

PlayStation 3
= 220.9 kg CO_2

Sound system
= 81.65 kg CO_2

= 28.82 kg CO_2
PC speakers

Scanner = 48.03 kg CO_2

clock radio = 48.03 kg CO_2

TOTAL ANNUAL GREENHOUSE EMISSIONS = 1160.88 kg CO_2
RUNNING COSTS = $174.13

= 4.80 kg CO_2
Mobile phone

iPod = 0.72 kg CO_2

Genetically modified organisms

Blackberries are delicious. So are raspberries. Imagine combining the two to produce a new 'super-berry'. An American horticulturalist called James Henry Logan accidentally did this very thing. Logan was crossbreeding different types of blackberry to try to produce a better plant, but raspberries planted nearby got involved. The result was the loganberry—a hybrid of the raspberry and blackberry.

Hybrid and crossbred plants and animals can occur naturally, but they can also be produced by humans. Farmers and horticulturists have crossbred (or 'hybridised') plants to produce new varieties with desirable features, such as better flavour in fruit or variation in flower colours. Peppermint, the

Eco-lingo

horticulture   *This is the cultivation (growing) and study of plants, particularly in gardens and greenhouses set aside for the purpose.*

hybrid of spearmint and water mint, is another tasty example. However, crossbreeding and hybridisation only works well when species from the same biological family are combined. Peppermint is the hybrid of two mints, loganberries are the hybrid of two types of berry, and 'zebroids' are hybrids of zebras and other members of the horse (equine) family. That's why hybrids of vastly different species, like hippogriffs (the hybrid of a horse and griffin, which itself is the hybrid of a lion and an eagle), don't exist, except of course in mythology and Harry Potter novels.

Specialised scientists, called genetic engineers, can now swap genes between unrelated species. Plants can be spliced with a fish gene to make them less sensitive to cold weather, for example. Crops can be engineered to be pest-resistant. They can even be engineered to be immune to the herbicides used on crops to kill weed plants. There is also potential to engineer crops to have better nutritional value or even to contain medicines.

It's in your genes!

Have you ever wondered why some people have blue eyes or why certain illnesses run in families? The answer is in our genes. Genes are the instructions that are inside the cells of all living things. They are the blueprint for each individual plant or animal, determining how large it can grow, what it will look like, its character traits and what it instinctively does in order to survive. When plants and animals reproduce, their genes are passed on to the next generation. So if you're short, bad-tempered and have freckles, blame your parents!

Genetic engineering: the pros and cons

When we make changes to the genetics of living things, we're basically changing their potential. As such, genetic engineering has set off a heated debate between environmentalists, farmers, scientists, biotechnology companies (who make the genetically modified plants) and even HRH Prince Charles! Is it a question of advancing science? Or is it a question of what is right and wrong? Here is a look at the arguments for and against genetic engineering and, in particular, growing genetically modified (GM) food crops.

Many scientists believe that GM foods should undergo the same level of testing as new drugs, with independent scientific studies and extensive human trials. We may yet find out that they're safe. However, in the meantime, we're effectively the guinea pigs. Environment groups like Greenpeace are campaigning for better labelling laws so that consumers know when they are buying products made with GM content and can make their own choice.

For genetic engineering

- Genetic engineering can increase crop production, meaning that more people can be fed from the same amount of land. Potentially, the world's poorest, starving people could be fed.

- It produces a greater yield from the use of land, water (irrigation) and fertiliser.

- Genetic improvements can lead to produce with better flavour, increased nutritional value and/ or better texture.

- Genetic engineering may produce tougher crops that can cope with the weather extremes brought about by climate change, and still produce a good harvest.

- Crops engineered to be pest-resistant need less pesticide chemicals.

- Genetic engineering could make farming more profitable for farmers and biotechnology companies.

Against genetic engineering

- Pest-resistant crops engineered to kill a target pest insect can also kill other insects, some of which may be beneficial.

- Crops engineered to be resistant to weed-killers will encourage overuse of herbicides, wiping out all other plant life except for the crop plant. This will remove food sources for local wildlife, such as birds and small mammals.

- GM crops are hard to contain. GM plants can contaminate non-GM crops and honey production, posing a threat to the organic farming industry.

- Once released into the environment, GM plants are difficult to 'recall'.

- GM crops have had very little testing. The long-term effects of eating GM food are unknown.

Germs

'Germ' is the common name we give to micro-organisms—microscopic living things, including bacteria and fungi. They're also nicknamed 'microbes' and they play vitally important roles in biological systems. But germs are something we love to hate—particularly the ones that make us sick. Cleaning-product advertising would have you believe that there's an army of evil bacteria out there, just waiting to give you a disease. This has made some people almost obsessed with killing germs as part of their household cleaning routine. In fact, Australians now spend around $45.8 million at supermarkets each year just on disinfectants. Aside from disinfectants, more and more cleaning products are now boasting that they are germ-killing or 'anti-bacterial'. In reality, we may be doing far more harm than good to our health by using these products.

Bacteria: friend or foe?

The answer is 'both'! There are hundreds of thousands of different types of bacteria, microbe and fungi. Microbes in the soil do all the hard work of breaking down dead materials into soil nutrients. Without the good bacteria in your digestive system (called 'gut flora' and weighing about a kilogram in an adult), you wouldn't be able to digest food properly. In fact, a decent amount of bacteria in our bodies is vital for human health. However, some types of bacteria are 'pathogens' and cause illnesses and infectious diseases.

In rich countries, there is extensive overuse of antibiotics, antibacterial soaps and disinfectants because we're so scared of getting sick. These products can kill the good bacteria needed for healthy bodies and healthy ecosystems. They can also contribute to the development of 'superbugs', bacteria that have built up resistance to germ-killing products.

In the home, a little bit of bacteria is a good thing. Our immune systems are kept strong by fighting off a small amount of disease-causing germs. However, it's still important to practise good hygiene habits to keep yourself from getting sick.

Think about it

Have you ever heard of the 'five-second rule'? The general idea is that you can eat food dropped on the floor if you pick it up within five seconds. It's a myth. Don't risk it, even if it's a lolly that you really want to eat!

The human body contains about ten times as many bacteria as human cells. There are an estimated 500–1000 different species in our bodies, helping us digest food and stay healthy. In fact, if aliens were to visit the earth and study humans, they might classify us as walking, talking ecosystems, rather than a single species!

Always wash your hands with soap and water before eating or preparing food, after going to the toilet and after sneezing into your hand or blowing your nose.

Remember that our efforts to kill disease-causing bacteria can also kill good bacteria. For example, antibacterial agents in laundry detergent can harm soil microbes if the laundry grey water is used to water the garden. Practise good hygiene and avoid the germs that can make you sick, but respect the role that bacteria and other microbes play in keeping ecosystems and the broader environment healthy.

Germs in food

When it comes to food, disease-causing bacteria can grow and thrive on food, which is why it's important to cook and eat with clean pots, plates and utensils, and to avoid eating food that may have gone off. Heating food to over 70°C kills bacteria, so thoroughly reheat leftovers before eating them. Don't eat food that may have been contaminated—for example, by falling onto the floor. Also never eat any food that you've found. You don't know its history.

France: the birthplace of germ-free food packaging

They say that an army marches on its stomach—meaning that, in order to fight, soldiers need to be fed. In the late eighteenth and early nineteenth centuries, this was well understood by Napoleon Bonaparte, who was busy taking over Europe. He offered a cash reward of 12 000 francs for anyone who could find a way to preserve food and ensure a safe food supply for the army. Nicolas Appert, a confectioner from Paris, came up with a method of sealing food in glass bottles, then dunking them in boiling water for a while, and won the prize. This was several decades before a fellow Frenchman, Louis Pasteur, proved that heat kills the bacteria responsible for spoiling food. Using the same basic process with metal cans instead of glass jars, the problem of glass breaking was solved. Thus the modern can was born in the early nineteenth century, funnily enough at about the same time that the cancan was born in the ballrooms of Montparnasse, another part of Paris.

Global warming

We all know how uncomfortable it is to try to sleep in a bed with one blanket too many. Overall, our planet is getting hot, sticky and uncomfortable in a similar way, but with more serious results. Global warming is the overall increase in the earth's temperature. It's largely caused by the blanket of greenhouse gases that insulates our planet. (More about greenhouse gases shortly.) Over the past century or two, this blanket has got thicker, trapping more heat. This in turn has caused changes in the planet's climate patterns.

Taking the planet's temperature

When people are sick, you can get them to sit still with thermometers in their mouths. Measuring the temperature of the planet is much harder. Temperatures are taken in a number of ways:

- **Weather stations** around the world measure the temperatures at the surface of the earth with special thermometers.
- **Weather balloons** measure temperatures higher in the atmosphere.
- Special **buoys** measure the temperatures in the ocean.
- **Weather satellites** can also measure heat radiated from the earth's surface.

These temperature readings are put together and an average is calculated. What scientists have found is that the global average surface temperature has increased by about 0.7°C over the past hundred years and the trend is towards further heating. At the same

The fifteen hottest years on record

As at 2008, the hottest years based on global average surface temperatures were:

1	1998	2	2005
3	2003	4	2002
5	2004	6	2006
7	2007	8	2001
9	1997	10	2008
11	1995	12	1999
13	1990	14	2000
15	1991		

Source: Met Office Hadley Centre and the Climatic Research Unit (CRU) at University of East Anglia

time, atmospheric scientists have observed that concentrations of carbon dioxide are now much higher, and are increasing more quickly, than at any time during the last 600 000 years. They predict that the earth's surface temperature is likely to rise by 1.0°C–6.4°C by the year 2100, depending on how much greenhouse pollution we're producing.

Potential effects of global warming

Understanding and acting to prevent global warming are vitally important because the consequences of this warming could be serious. Scientists say we're in a climate crisis. If the climate continues to warm as predicted by climate scientists, these could be some of the effects:

- Some of the ice in the polar icecaps would melt. We are already seeing this in the Arctic Circle.
- Sea levels would rise.
- Low-lying islands and mainland coastlines could be flooded.
- Weather patterns could change dramatically, with increases in drought, hurricanes and floods.
- Agriculture and farming could be affected, resulting in food shortages.
- Ecological systems and important habitats could similarly be affected, causing environmental decline and more extinctions.
- Waterborne and insect-borne diseases would increase in some areas.

Current federal government predictions for Australia are that by 2030 we will face:

- about 1°C warming
- up to 20 per cent more months of drought
- up to a 25 per cent increase in days of very high or extreme fire danger
- more storm surges and severe weather events.

Jason and the Argo Floats

In Greek mythology, the hero Jason set out with a group of adventurous friends, called the Argonauts, on a ship called the *Argo*. Their quest was to capture the golden fleece. Climate scientists recently realised that, while they had information on land temperatures, they knew little about the role of the ocean in climate change and how ocean temperatures are changing. So they embarked on a quest of their own: to put special temperature and salinity monitors into oceans all over the world. These special floating robots are called Argo Floats. They are dropped into the seven seas by container ships and scientific vessels.

Over 3200 Argo Floats are currently active in the world's oceans. They take measurements near the ocean surface, but are also able to sink to specific depths and take further measurements. Each float has a satellite antenna at its top, which beams information back to scientists. Meanwhile the 'Jason' satellite system is orbiting the earth, an eye in the sky monitoring the ocean surfaces. At any time, scientists and ordinary people worldwide can access this information. See for yourself at <www.argo.net>.

Argo floats

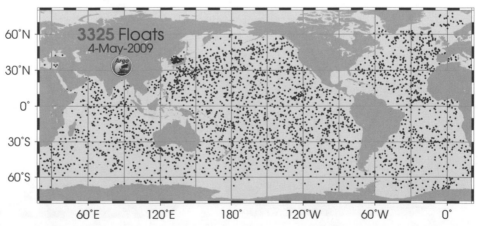

Source: Argo <www.argo.ucsd.edu>.

Greenhouse effect

The traditional greenhouse is a glass garden house, designed so that plants that prefer warmer weather can be grown in colder climates. The glass allows sunlight and radiant heat into the greenhouse, but stops the heat from escaping. As a result, the air inside the glasshouse is kept at a warmer temperature than the air outdoors.

In a similar way, a layer of greenhouse gases in the atmosphere allow sunlight in, which warms the earth's surface. Some of this heat is re-radiated back into the atmosphere. The layer of greenhouse gases in the atmosphere acts like a blanket that stops much of the heat from escaping to space, keeping the temperature at the earth's surface nice and comfortable for all the planet's life forms. Without the greenhouse effect, the earth's average surface temperature would be about −19°C—much colder than the average 14°C we currently enjoy. The big

The main greenhouse gases

The most significant greenhouse gases in the atmosphere include:

- water vapour
- carbon dioxide
- nitrous oxide
- methane
- ozone.

environmental problem is that an *enhanced* greenhouse effect is happening. It's too much of a good thing!

Greenhouse gases (such as carbon dioxide and methane) are naturally occurring, resulting from the gas exchange of plants, the excrement (poop!) of animals, bushfires, volcanic activity and the rotting of dead plants and animals. Photosynthesis uses these gases to build carbohydrates in plant tissues. This is part of the 'carbon cycle' outlined on page 20.

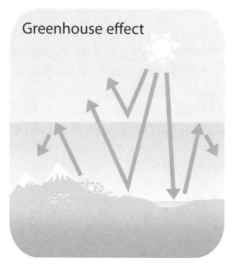

Greenhouse effect

Enhanced greenhouse effect

Since industrialisation, humans have been logging forests and burning huge amounts of fossil fuels, such as coal, oil and natural gas, to provide power. The burning of fossil fuels unlocks the stored carbon, producing an oversupply of carbon dioxide and other greenhouse gases to the atmosphere. They are adding to the planet's blanket, and the blanket's getting too thick.

The sad truth is that global emissions of greenhouse gases need to be drastically slashed to stop global warming and climate change. Renewable energy offers many viable alternatives, and we can also all cut back on the things we do that add to the greenhouse effect.

Measuring greenhouse gas emissions

There are many different greenhouse gases, each with a different ability to warm the planet, so scientists felt it would be useful to come up with a standard way of measuring them. Greenhouse emissions are talked about in terms of kilograms or tonnes of carbon dioxide or CO_2, the main greenhouse gas aside from water vapour. Other greenhouse gases are expressed as 'carbon dioxide equivalents', which are calculated by multiplying the amount or weight of each gas by its ability to warm the planet compared with carbon dioxide. For example, methane gas is twenty-one times more powerful a greenhouse gas than carbon dioxide, so 1 kilogram of methane is 21 kilograms (carbon dioxide equivalent or 'CO_2-e') of greenhouse emissions.

What does a kilogram of carbon dioxide look like?

Many people find the greenhouse effect difficult to understand. Part of the reason for this is that greenhouse gases are mostly invisible. The Victorian government's 'You have the power. Save energy' campaign has come up with a way to help people picture an amount of carbon dioxide. Campaign staff worked out that it takes about 50 grams of carbon dioxide to fill a party balloon. So you can think of 2.8 kilograms of greenhouse gas emissions—the amount produced by burning one litre of petrol in a car—as 56 black balloons worth!

Climate and carbon clues

Scientists studying greenhouse gas emissions and climate change need to know what was in the air tens, hundreds and even thousands of years ago. But how do you do this without a time machine? Scientists cut long cylinders of ice, called 'ice cores', from very old glaciers and looked for air bubbles trapped in the ice many, many years ago. This has given them a record of greenhouse gas levels in the atmosphere dating back 160 000 years.

Greenhouse gases by numbers ... and pictures

Numbers tell a story. They can also paint a picture, in the form of a graph. And a picture conveys a thousand words. Here are a few graphs and numbers that illustrate our global greenhouse problem, where it is coming from and what shape it takes.

Which countries of the world produce the most greenhouse emissions?
The following graph gives a rough overview of total carbon dioxide emissions by region.

You can see that North America and China are the biggest emitters. But that is only part of the picture ...

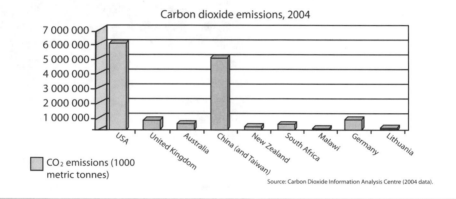

Carbon dioxide emissions, 2004

CO₂ emissions (1000 metric tonnes)

Source: Carbon Dioxide Information Analysis Centre (2004 data).

When you take into account the size of the human population of the countries producing these emissions, a different picture emerges. When calculating the greenhouse emissions of a country or region averaged over its population, North America is still a big emitter, but Australia is too. China, by contrast, with its large population, produces fewer emissions per person.

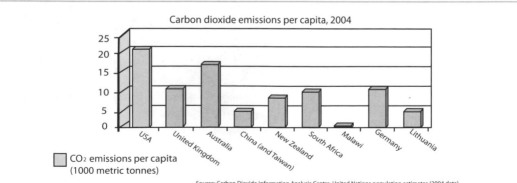

Carbon dioxide emissions per capita, 2004

CO₂ emissions per capita (1000 metric tonnes)

Source: Carbon Dioxide Information Analysis Centre, United Nations population estimates (2004 data).

What human activities produce greenhouse emissions?

- **Energy supply** (making electricity)
- **Transport**, including planes, trains and automobiles, as well as the freight of goods
- **Buildings**
- **Industry**
- **Forestry, deforestation and land-use change**
- **Agriculture** (emissions from crops and livestock—yes, that includes cow burps and farts)
- **Waste** (rotting rubbish) and **waste water**

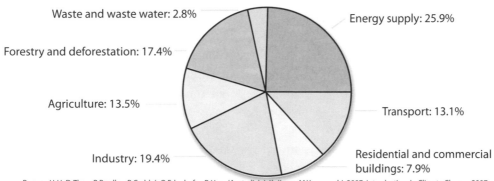

Greenhouse gas emissions by sector, 2004

Waste and waste water: 2.8%

Forestry and deforestation: 17.4%

Agriculture: 13.5%

Industry: 19.4%

Energy supply: 25.9%

Transport: 13.1%

Residential and commercial buildings: 7.9%

Rogner, H-H, D Zhou, R Bradley, P Crabbé, O Edenhofer, B Hare (Australia), L Kuijpers, M Yamaguchi, 2007: Introduction. In Climate Change 2007: Mitigation. Contribution of Working Group III to the Fourth Assessment Report of the Intergovernmental Panel on Climate Change [B Metz, OR Davidson, PR Bosch, R Dave, LA Meyer (eds)], Cambridge University Press, Cambridge, United Kingdom and New York, NY, USA.

What about me? How does my household contribute to the greenhouse effect?

We contribute to the greenhouse effect through our direct use of transport, which burns fuel, and our use of energy, including electricity. But we also consume food and material goods, which themselves produce greenhouse emissions on their journey to our homes. The following graph shows the Australian Conservation Foundation's estimates of the sources of greenhouse emissions produced by the average Australian household.

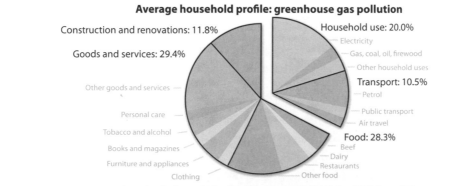

Average household profile: greenhouse gas pollution

Construction and renovations: 11.8%

Goods and services: 29.4%

Other goods and services

Personal care

Tobacco and alcohol

Books and magazines

Furniture and appliances

Clothing

Household use: 20.0%
- Electricity
- Gas, coal, oil, firewood
- Other household uses

Transport: 10.5%
- Petrol
- Public transport
- Air travel

Food: 28.3%
- Beef
- Dairy
- Restaurants
- Other food

Source: Australian Conservation Foundation, Consuming Australia: Main Findings, ACF, Melbourne, 2007.

Habitat

The ideal habitat is an environment where you feel healthiest and happiest. In ecology, habitat is the natural environment in which a particular plant or animal species lives. It has the right temperature conditions, the right shelter and enough water and food to give the species the best chances of growing, thriving and reproducing. Habitats can be large and complex. For example, birds may have particular nesting habitats, but may also migrate over great distances. Or habitats might be tiny microhabitats, like a piece of dead wood that provides a home to insects. A healthy and adequately sized habitat is crucial to the wellbeing and survival of a species. Unfortunately, the habitats of many plant and animal species are under threat as a result of human activity and interference.

Threats to habitat

The ultimate cause of loss of habitat is the earth's growing human population. The more people there are, the more land is needed to grow food, the more space is needed for housing and the more pollution is produced.

- **Land-clearing and deforestation** removes natural vegetation, sometimes endangering plant species. However, it's also killing and endangering the animals to which these habitats provide food, water and shelter. Often the first animals to suffer are the large mammals, particularly the meat-eaters at the top of the food chain. These animals need large habitat areas to provide enough hunting ground with enough prey to feed them. Often the areas set aside to preserve the habitat of these animals are large enough to provide shelter, but are inadequate hunting ranges.

- **Pollution**, such as acid rain, water pollution and hazardous waste, can make a habitat an unhealthy place to live.

- **Global warming and climate change** are having an impact on the natural environment. This can damage habitat areas. For example, the ice sheets that polar bears hunt on are melting sooner, and coral reefs can be killed by small changes in temperature. The timing of seasons is changing, affecting the breeding and reproductive cycles of some species. Tropical weather patterns are slowly inching away from the equator. Habitat ranges are shifting as temperatures rise, often forcing animals to move to cooler areas.

Protecting and preserving habitat

By protecting and preserving remaining habitats and regenerating some of those that have been lost, we can preserve and protect the animals that live there. Some conservation projects are developing **wildlife corridors**, regenerated strips of vegetation that connect previously isolated patches of remnant habitat. These wildlife corridors extend the range of different species so that breeding populations can mix and avoid the problems of inbreeding. City planners are also starting to do their bit by planning urban 'bush parks', inner-city sanctuaries for small native animals and birds. We can even provide some 'backyard habitat' for smaller creatures by planting animal-friendly gardens.

Eco-activity: attract wildlife to your garden

You can create some inner-urban habitat for wildlife by making your garden wildlife-friendly.

- *Plant native trees and shrubs to attract and feed native birds and butterflies.*

- *Get a cat-proof birdbath to provide a safe water source for birds. Either hang the bath from a tree or put it on a high pedestal and regularly change the water.*

- *Create shelter and nesting sites for birds by placing bird boxes in trees. Surround the trees with shrubs to create a protective thicket.*

- *Provide hollows and sunbathing spots for lizards by partially burying pipes in garden beds, using natural mulch and including rocks and stones in the garden bed. You can place these lizard-friendly areas near your compost bin to provide the lizards with an extra food source.*

- *Plant nectar-producing species such as bottlebrushes and banksias to attract butterflies, insects and small birds.*

- *Garden ponds can be turned into frog habitats. Plant shrubs that attract insects, which provide food for the frogs. You may wish to include small native fish in the pond to prevent mosquitoes breeding in the pond.*

The range of wildlife that you can attract to your garden will depend on the area you live in. Consequently, this will affect the kind of plants that you can use to create backyard habitats. For more information and specific advice on what you can plant around Australia, go to the Flora for Fauna website at <www.floraforfauna.com.au>.

Health hazards

At the end of the day, humans are a species of animal and the earth is our habitat. Like all living things, our health and wellbeing can be influenced by our living environment. In fact, global warming and pollution aren't just environmental issues; they're important public-health issues that need consideration and action. So looking after the environment is not just about saving the whales and planting trees; it's also about looking after ourselves.

Climate change and health

If there was a chemical spill in an industrial area, you wouldn't be surprised to hear of people getting sick in the local area. Some environmental health hazards have an immediate local impact. But the health effects of global warming and climate change are felt around the world, regardless of where the greenhouse emissions that caused them came

from. These health problems include deaths and illness from climate-related disasters (such as floods, hurricanes, heatwaves and bushfires), heat stress, and diseases spread by insects as their range changes with the climate.

Environmental toxins

The quality of our local environment is also important. If potentially harmful toxins get into our air, water, homes or food, our risk of getting sick increases. These toxic pollutants come from a number of sources, such as factories and their wastes, mining, burning fuel and petrol, hazardous chemicals that are not properly handled and pesticides. Among humans, they can trigger allergies, cause cancer and contribute to a wide range of health problems. The good news is that we can reduce the risk of getting sick by limiting our exposure to toxins that might harm us.

Recent years have seen increases in asthma, eczema, hay fever and allergies around the world, with the highest numbers of cases in the world's richer countries. While scientists don't fully understand the link between asthma and wealth, they do know that there are a number of environmental asthma triggers, including pollution, wood smoke, dust, chemicals and strong smells, changes in weather and temperature, and

Eco-lingo

pollutant *This is a contaminant that, when introduced to an environment, can cause harm, discomfort or instability to the living things in that environment.*

Did you know ... ? NASA scientists working towards healthier air in space shuttles found that some plants remove chemicals like benzene and formaldehyde from indoor air. Plants recommended for improving indoor air quality include the happy plant, peace lily, weeping fig, aloe vera and gerbera.

food additives—things that are part of our modern lives in big cities.

Indoor air quality

The average person spends up to 90 per cent of their time indoors, so we have to keep the air inside our homes clean and healthy. Polluted indoor air is a health risk, contributing to problems such as headaches, fatigue, dizziness, respiratory problems and eye, nose, throat and skin irritation. While we don't enclose factories or start cars inside our houses, there are other forms of air pollution that occur in the home.

The main indoor air pollutants are:
- **combustion gases** from cigarette smoke, wood heaters and cooking
- **chemical pollutants** from toiletries, fly spray and other insecticides, paints and cleaning products
- **'offgas' or 'outgas' pollutants** from new products, paint, glossy books and other printed material, carpet and furniture. Offgas pollutants give products 'that new smell' and are generally solvents and other chemicals used in the manufacture of the product that gradually escape from the product over time
- **natural pollutants,** which are naturally occurring, but unhealthy nonetheless. These include dust mites, pet hair, mould and fungi
- **fine airborne particles**. Some materials can go from 'innocent' to 'irritant' if they're in a fine, powdery form and become airborne. Take care when using powdered products, such as body powder or washing powder.

Eco-activity: indoor air pollution checklist

How does your indoor air fare? Tick the box for each of the following things that are in your home. The more you have, the more likely your home has poor indoor air quality. See if you can get rid of some of the items on the list and regularly open windows to let fresh air in.

☐ *Plug-in or spray air fresheners*

☐ *A member of your household who is a smoker*

☐ *Chlorine bleach*

☐ *Gas stoves or heaters without a flue or chimney*

☐ *Open wood fire*

☐ *A car parked in a garage with a connecting door to the house*

☐ *Insect spray*

☐ *Paint stripper, nail polish remover or house paint*

☐ *Indoor pets (dogs, cats, birds, mice)*

☐ *Some spots of mould on walls or the ceilings*

☐ *Carpet (in more than a quarter of the house)*

☐ *Recently painted or renovated rooms*

☐ *New carpet or furniture that has a chemical smell*

☐ *Aerosol spray deodorant or hairspray*

Introduced and invasive species

From marsupials and drought-tolerant plants in Australia to polar bears and mosses on Canada's tundra, our planet's different landscapes have particular plants and animals that belong there. These local species suit the local conditions, the soil and weather patterns. An introduced species, on the other hand, is one brought by humans into a particular region.

Eco-lingo

native   This refers to species from a particular country or region (for example, the two-humped Bactrian camel is native to north eastern Asia).

introduced species   This is a non-native animal or plant brought to a region by humans (also called an **'exotic'** or **'alien'** species).

domestic   This term is used for tamed animals that live with humans and are dependent on them. Examples include cows, horses, chickens, sheep and pet dogs and cats.

wild   This term describes animals that live separately and independently from humans.

feral   Domestic animals that have become wild are described as 'feral'.

weed   This is a plant growing where it is not wanted or where it causes problems.

invasive   This term is used for a species that is able to establish and grow aggressively into an area.

In their natural habitats, individual species play small but important roles. But if you put them into an environment where they don't belong, they can die or, worse still, completely upset the local ecosystem and become invasive. An invasive species can eat too much prey or vegetation for the landscape to support it. Invasive species can also compete with native species for space, water, food and sunlight. They can become a great burden on both the natural environment and agriculture. They can even cause extinctions.

How are they introduced?

New species can be introduced both intentionally and accidentally.

Ways species are intentionally introduced

- Some species are introduced to provide particular **foods**. Early European settlers found Australia's unique biodiversity completely unfamiliar. They were used to eating and using produce from English and European farms and brought these species with them. Rabbits came to Australia with the first fleet to provide a protein source that would grow quickly and reproduce.
- **Acclimatisation societies** were common in the colonial era in the Americas and Australasia. Western settlers were perhaps homesick for familiar plants, flowers and animals, or thought that native species were somehow inferior to the plants and animals from home. Alternatively, they

simply felt that the colony's local environment would be in some way enriched by the introduction of plants and animals from overseas. These societies would set about establishing introduced species in the colonies.

- Some species were introduced to provide **sport**. Rabbits, foxes, deer and pheasants were introduced in the nineteenth century to provide game for recreational hunters.
- **Biological pest control** was another reason for importing non-native species. Cane toads and Indian mynah birds were introduced in Australia to control pest insects, but became pests themselves!

How species are accidentally introduced

- **Soil** can carry weed seeds, eggs, micro-organisms and small animals. For example, one researcher collected seeds from the sludge run-off from a car wash in Canberra and was able to germinate 259 different plants from them, many of them weeds.
- Just as pets can escape and go feral, plants can escape from gardens. **Garden escapes** are a major source of environmental and agricultural weeds.
- Some introduced species were **stowaways**, like the rats and weevils that hitched a ride with the First Fleet. In particular, the ballast water (the water taken into a ship to keep it stable when it has no cargo) that is dumped when a ship is loaded can contain exotic and potentially invasive

marine species, such as the northern Pacific seastar.

- **Tourists** can also bring seeds, microbes, eggs, insects and other tiny biodiversity problems into a country. These plant and animal hitchhikers may be hidden in souvenirs, food products and other items made from living or once living materials. Examples include fruit fly larvae in fruit, and wood-boring insects in wooden souvenirs. That is why the quarantine laws of many countries ask tourists to declare any potentially risky items or food in their luggage.

Austin powers

The Austin family has a chequered past. On the negative side, Thomas Austin is credited with starting Australia's rabbit plague. In 1859 he released twenty-four breeding rabbits onto the land around his homestead, Barwon Park, in Winchelsea, Victoria. He was an enthusiastic member of the Acclimatisation Society of Victoria. People like Thomas Austin were trying to recreate England in Australia, and allow for a bit of fun hunting. They had no idea that rabbits and foxes would one day wreak havoc on the landscape. On a more positive note, Thomas Austin's wife Elizabeth started the Austin Hospital, which is now one of Melbourne's leading teaching and research hospitals.

Controlling introduced species

Introduced and invasive species are a worldwide problem, particularly in this modern age, when ships and aeroplanes can travel easily from country to country. There are two fronts in the battle against invasive species: preventing their entry into a country or region, and controlling or eradicating those that have already entered.

- **Quarantine authorities** police airports and shipping terminals, checking the people, luggage and goods that enter. You may have seen sniffer dogs at the airport. Yes, some are looking for bombs or drugs, but others are trained to sniff out fruit, meat, eggs, plants and even smuggled animals. There are also expert waterfront workers who check the ballast water of container ships for pests and the contents of shipping containers themselves. For example, they may check for seed-containing soil on imported second-hand farming machinery.
- **Biological control** is sometimes used to reduce pest numbers. This uses the help of the pest species' enemies. For example, rabbit-borne diseases myxomatosis and calicivirus have been released in Australia to reduce rabbit numbers.
- **Poisons** are also used, including herbicides to kill weeds and (more controversially) poisoned bait to kill animals. Many people and animal welfare groups are concerned about the ways animal pests are controlled and killed.

- **Weeding** by hand is used in gardens and on some organic farms.
- Some weeds are **burnt off**.
- **Education** can help tourists, householders and farmers to act more responsibly and adopt better ways of working and behaving. For example, weed education programs can help people choose garden plants that aren't invasive, and farming education programs can teach farmers how to identify and eliminate pests before they spread.

A nose that knows

In Australia, the Australian Quarantine and Inspection Service (AQIS) enforces the country's quarantine laws, which help prevent the importation of invasive species and which prohibit the smuggling of endangered plant and animals and their products.

Some of AQIS's workers have four legs and are trained to be nosy. Beagles were chosen to be 'friendly' detector dogs. Their sense of smell is thought to be 100 times more acute than that of humans.

Source: AQIS

Feral Aussies

Australia is home to 10 per cent of the world's biodiversity. Its isolation from other continents and its unique conditions have produced weird and wonderful flora and fauna. However, the unique Australian environment has not responded well to many exotic species from overseas. Conversely, some Australian plants and animals have become troublemakers overseas.

Troublemaking exotics in Australia

- Cats were brought into Australia to control mice and other pests and are now household pets. Cats are predators. Domestic, stray and feral cats all kill native birds, small mammals, reptiles and insects.

- Foxes were first released in Australia near Melbourne for fox hunting in 1855. Within fifty years they had spread to Western Australia. Foxes kill small native animals.

- Feral pigs are destructive animals. Wild pigs are ravaging the floor of the Daintree Forest.

- The northern Pacific seastar is a voracious predator that feeds on a wide range of native marine animals. It's believed that the seastar is affecting oyster farm production in Tasmania.

- The European blackberry was introduced to Australia in the mid-nineteenth century and promoted as a good plant to control erosion, produce nice hedges and provide food. It's now a major weed of both pastures and natural ecosystems.

Unwanted Aussies overseas

- The melaleuca tree ('paperbark' or 'tea tree') is a major threat to the Everglades ecosystem in Florida, USA.

- Australia's national floral emblem, the golden wattle, is devastating the countryside in South Africa.

- Brush-tailed possums were introduced to New Zealand in the 1850s with the hope of establishing a local fur industry. Now they're a threat to native wildlife as they eat the eggs and chicks of native birds and native insects. They also help to spread a bovine disease, threatening the beef and dairy industries.

- The brown tree snake, an accidental import to Guam, has decimated native bird populations. The Guam rail, one of its victims, is now extinct in the wild.

- *Grevillia robusta* (silky oak) was introduced in Hawaii for timber. It's now taking over Hawaiian dry forests and suppressing native tree species.

Learn more

To find out more about the Australian Quarantine and Inspection Service, go to <http://www.daffa.gov.au/aqis/quarantine>.

Invasive species by numbers

There are over **2800** weeds (or unwanted plants) in Australia. About **700** of these are ordinary garden plants that have escaped from our backyards.

Weeds cost Australia about **A$4 BILLION** each year due to lost agricultural production and the costs of weed control.

In 1935, about **100** cane toads were brought from Hawaii. They were bred, and a few thousand were released in northern Queensland in the hope they would control the cane beetle. They didn't! There's now an estimated **200 MILLION** cane toads in Australia.

Female cane toads lay **8000–30 000** eggs at a time. In stark contrast, most Australian native frogs typically lay **1000–2000** eggs per year.

Of the total weight of fish in some parts of the Murray–Darling River Basin, up to **90%** is non-native carp. They may not be tasty enough to be dished up in restaurants, but they can be used to make fertiliser and soil conditioner products!

A single breeding pair of rabbits can multiply to **184** rabbits in just **18** months.

There are more than **500 000** feral camels roaming around in the Australian outback. Some estimates put the number as high as **700 000**, with the population doubling every **8** years.

A New South Wales government report recently said that feral pigs were a threat to **81** threatened species in that state alone.

The Chinese mitten crab (*Eriocheir sinensis*) is a non-native species causing trouble in Europe and North America. The female carries between **250 000** and **1 MILLION** eggs.

Lantana is a pretty flowering garden plant … and an invasive weed. There are about **650** varieties of lantana in over **60** countries or island groups.

If plants were characters in Hollywood movies, then Lantana would be the femme fatale—the highly attractive but ultimately destructive lady. Lantana is a perfumed and beautifully coloured flowering plant originally from Central America. In the seventeenth century, when European empires were expanding and founding colonies around the world, items brought back from the Americas were the hip and happening trend. Lantana was brought to Europe, where it became a popular ornamental plant.

As the empires spread, they took their favourite plants with them, and so Lantana was spread around the world's warm regions. It was introduced in Australia in the mid-nineteenth century but quickly got out of hand. Lantana is a 'biodiversity bully'; its spread threatens the survival of other native species. Lantana forms dense thickets that smother other vegetation. It's also poisonous, killing thousands of animals each year.

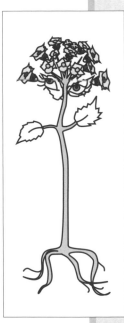

Online profile: Lantana camara

About me: I'm an alluring kind of gal. I'm nice to look at and nice to smell, but be warned: I'm one tough customer. Diseases and pests don't bother me much; I don't need much water, and I can handle the heat. I'm hardy and I spread like wildfire—before you know it, I've taken over. I can't help it if I'm a little poisonous; I do what it takes to survive.

Friends: The birds are my friends: they spread my seeds, helping me in my efforts to take over the tropical world!

Interests: I watch the stock market. I like hostile takeover bids.

Favourite album: *Dangerous* by Michael Jackson

Favourite song: 'Can't Get You Out of My Head' by Kylie Minogue

Favourite band: Savage Garden

Favourite TV show: *Totally Wild*

Favourite movie: *The World is not Enough*—I love a good James Bond movie; they're the natural habitat of dangerous women!

Aliases: Like all good femme fatales, I go by a few different names, which can make it hard for gardeners to work out who I *really* am. My other names include yellow sage, red flowered sage, tick berry, wild sage, prickly lantana, chiPoniwe, mikinolia hihiu, curse of India (I think that's a bit harsh, even if it is true), landana, lanitana, rantana, rahndana, tukasuweth, te kaibuaka, talatala, kauboica, and many more!

Kyoto

The year 1992 was an interesting one for Planet Earth. The summer and winter Olympics were held in the same year for the last time. Disneyland Paris opened. Billy Ray Cyrus had a hit song called 'Achy Breaky Heart' and a newborn daughter called Destiny Hope (later known as Miley Cyrus).

It was also the year of the United Nations Conference on Environment and Development, better known as 'Earth Summit', where representatives from 172 governments and 2400 non-government organisations got together in Rio de Janeiro, Brazil, to discuss ways of achieving a balance between economic growth and development and a healthy planet.

Earth Summit resulted in a number of agreements, including the United Nations Framework Convention on Climate Change (UNFCCC), an international treaty to develop measures to stabilise greenhouse gas emissions in an effort to avoid climate change.

The Kyoto Protocol is the follow-up to the UNFCCC and is an international pact to cut greenhouse gases. The Kyoto Protocol was signed by dozens of countries at the 1997 United Nations climate change conference held in Kyoto, Japan. The governments agreed to reduce the total amount of greenhouse gases produced by developed countries by 5.2 per cent of 1990 levels during the five-year period of 2008–2013. Kyoto Protocol included set mandatory (legally required) limits on greenhouse gas emissions.

Once home from Japan, the next step for signatory countries was to ratify the protocol, formalising it within their own national laws. At least fifty-five countries representing at least 55 per cent of the emissions specified in the agreement were required to ratify the protocol in order for it to come into legally binding force.

By March 2009, 183 countries, including Canada, New Zealand, Japan, the countries of the European Union, Russia and, more recently, Australia had ratified Kyoto. The USA is the only nation that has signed but not ratified the agreement. The government of the USA (one of the most greenhouse polluting nations) under the presidency of George W Bush had argued that Kyoto is too expensive and that it omits developing nations, such as China. Some people have compared signing but not ratifying the Kyoto Protocol to getting engaged but refusing to get legally married. Newly elected President Barack Obama has promised that his administration will do more to reduce the USA's greenhouse emissions and to tackle climate change.

The signatory countries will change their laws, undertake energy reform and industrial reform, develop renewable energy and introduce community education programs to meet their target greenhouse gas reduction. They will also use market-based tools, such as carbon credits, emissions trading schemes and taxes.

Eco-lingo

treaty   *This is a formal contract or agreement.*

protocol   *This is the name for a formal agreement between nations or states.*

What developed faster: international climate change policy or Miley Cyrus?

International climate policy	Year	Miley Ray Cyrus
Earth Summit held in Rio de Janeiro; the United Nations Framework Convention on Climate Change is born.	1992	Destiny Hope (Miley) Cyrus is born on 23 November to Billy Ray Cyrus and Tish Finley.
	1993	
	1994	Miley becomes a big sister (already having older half-siblings).
	1995	Miley learns to ride horses, growing up on the family farm, surrounded by animals.
	1996	
The third Conference of the Parties to the UNFCCC is held in Kyoto, Japan. The Kyoto Protocol is negotiated and signed. Meanwhile, the US government gets cold feet, saying it will not ratify the agreement without emissions reductions or targets for developing countries.	1997	Miley celebrates her fifth birthday.
Hottest year on record	1998	
	1999	
	2000	She becomes a big sister again.
The new US President, George W Bush, gives Kyoto the thumbs down. Other nations ultimately go ahead without US support.	2001	
Australia, under Prime Minister John Howard, sides with the USA, putting Kyoto in jeopardy. This places Russia in the hot seat, knowing its choice will make or break Kyoto.	2002	Miley turns ten years old.
Several countries put pressure on Russia to ratify Kyoto.	2003	She appears in the movie Big Fish as 'Ruthie', and in her dad's TV series Doc.
A deal is done. Russia ratifies Kyoto, while the European Union puts its support behind Russia's bid to become a member of the World Trade Organization.	2004	Miley is given her first guitar and later becomes a spokesperson for Daisy Rock Guitars.
The Kyoto Protocol enters into force on 16 February 2005. Australia, Canada, China, India, Japan, South Korea and the USA get together and sign the Asia-Pacific Partnership on Clean Development and Climate, an agreement that isn't legally binding. Second hottest year on record	2005	She wins the title role in the new Disney series Hannah Montana.
	2006	The Hannah Montana soundtrack, in which Miley Cyrus sings nine of the thirteen tracks, is released, eventually reaching number one on the US Billboard 200 album chart.
Australia, under new Prime Minister Kevin Rudd, ratifies the Kyoto Protocol.	2007	Miley appears in the movie High School Musical 2. She releases her first solo album, Hannah Montana 2: Meet Miley Cyrus, for which she co-wrote seven tracks, and embarks on The Best of Both Worlds concert tour.
	2008	Video and audio recordings of The Best of Both Worlds tour performances are released as a feature film and CD and are very successful.
The USA gets a new President, Barack Obama, who promises to do more about climate change than his predecessor. The 2009 United Nations Climate Change Conference is scheduled for December in Copenhagen, Denmark. The conference goal is to establish an ambitious global agreement to follow the expiry of the first commitment period under the Kyoto Protocol.	2009	Miley stars in the feature film Hannah Montana: The Movie and, naturally, sings for the movie's soundtrack album.

Land-clearing and deforestation

Ten thousand years ago, forests covered a third of the earth's land. Then came agriculture. Growing and harvesting crops and keeping domesticated livestock made food supplies more reliable for humans and allowed communities to build permanent settlements, replacing their nomadic lifestyle. The space needed for farming came from clearing areas of natural vegetation, including forests, scrub, bushland and prairies. Land has also been cleared for forestry and to make way for urban sprawl.

We've now lost a quarter of our planet's forests and only 12 per cent are still in their natural state. Each year, we're still loosing at least 16.2 million more hectares of our forests through logging and land-clearing, placing around 10 per cent of the world's tree species in danger of extinction.

It's not just the trees themselves that are becoming endangered through land-clearing. The habitat for a variety of wildlife is also destroyed. This places some species at risk of becoming extinct. In Australia, for every 100 hectares of woodland cleared, 1000–2000 birds lose their homes. Similarly, 200 reptiles are killed for every hectare of mallee country cleared. Land-clearing also causes dryland salinity.

Land-clearing and deforestation are contributing to air pollution and climate change. Bulldozed, rotting and burning forests and bush 'unlock' the carbon stored in plant tissues and release massive amounts of greenhouse gases and other pollutants into the air. The air over Indonesia and neighbouring countries is often thick with smoke haze from fires used to clear land for plantations. Sometimes the haze is so bad that schools and offices are temporarily closed, people are forced to wear face masks, and the young and elderly are advised to stay indoors.

Deforestation, erosion and high rainfall combine with devastating effects. Much of the soil washed from cleared land by rainfall ends up dumped in rivers. This is causing water levels to rise and the rivers to flood. In 1998, China's Yangtze River burst its banks in the southern province of Hunan, killing more than 4000 people. This prompted the government to ban logging in sensitive areas and intensify their replanting program. In parts of South-East Asia, much of the problem lies outside the law. It has been estimated that nearly three-quarters of log production in Indonesia comes from illegal logging.

Over the past 200 years, Australia has lost well over half of its rainforests and more than 30 per cent of other forests and woodlands. But the kind of land-clearing that really gets people upset is the clear-fell logging of old growth forests. Some of Australia's beautiful hardwood forests, such as Tasmania's Styx Valley, are being logged for woodchips to make paper and packaging. Some of the trees in the Styx Valley are 500 years old and over 100 metres high. These unique forests could be preserved and developed as tourist attractions. Already, the giant redwood forests in the USA attract visitors. Instead, we're taking this amazing natural resource and liquidating it for the quick woodchipping dollar.

Animals threatened by deforestation

In Australia

- Long-footed potoroo
- Leadbeater's possum
- Tiger quoll
- Yellow-bellied glider
- Glossy black-cockatoo
- Sooty owl
- Regent honeyeater
- Spotted tree frog

Around the world

- Siberian tiger
- Woodland caribou
- Spectacled bear
- Pygmy hippopotamus
- Woolly spider monkey
- Orang-utan
- Squirrel monkey
- Ruffed lemur

Old growth forests are complicated ecosystems that take centuries to establish. Tree hollows occur in only very old trees. Around 400 of Australia's land-dwelling animals (including birds, marsupials and other mammals, amphibians and reptiles) use these tree hollows. Crazy as it seems, some forestry companies are clearing old growth forests to plant 'regrowth' forests. Once the land is cleared, the forestry companies lay bait laced with 1080 poison to kill any animals that might dare to eat the new seedlings. These new forests will have no tree hollows or fallen hollow logs to provide homes for animals.

Tropical rainforests are also disappearing at an alarming rate. Rainforests help to stabilise the global climate, purify the air and water, and contain more than half of all the world's plant and animal species. This biodiversity contributes billions of dollars to the world's economy through the production and sale of the products that come from rainforests. The plants alone produce a range of hardwoods, rubber, essential oils, fruit, spices, coffee and medicines. Tropical rainforests still hold hundreds of undiscovered species and many more that haven't been fully investigated. Rainforests are rapidly being destroyed. It's hoped that these forests may provide treatments and cures for cancer, AIDS and other illnesses. Yet this huge medical potential may go untapped, and these plants and animals may never be discovered.

Landfill

You put your rubbish in the rubbish bin. When the rubbish bin gets full, you empty it into your wheelie bin. On rubbish day, the wheelie bin gets put on the kerbside so that a garbage truck can empty it, and then the garbage truck drives off into the distance. Have you ever stopped to wonder happens next?

Once the truck is full of rubbish, it heads to a landfill site, also known as a rubbish dump or tip. A landfill is an area of land set aside for disposing of rubbish permanently. Waste is basically buried—deposited in layers along the 'working face' of the landfill, then compacted and covered with soil (usually daily).

The trouble with landfills is that they come with both environmental and financial costs. They cost a lot to build, run and (once closed) rehabilitate. These costs are paid for by businesses and industries that send their waste there, and by householders who pay rates to the local councils that provide garbage-collection services.

Landfills can also pollute the local environment. As materials break down and the landfill site is exposed to weather, landfills produce the by-products of landfill: gas and leachate, the toxic liquid produced as rainwater seep through the rubbish. The main component of landfill gas is methane, which is a greenhouse gas, an explosion risk and very smelly for anyone living nearby. Landfill sites also attract rats and other vermin, and produce a lot of dust and noise. No one wants to live near one, so there is usually a lot of community opposition to government plans to build new landfill sites. This is what we call the NIMBY attitude: 'Not In My Back Yard!' When landfill sites are close to urban centres, the garbage trucks don't have to drive as far, using less fuel and producing less greenhouse emissions. But when they're too close, it's the residents who kick up a stink!

Modern landfill operations have special liner and drainage systems, which remove the toxic leachate. Landfill sites can also tap the gas and burn it to produce electricity, a greener electricity source than coal-fired power stations. However, even when a landfill site is well managed and producing green electricity, it's still a dead end for the materials that end up there. Each year, billions of aluminium drink cans that could have been recycled end up in landfill. Ideally, we should recover and make better use of the resources that end up as waste. While the organic matter in landfill will eventually break down, the plastic in landfill will remain there for hundreds of years. So landfills don't completely solve the problem of rubbish; they leave it for future generations.

When a landfill becomes full, it is covered or 'capped' and the land can be used for other purposes, such as sport fields, parks or golf courses. In some cases, it can even be built on, provided the build-up of methane is still captured and removed to reduce the explosion risk.

Landfills tell stories

Disposal in landfill is a method of dealing with waste that has been around for thousands of years. In fact, archaeologists (scientists that study ancient cultures by examining their material remains) and anthropologists (scientists that study humankind) look for and study ancient household rubbish dumps, called kitchen middens. The bits of bone, shell, pottery and other artefacts tell us a lot about ancient societies and civilisations: what they ate, what they produced, the tools they used, what they used as money and how they lived. Similarly, our landfills say a lot about our society. Archaeologists a thousand years from now might study our landfills and conclude that people in the early twenty-first century were obsessed with Tamagotchi toys, used a lot of packaging and broke a lot of stuff.

A modern landfill in cross section

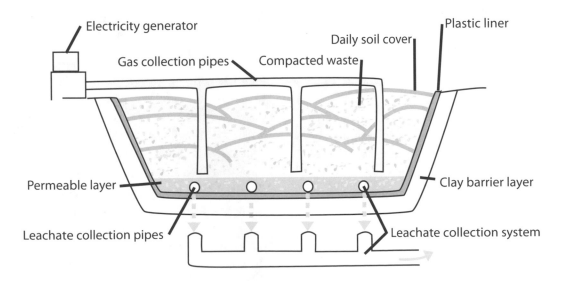

Lifestyle

A sporty person has an active lifestyle. A computer geek is more likely to have a sedentary lifestyle (a clever-sounding way of saying that he or she sits a lot!). Your lifestyle is your pattern of living: what you do during the day, what you eat, what you buy, what you do for fun, where you live and how you get around.

Early in the book we looked at the ecological footprint (see page 38), which is a way of measuring the environmental impact of a particular lifestyle. More importantly, we looked at lifestyle choices that can reduce our ecological footprint.

It's important to remember that not everyone in the world enjoys the same kind of lifestyle that you do. We enjoy a high standard of living in Western countries, but children in many developing nations have very different lifestyles, and much smaller footprints!

Learn more

See what life is like in other developing countries by downloading individual country profiles on the World Vision Australia Schools Resources website at <www.worldvision.com.au/learn/schoolResources/country profiles.asp>.

Walking in someone else's shoes

When someone asks you to consider something from someone else's point of view, they say, 'Put yourself in their shoes'. Here we take a walk in the ecological footprint of two very different young people.

Harry lives in Adelaide, South Australia. He rides his bike to school each day, except on Fridays, when his Mum drives him to football practice after school. He has a shower every day (twice on Fridays). His house is full of electricity-using gadgets, and he loves going online to play RuneScape with friends. His two chores are taking care of the household recycling and, in summer, watering the garden using water from the rainwater tank (many Adelaide homes have had them for years). His favourite food is chocolate ice-cream. When he grows up he wants to be a sports journalist and says that being a TV sports commentator would be the coolest.

Asale has never seen, let alone tasted, chocolate ice-cream. Instead, she has two bowls a day of corn porridge, cooked with vegetables and sometimes a bit of fish or meat. She lives in rural Malawi in Africa. Her brother goes to school. Asale went to school for a little while but was needed at home after her mother died. Her chores take up much of her day and include growing vegetables for the family, fetching wood and water, and looking after her younger brothers and sister. Asale wants to learn to read and write.

Eco-activity: Dear Diary

Many of our daily lifestyle habits have an impact on the environment. The trouble with habits is that you do them automatically, without really thinking about them or their consequences.

One way to become more aware of how your lifestyle affects the environment is to keep an eco-diary. Photocopy this page (or create an electronic version on a computer) and fill out the things you do, buy or consume in a single day. Also write down any ideas you may have that might lessen the impact of these activities in the future.

Waste

Write down each item you throw out or recycle.

_____

_____

_____

Energy

Write down everything you do today that uses energy, including electricity. Think of things like turning on a light, watching TV, recharging a game console, turning on a heater, using a hot-air hand-dryer or using a microwave.

_____

_____

_____

Water

Write down every time you turn a tap on or use water in some way, including flushing the toilet, washing hands, having a drink or having a shower (and write down how long you take, if you have a shower timer).

_____

_____

_____

_____

Getting around

Did you go anywhere today: school? shopping? a friend's house? How did you get there?

_____

_____

_____

Shopping

Write down all of the things you bought. Revisit this list later and write down how quickly and how much you used them, and whether you think they were worth the money and resources needed to make them.

_____

_____

_____

_____

Litter

Take a simple apple core. The person who ate the apple is about to decide the core's destiny. Will he or she put it in a rubbish bin and send it to landfill, put it in a compost bin and turn it into plant food, or dump it on the ground and turn it into a smelly, slimy, bug-infested piece of litter? What makes something a piece of litter? Being in the wrong place at the wrong time.

Litter is often talked about, and most people agree it's a problem, yet amazingly people still do it! One of the reasons we're concerned about litter is that it can lead to increased health risks. Litter adds to local pollution, attracts vermin (such as rats) and provides a breeding ground for bacteria. Broken glass and syringes can cause cuts and other puncture wounds. Litter can harm wildlife. Smouldering cigarette butts can also be a fire hazard. And for those with an inner neat freak, litter simply doesn't look good.

A little litter goes a long way, given the right conditions. Wind can carry lightweight litter items, such as empty plastic bags, over great distances. Rain can wash the litter off streets, into stormwater drains and eventually into rivers, waterways and the sea. In fact, it's been estimated that around 95 per cent of the litter on the beaches of Melbourne, Victoria, comes from suburban streets.

Common litter items are cigarette butts, plastic bags, lolly wrappers, bottle tops, straws, cans and bottles, takeaway coffee cups, chip bags and cigarette packaging. Even popped balloons and their strings from balloon releases can end up in the environment as litter and harm wildlife. Litter is also a financial problem, with local councils having to spend millions of dollars each year on preventing and cleaning up litter.

> *I am a Waste Wise Witch. Being a Waste Wise Witch is good because it is fun and I love helping the environment. We help the environment by picking up rubbish and then some Waste Wise Witches and Wizards do recycling bins. Other kids could be waste wise too.* Kelly, 10

Did you know ... ? An estimated 8000 people volunteered to pick up other people's litter on Clean Up Australia Day in March 2008. That's just in one country. Clean Up the World Weekend is held each year in the third weekend of September, involving an estimated 35 million volunteers from more than a hundred countries.

Eco-action: a little less litter

- *Look after your local environment and don't litter. Remember that dropped rubbish is still litter even if it's small (bottle lids), it's not noticeable (chewing gum stuck under a seat) or it's biodegradable (banana peel). Use a bin instead.*

- *Many bushland parks and nature reserves have a 'carry in, carry out' policy when it comes to visitors and their rubbish. Take a small bag or container with you to take litter home in if you're going somewhere where you're unlikely to find a bin.*

- *You can even go one step further and pick up other people's litter while you're out and about.*

Litter hot spots

According to the Keep Australia Beautiful National Litter Index 2007/2008, an Australia-wide litter count, the worst locations with the highest amounts of litter are:

- Retail areas
- Industrial areas
- Shopping centres
- Car parks
- Beaches
- Highways

Lethal litter

- Plastic shopping bags are blown into the sea where they do a very good impersonation of a jellyfish. Huge knots of this plastic have been found in the bellies of dead whales and other large marine mammals that have mistaken them for food.

- Fishing line, netting, rope and other litter from sport and commercial fishing can trap and strangle animals.

- The 'honeycomb' plastic that holds a six-pack of cans together is also lethal. The strong plastic rings can strangle and slit the throats of small marine animals, including fairy penguins.

- A post-mortem on a sperm whale found dead on a North American beach found that the whale had starved to death because a plastic gallon bottle had plugged its small intestine.

- Cigarette butts include the filter, which traps some of the most toxic components of cigarette smoke. Cigarette butts are like fibrous pellets of poison and can kill birds, turtles and other marine animals that swallow them. Studies have also linked cigarette butt pollution to tumours in marine animals. On land, flicked cigarette butts can also cause bushfires, which can kill animals and burn their habitat, not to mention the toll on human lives and settlements.

What sort of litterbug is that?

'Litterbugs', the nickname given to people that litter, are more common than you would think. An Australian company, Community Change, with the help of funding from Australia's beverage industry, did some research into who litters, and into how, what and why people litter. Here's a list of the common types of litterbugs, based on the littering behaviours identified by the people at Community Change. You may recognise a couple.

The litterbug line-up

- **The foul shooter:** Like a sloppy basketball player, he aims at the bin, but doesn't care if he misses.

- **The sweeper:** She takes her place at a recently vacated outdoor café table and sweeps any remaining rubbish onto the ground.

- **The inch worm:** This litterbug deposits the litter item close to his body on the ground or a park bench and, inch by inch, slowly moves away from it.

- **The undertaker:** This person buries the litter, commonly a cigarette butt buried in the sand at the beach.

- **The flagrant flinger:** Litter is unashamedly thrown or dropped without any apparent concern, occasionally as an act of rebellion by a teenager who likes to show off!

- **The 90 percenter:** This litterbug bins most of the obvious rubbish but leaves behind smaller items.

- **The wedgie:** Pieces of litter are stuffed into cracks or small spaces.

- **The grinder:** Her boots were made for walkin' ... and grinding cigarette butts to smithereens.

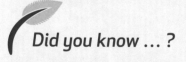

Did you know ... ?   The United Nations Environment Programme (UNEP) has estimated that over 13 000 pieces of plastic litter are floating on every square kilometre of ocean surface.

Litter on the high seas

Burial at sea is all well and good for sailors, but unfortunately it's happening to rubbish too. About eight million items of marine litter have been estimated to enter the world's oceans and seas every day.

Some of it sinks to the sea floor; some floats on the surface. Either way, marine litter is an environmental problem that pollutes marine ecosystems, injures and kills sea life, smothers areas of seabed, provides a floating path for the spread of invasive species and helps toxic substances accumulate (build up) in the marine food chain.

The bad news for humans is that marine litter affects us too. It can contaminate beaches and harbours, damage boats, ships and fishing equipment, pose health and safety risks to people at sea and cause poisons such as heavy metals to build up in some types of seafood.

Trash vortex!

Floating in the doldrums of the North Pacific is a huge floating toxic swamp of rubbish called the Great Pacific Garbage Patch—also known as the Asian Trash Trail, the Eastern Garbage Patch, the Plastic Soup or the Pacific Trash Vortex. It's the result of litter, flotsam and jetsam, the durability of plastic, and ocean currents. This area of ocean— the North Pacific Subtropical Gyre—has slowly circulating ocean currents, so the floating, mostly plastic litter that makes its way there becomes trapped. Although its exact size is hard to measure, the lowest estimates are about 700 000 square kilometres, making it literally bigger than Texas!

Sources of marine litter

From the sea	From the land
• Commercial shipping, ferries and cruise liners	• Waste dumps located near the coast
• Fishing vessels	• Waste from other sources transported along rivers, canals and other inland waterways
• Military fleets and research vessels	• Release of untreated waste water, including urban stormwater
• Pleasure craft	• Industrial facilities (solid waste from landfills, and untreated waste water)
• Offshore oil and gas rigs	• Tourism (visitors to the coast, beach-goers)
• Fish farming installations	

Source: UNEP Regional Seas Program

Natural disasters

The next few pages are officially a disaster area—probably like your little brother's bedroom. Natural disasters happen when the forces of nature are at their most powerful and doing the most damage. They harm the natural environment and human-made structures and settlements alike.

The natural disasters that you'll hear the most about are the ones that kill the most people or that inflict the most expensive damage. For example, Hurricane Katrina, a hurricane that tore through the Gulf of Mexico and into southern USA in August 2005, was not the strongest on record, but it cost many lives and caused billions of dollars in damage to the city of New Orleans—a modern, prosperous city.

Some natural disasters take us by surprise. Earthquakes, and the tsunami they can cause, come with little or no warning. Some natural disasters happen in predictable areas, times of year and patterns, such as 'Tornado Alley' between the Rocky Mountains and Appalachian Mountains in the USA and the summer bushfire season in Australia. Being predictable, people can make plans to avoid these disasters, prepare for them or manage their effects.

Natural or unnatural disasters?

Some natural disasters are starting to show signs of human influence. Climate change is changing the frequency and strength of certain weather disasters. Plus, land-clearing, deforestation, mining and other human activities are affecting the stability of some land areas, increasing the amount of damage that can be done by natural disasters. For example, logging removes the trees that might slow down an avalanche or whose roots would hold down the soil in heavy rainfall.

Natural disasters can be scary, but it's important to learn about them. That way, we can be prepared and know what to do when they happen. In the case of those that stem from climate change, we may even be able to help prevent them from getting too much worse.

Land movement disasters

- **Earthquakes** are caused by movements of the earth's crust, generally along 'fault lines'. They are felt as a shaking of the ground, which can damage the buildings, roads and other structures nearby.

Did you know … ?

Munich Re, an insurance company, estimates that the world's natural disasters in 2008 cost US$200 billion, more than 2007's US$82 billion, but below the record of US$230 billion for 2005, the year Hurricane Katrina hit the USA.

Sometimes they rupture gas pipes, causing fires. Earthquakes can occasionally be triggered by large explosions, such as those in mining operations.

- **Volcanoes** are openings in the earth's crust that allow molten rock, ash and hot gases to escape from beneath. Over time, layers of cooled molten rock build up, producing a mountain shape. When enough pressure builds up under the volcano, it erupts. Volcanoes are generally found where the planet's tectonic plates (like large pieces of the earth's crust) meet, or at 'hotspots' within plates. The idea of living near a volcano might seem crazy, but the fertile soil in volcanic areas can tempt people to live near those volcanoes that only erupt rarely.
- **Avalanches** are sudden and dramatic flows of snow down a mountainside. They happen when snowpack (the build-up of layers of fallen snow) becomes too heavy for the mountainside and its vegetation to support its weight.
- **Landslides** and **mudslides** occur when a large area of ground, rock or earth moves or subsides. They are basically the effect of gravity on unstable ground. Natural causes of landslides include erosion, softening of the ground by water (such as excessive snow melt or rainfall), loss of plant root systems that give soil structure, earthquakes and volcanic eruptions. However, humans can cause or assist landslides by creating vibrations with machinery, removing deep-rooted plants, changing the contours of the land so that drainage and stability are affected, or by causing explosions, such as in mining.

Water disasters

- **Floods** can be caused by rising water levels or periods of heavy rainfall, including cyclones and other extreme weather events. Like weather-related natural disasters, flooding is expected to increase as a result of climate change, global warming and melting icecaps. Floods make sanitation difficult, mixing sewerage with drinking water and spreading diseases, such as cholera and typhoid. Stagnant flood waters also provide breeding grounds for mosquitos, which spread other diseases, such as malaria.
- **Tsunamis** bring a damaging rush of water, followed by the consequences of flooding. They are caused by earthquakes.

Did you know ... ? All weather disasters are expected to increase, either in severity or frequency or both, as a result of climate change.

Weather disasters

- **Heatwaves** can cause crop failure, wildfires, and illness and death in plants, animals and people.
- **Drought** occurs as a result of inadequate rainfall. It causes crop failure and famine.
- **Thunderstorms** or electrical storms are known for their lightning and thunder. The lightning can start wildfires. Thunderstorms may be accompanied by high winds and heavy hail or rainfall, which have their own damaging effects.
- **Winter storms** or **blizzards** are severe storms with very cold temperatures, strong winds and heavy snowfall. In some areas, they may be followed by a high risk of avalanches. Even just unusually cold temperatures alone can affect frost-sensitive crops.
- Strictly speaking, a **cyclone** is a low-pressure weather system, but we usually use the word to mean a rotating storm system with heavy rain and winds that blow towards a low-pressure eye of the storm. Cyclonic storms in the Southern Hemisphere are often called **tropical cyclones**; in the North Atlantic and West Pacific oceans, they are called **hurricanes**, and they are called **typhoons** in the East Pacific Ocean.
- **Tornadoes** are long, thin vertical tunnels of rapidly spinning air, earning them the nickname 'twisters'.

Eco-action: give the gift of global aid

The 2004 Boxing Day tsunami devastated India, Sri Lanka, Indonesia and Thailand, killing over 225 000 people and making millions more homeless. The tragedy captured the hearts of many Australians, particularly those who had enjoyed holidays in these countries. Australians collectively donated about A$353 million to help the victims of the disaster.

There are many worldwide charities dedicated to helping the victims of natural disasters and the millions more who continually struggle with poverty, war and injustice. Some are:

- *World Vision,* <www.worldvision.org.au>
- *the Red Cross,* <www.redcross.org.au>
- *UNICEF (the United Nations Children's Fund),* <www.unicef.org.au>.

Some charities offer a cool way for people to make a donation instead of getting a gift for a person who has everything! You can give a charity gift on their behalf. Through the Oxfam Unwrapped program, for instance, you can give a mosquito net to protect a disadvantaged family from malaria ($20), a goat to provide milk and cheese ($39), water for a school in Laos or Cambodia ($98) or even a pedal-powered bicycle ambulance ($296) for a village in Malawi or any one of a number of other life-saving presents. Go shopping at <www.oxfamunwrapped.com.au>.

Bushfires and wildfires

Humans have a love–hate relationship with fire. Its intense release of the energy can be both helpful and harmful. Cooking and heating with carefully controlled fires dates back to prehistoric times. However, when fires get out of control they can threaten and destroy life (human, animal and plant life), damage property, contribute to pollution and harm the environment.

Wildfires are uncontrolled fires in areas of vegetation, such as wilderness, forests or the bush. In the Australasian region, they're called 'bushfires'. The basic things needed for a fire to start and burn are a supply of fuel (materials that burn fairly easily), enough oxygen (fires can't burn without oxygen) and an ignition source, such as a spark, an existing flame or lightning. Other factors, such as very hot weather and dry windy conditions, can make bushfires larger and more intense, increasing their damage and spreading them over great distances.

Bushfires are often linked to the weather disasters of drought, heatwaves and windy thunderstorms. In fact, many of the world's worst wildfires have followed periods of drought and high temperatures. Drought and heatwaves provide the right conditions for bushfires, drying the land and plant life, making it a highly flammable fuel. In such dry conditions, it can take only a tiny spark to start a bushfire, such as a still-burning cigarette butt, sparks from power tools, barbecues, fireworks or campfires. Lightning strikes and sparks from faulty or broken powerlines can also start bushfires.

Shockingly, some bushfires are deliberately lit by people who have a nasty desire to cause harm or experience danger. This is a criminal act, known as 'arson', and convicted arsonists go to gaol. If people are killed by deliberately lit fires, arsonists are also charged with manslaughter. Following the 'Black Saturday' bushfires in Victoria (which included deliberately lit fires), the Australian Prime Minister, Kevin Rudd, described the arson attacks as 'mass murder'.

Like weather disasters, wildfires are expected to increase, either in severity or frequency or both, as a result of climate change. Many Victorians who had experienced both the 1983 Ash Wednesday and the 2009 Black Saturday bushfires said that the 2009 fires were faster and more intense than any other. Many experts called these fires, coming after an extremely long drought, a different kind of bushfire—one intensified by climate change and possibly a taste of things to come.

Types of wildfire

- Bushfire
- Grass fire
- Forest fire
- Peat fire
- Brush fire

Did you know … ? Cyclone winds blow in a clockwise direction in the Southern Hemisphere and an anti-clockwise direction in the Northern Hemisphere.

USA, 1910
After nine days of blizzard conditions, the town of Wellington, Washington, in the Cascade Mountains was deep in snow. Warm wind and rain caused a slab of snow to break off Windy Mountain. The resulting avalanche hit the town, causing ninety-six deaths.

Around the world: eco-disasters

Italy, 79 CE
Mount Vesuvius famously erupted in 79 CE, burying the Roman cities of Pompeii and Herculaneum. It has erupted many times since then and is considered one of the highest risk volcanic areas, since it is one of the few volcanoes to have erupted in the last century and it has about three million people living near it.

Gulf of Mexico, 2005
Hurricane Katrina, which left the city of New Orleans underwater in its wake, was the USA's most expensive hurricane in history, causing over US$80 billion worth of damage (2005 estimate). More than 1800 people lost their lives.

Russia, 1904
A tornado swept through the suburbs of Moscow, destroying over 3000 homes.

rope, 2003
e record-breaking summer heatwave
used wildfires in Portugal, crop losses in
uthern Europe and an estimated 35 000
aths, mostly of elderly people, from heat.

China, 1931
The Central China floods of 1931 were possibly the deadliest natural disaster on record. A series of abnormal weather events (heavy winter snowfall, high rainfall and a series of cyclones), following a drought, all caused river levels to rise. The Yellow, Yangtze and Huai rivers all flooded. Estimates of the human death toll range up to four million.

ngladesh, 1970
e devastating Bhola tropical cyclone hit
ngladesh (then East Pakistan) and West
ngal in India. It was the world's deadliest
pical cyclone on record. The cyclone and
e storm surge it caused killed up to half a
llion people, or more, in these low-lying
ds.

Philippines, 2006
The Philippine province of Southern Leyte experienced a massive mudslide on 17 February 2006. The mudslide was believed to have been caused by ten days of heavy rain, a minor earthquake and logging and mining previously done in the area, destabilising the soil. Over a thousand people died.

Indonesia, 1883
Krakatoa is a volcanic island. Its eruption in 1883 was one of the most powerful of modern times and could be clearly heard 3500 kilometres away in Perth, Australia. More than 36 000 people died. Clouds of ash in the atmosphere disrupted normal weather patterns and caused temperatures worldwide to drop by a degree or so. The island is still active, and scientists warn people not to come within 3 kilometres of it.

dian Ocean, 2004
e Boxing Day tsunami was caused by an undersea
rthquake with a magnitude of 9.3. The resulting
nami devastated the coastlines of countries
rdering the Indian Ocean, killing more than
5 000 people in eleven countries. The hardest
countries were Sri Lanka, India, Thailand and
donesia.

Australia, 2009
The Black Saturday bushfires that were at their worst on 7 February (but continued burning for over a month) killed 173 people, hospitalised hundreds more, destroyed more than 2000 homes and burnt a total area of well over 4000 square kilometres.

stralia, 1983
e Ash Wednesday bushfires of 16 February burnt
30 square kilometres in a single day in South
stralia and Victoria. Seventy-five people lost their
es.

stralia, early 2000s
ny parts of Australia experienced drought conditions
5–10 years, severely affecting farming and river health.

Oil

'Oil' is the name given to many liquids that are thicker than water, that don't dissolve in water and that burn. They can come from plants (such as the olive oil in your salad dressing), animals (including the emu oil used in traditional Aboriginal medicine or lanolin from animals with wool) or from mineral deposits (petroleum).

Oil is useful stuff. Some oils dissolve substances that don't dissolve in water. Some oils are used in food, others in beauty products, and they are the raw material for making plastic. But the major use for oil is as a fuel. It's a convenient liquid form of energy that can be piped over great distances, carried across oceans in oil tankers, pumped at petrol stations and used to heat homes, produce electricity, power motors and move cars and aeroplanes. The vast bulk of the oil we use comes from crude oil, a mineral resource extracted from reserves in the earth's crust.

Jurassic juice

Crude oil is basically millions of years of sunlight that fell on the earth tens of millions of years ago, concentrated into a liquid. Prehistoric oceans were teaming with living things that got their energy from sunshine and stored it in their tissues. After they died and settled on the ocean floor, layers of sediment buried them. Millions of years of time, heat and pressure turned this dead organic matter into oil, as shown in the diagram of fossil fuel formation on page 69. We now rely heavily on oil and its products, both as an energy source and as a raw material for making a huge range of materials, products and substances.

Petroleum in products

All these products can contain materials made from (petroleum) oil:

- CDs and DVDs
- lip gloss
- cleaning products
- pens
- mobile phones
- calculators
- computers
- shampoo
- deodorant
- stockings
- Polarfleece jackets
- sleeping bags
- aspirin
- fertiliser
- bug spray
- cars
- toys
- drink bottles

Think about it

What is the best use of corn: food, fibre or fuel? Keep in mind that the grain needed to make enough ethanol to fill a 95-litre four-wheel drive petrol tank could feed one person for a year.

> **Did you know ... ?** The oily road run-off from a city of 5 million people could release as much oil into the ocean over a year as one large tanker spill.

Oily issues

The trouble with oil is that, despite its uses and convenience, its extraction and use, and our reliance on it, have some serious environmental consequences. The main problems associated with oil are that:

- the extraction and refining of crude oil damages local environments and produces pollution
- burning oil as a fuel is one of the major sources of climate-changing greenhouse gases
- petrol derived from crude oil is burnt to provide power in cars, producing smoggy and unhealthy urban air
- the world has a limited amount of crude oil. It is not renewable. Plus, worldwide demand for oil is increasing rapidly.

Oil spills

Oil spills from oil tankers and pipelines wreak havoc on the marine environment. Oil smothers and poisons the animal and plant life that lives in and around the sea. One of the most famous oil spills was the 42-million-litre *Exxon Valdez* spill of 1989. This spill harmed or killed thousands of aquatic mammals and hundreds of thousands of seabirds, and shut down the local fishing industry. Seabirds were coated in oil, which ruined the waterproofing effect of their feathers. They died from exposure to the cold.

Even low-level oil pollution can damage wildlife. The relatively small 6800-litre diesel fuel spill near the Galapagos Islands in January 2001 at first appeared to cause little harm. A recent study, though, has found that 62 per cent of the iguanas on one of the affected islands died within a year of the accident. Since 1970, there have been over fifty spills as big as the *Exxon Valdez* spill. The worst oil-spill disaster was the 1991 Gulf War.

Is plant power the answer?

As the world starts thinking about what might happen if we run out of oil, many scientists, politicians and ordinary people are looking hopefully at renewable oil from plants. People are now getting excited about biodiesel cars and plastic bags made from cornstarch. Unfortunately, there's a downside to plant power. For example, as people start producing car fuel from ethanol, which is made from corn, it pushes the price of corn up. This makes corn too expensive for the world's poorest people, many of whom rely on corn (or maize) as their main food. In Indonesia, native rainforests are being cleared to make way for palm oil plantations. This land-clearing produces huge quantities of greenhouse gases and is threatening the survival of the region's orang-utans. So there are still good reasons to use less oil, regardless of where it comes from.

Overhunting

It's a tough world out in the wild. Different species have different attributes and abilities that help them to survive. Some are hunters, with a killer instinct that helps them to catch their prey. This might seem vicious, but the alternative is staying hungry. You can see the hunting instinct in action when lions chase antelope in wildlife documentaries, or even when your pet kitten stalks your pet goldfish.

In nature, there's a delicate balance between the hunter (predator) and the hunted (prey). The numbers of a particular species grow as long as there's enough food to eat. So, too, predator numbers grow as long as there's enough prey. When they run out of prey, the predator numbers drop off. This gives the prey species a break—a chance to grow, have babies and re-establish their numbers.

Humans can be hunters, too. We also have the help of four-wheel drives and other off-road vehicles, weapons and machinery, which make it easier for us to take whatever we want from the natural world, with little resistance.

The trouble is that humans have become too good at hunting. Also, there are many of us to feed and clothe, and our numbers are continuing to grow. The animals we hunt aren't getting a break from being hunted.

Learn more

See the entry on endangered and extinct species (page 46) for more information on the extinction of animals.

Animals hunted to extinction

- Moa, a flightless bird
- Woolly mammoth
- Giant bison
- Giant armadillo
- Some species of ground sloth
- Tasmanian tiger
- Dodo bird

The domino effects of overhunting

Animals can be hunted to extinction. This can have flow-on effects in the ecosystems to which they once belonged. For example, the Mauritian calvaria tree stopped sprouting seeds soon after the dodo became extinct. It turns out that the calvaria seeds need to be eaten and digested in order to sprout–a job the dodo bird had been doing.

Learn more

See the entry on animal welfare (page 9), for more information on cruelty to animals.

How species become overhunted

Humans are continuing to hunt and fish a range of land and sea species unsustainably. There are a number of factors that contribute to a species becoming overhunted.

Subsistence hunting:
hunting to survive

In developing countries, humans mostly hunt to provide food for their often-starving families. In these areas, there was once enough 'bush meat' from wild animals to feed the people. However, without adequate birth control and the teaching of family-planning principles, and with habitat loss and land degradation from environmental problems such as drought, the human population has become too large for the land to support. Many forests and savannah lands have been picked clean of edible animals.

Commercial hunting and fishing

Hunting and fishing can be a way of making money. For commercial hunting and fishing to be sustainable and profitable into the future, animals can't be caught faster than the rate at which their young are born. Otherwise, the numbers of hunted animals start to decrease, becoming 'depleted'. Overfishing is particularly a problem. The United Nations Food and Agriculture Organization estimates that over 70 per cent of the world's fish species are either fully exploited or depleted. Governments set limits on the numbers of animals that can be caught. Legitimate commercial hunting and fishing operations work within the laws set by governments.

Illegal hunting for black market trade

Not everyone who hunts for a living, however, does so within the rules set by governments. There are some hunters and fishing operations that operate outside the law. They may take greater numbers of their target species than they're allowed, or hunt endangered species illegally. They generally care more about the money than conservation. As well as removing species from the environment in an unsustainable way, they sometimes catch live animals and keep them in appalling conditions before selling them.

Big game hunting: game on or game off?

While the sport of hunting can threaten endangered animals, in some cases it may help to secure a future for them. Some countries are allowing a small, closely watched and controlled amount of hunting in their wildlife reserves. Big game hunters pay huge amounts of money to be allowed to hunt protected animals. Yes, for the bargain (not!) price of US$10 000, you too can buy a licence to shoot one elephant. But you can only shoot one of the marked elephants, which are too old to reproduce. Many of these reserves put the money raised back into the upkeep of the land and the conservation of its animal inhabitants.

Ozone layer

The sun gives out lots of different wavelengths of radiation, including visible light and ultraviolet (UV) light. We love the sun's brightness and warmth, but some wavelengths of light are damaging. Think of the ozone layer as SPF 30+ sunscreen for the planet. The planet spends all its time in the sun, so without the ozone layer it would get very 'sunburnt'.

Air is a mixture of gases. The air 14–45 kilometres above the earth's surface has high amounts of ozone in the mixture. This layer of gas is called the ozone layer. It's higher up in the atmosphere than the height that aeroplanes cruise at. The ozone layer is vitally important because it absorbs over 90 per cent of the ultraviolet light shining from the sun towards the earth. We definitely want just the right amount of ozone in the atmosphere.

What's up with the ozone layer?

Some gases can destroy ozone. We call these ozone-depleting gases. The most famous (or perhaps infamous) ozone-busting gases are a family of human-made chemicals called chlorofluorocarbons (CFCs). CFCs have been used to make some types of plastics and foam packaging, in refrigerators and car airconditioners, and as a carrier gas in aerosol cans. When these gases escape into the air, they gradually float up into the atmosphere and are slowly eroding the protective ozone layer.

Ultraviolet light: friend or foe?

- Ultraviolet light can be used to kill in sterilisation systems.

- Too much ultraviolet radiation can cause eye cataracts, sunburn and skin cancers.

- It can also damage plants, both natural vegetation and crops.

- Ultraviolet light also puts a lot of stress on plankton, the tiny floating ocean plants that are at the base of the marine food chain.

When sunlight falls on CFCs in the ozone layer, the CFCs break down and release highly reactive chlorine atoms. The trouble with chlorine atoms is that they react with ozone, destroying the ozone, but they are not destroyed themselves. One free chlorine atom can munch through thousands of ozone molecules and itself remain intact. Our atmosphere still has a supply of these ozone-destroying chlorine atoms that will continue wreaking havoc for years.

In the late 1970s and early 1980s, it was becoming clear to scientists that the ozone layer was getting thinner. By the late 1980s, scientists had discovered a first 'hole' in the ozone layer over the Antarctic, larger than the area of Australia. Soon after, another hole was discovered, this time over the Arctic. These holes are really areas where the amount of

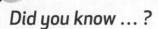

ozone is significantly lower than elsewhere. The holes change size, thickness and shape with the seasons, due to the weather and wind patterns around the poles and their long periods of daylight and darkness.

Holes over the barely populated poles are one concern. But more alarming is the gradual thinning of the ozone layer away from the polar regions. These are the areas where most of the world's food production occurs and where the most people live.

In 1987, governments from around the world began developing an agreement to phase out the use of CFCs in manufacturing. On 1 January 1989, the agreement—the Montreal Protocol on Substances that Deplete the Ozone Layer—came into force. However, the problem isn't yet completely solved. CFCs are still used in a few countries. Plus, old CFC-containing products, such as unwanted fridges or the airconditioners in scrapped cars, can still release CFCs. They must be carefully disposed of so that the remaining CFCs are captured.

The lower atmosphere

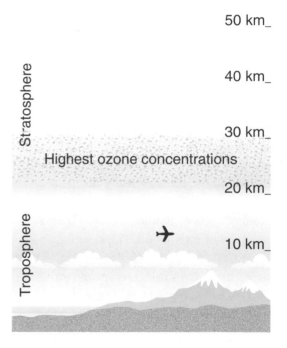

Packaging

Packaging gets a lot of bad press. We've seen lots of packaging in the mountains of rubbish sent to landfill tips. Much of the rubbish that pollutes our streets and harms wildlife is packaging litter. But this is only part of the picture.

Giving credit where credit is due, packaging has allowed food to be contained and preserved for longer than fresh food would otherwise keep. So, while packaging creates packaging waste, it also prevents food waste. Packaging has meant that food can be preserved for times when it is out of season, stockpiled in times of plenty, and transported to places with inadequate food supplies.

The problem with packaging is what happens to it when it's no longer wanted. Packaging is a big contributor to household waste. The good news is that many types of packaging are easily recycled; some can be made from renewable materials, and biodegradable varieties are being further developed.

Another problem is the practice of over-packaging products to make them look bigger, brighter or like they offer better value than they really do. Look at the perfume gift boxes in stores around Mother's Day and you'll see shoebox-sized gift sets containing a relatively small bottle of perfume and tube of body lotion. The key to making packaging more sustainable is finding the line between what's necessary and useful and what's unnecessary and excessive.

Think about it

Bananas and mandarins come with their own biodegradable packaging: it's called 'peel'!

Packaging through the ages

~11 000–9000 years ago	Fragments of early pottery and ceramics found in China dating this far back
~8000 years ago	Ceramics developed in the Middle East
~5000 years ago	Wood crates, barrels and boxes found in Egyptian tombs dating back to this period
~3500 years ago	The invention of the pottery wheel
~2500 years ago	Glass-blowing leads to glass containers
~2000 years ago	Cellulose fibre
~1750	Bone china, made using bone ash, is developed in England in an effort to make a local equivalent of imported Chinese porcelain
1930s–50s	Styrene foam
early 1950s	The aseptic carton or 'Tetra Pak' (carton board containing thin layers of plastic and aluminium)
1950s	Aluminium foil containers
1958	Heat shrinkable plastic film
1959	Aluminium can
1977	Plastic polyethylene terephthalate (PET) containers

Plastic

Imagine life without plastic: no plastic litter, no CDs or DVDs, no Nintendo DS consoles, no sports water bottles and no Bratz dolls, but also no lightweight car parts, solar panels, seat belts, Tupperware and life jackets. That was life up until a little over 150 years ago, when the English metallurgist and inventor Alexander Parkes created the first human-made plastic (which he named Parkesine—after himself!) Since then, product designers and manufacturers have found plastics irresistible.

Nowadays, plastics are used to make a huge number of different products. Plastics are generally cheap, versatile, lightweight, relatively strong, easily mouldable and durable materials. Their uses range from soft-drink bottles to temporary road barriers, and from building materials to lolly wrappers.

What are plastics?

Originally, the word *plastic* was an adjective used to describe the ability of some materials to be shaped or moulded. 'Plastics' is the general name given to a range of products and materials made from human-made polymers, recognising their mouldability. A number of natural polymers, such as amber and other resins, are also considered to be plastics. Plastics are made from long hydrocarbon molecules, which are mostly derived from fossil fuels, such as oil and natural gas. Plastics can also be made from plant oils.

Polymers

Polymers are like mega-sized hydrocarbon molecules, made from long chains of repeating identical units. In fact, the word *polymer* comes from the Greek words *poly*, meaning 'many', and *meros*, meaning 'parts'. Polymers are made in a chemical process called 'polymerisation', by bonding many of the same small molecules, called monomers, together to form a long chain-like molecule.

Common synthetic polymers include:

- nylon (used to make fishing line)
- polyester (used to make Polarfleece fabric)
- polystyrene foam
- PVC (or polyvinyl chloride, used to make water pipes).

Plastics and the environment

For all their versatility and other advantages, plastics have a dark side: they come with a range of environmental impacts. Like all petrochemical and fossil-fuel products, their production produces greenhouse emissions and toxic pollution. Ultimately, there are a limited number of fossil-fuel resources that can be tapped, and many competing uses for them. With oil prices rising and demand for oil from China and India growing, petroleum-derived plastics won't always be a cheap option. In short, such plastics are not renewable. They also use a significant amount of energy in their manufacture. Bioplastics, made from plant ingredients such as cornstarch and plant oils, are being developed as a renewable, potentially less-polluting alternative.

There are substances in some kinds of plastic that do a very good impersonation of hormones. These substances are often called endocrine disrupters because some scientists suspect that they can influence and damage the endocrine and reproductive systems of the animals and humans that ingest them. Small amounts of plastic chemicals can sometimes leach into the foods they package. Endocrine disruptors used in some plastics include:

- the highly toxic heavy metals lead and cadmium, which are sometimes used as stabilisers in the production of PVC
- phthalates, which are used as plasticisers to make a brittle plastic more flexible or hard plastic softer
- bisphenol A (BPA), which is used to strengthen some plastics.

Finally, plastic waste and how it is treated are also eco-issues. Given that many plastics are made from fossil fuels, it seems logical that plastic waste can be burnt to produce energy. Unfortunately, burning plastic also produces a range of toxic pollutants. Most plastics are not biodegradable, take hundreds of years to break down in landfill, and persist in the environment if littered. While many types of plastics claim to be recyclable, in reality only a few types are commonly recycled, although the recycling of plastics is generally improving. Biodegradable plastics are also being developed, but there is some concern in the packaging industry that degradable plastics could contaminate and hamper the recycling of conventional plastics.

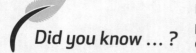

Did you know ... ?   In 2005, 28 million US tons (25.4 million metric tonnes) of plastic were produced in the USA. Of that, 27 million tons ended up in landfill.

Plastic bags

We hate seeing them blowing around the streets; we hate the harm they do to wildlife, and we hate the fact that they'll still be here doing a poor job of biodegrading long after we've gone. Plastic bags started out as a convenience item, designed to get shopping home without the bag ripping or getting wet and falling apart. However, they've since become a pet hate of environmentalists and non-greenies alike.

There has been a lot of talk about how to reduce our use of plastic bags and the litter they make. Some people think that our governments should be doing more, or that supermarkets should use alternatives or provide biodegradable bags. It's even been suggested that plastic supermarket bags should be taxed or carry a deposit that is refunded when people return them for recycling. It's easy to forget that plastic bags are only a problem because people insist on using them.

In 2002, the Irish government put a 15 euro-cent levy (around 25 Australian cents) on every plastic shopping bag taken from stores. Within five months, plastic bag use had dropped by around 90 per cent. This was not because everyone on the Emerald Isle suddenly became a greenie. It was more because people didn't like being hit in the hip pocket. It took a financial disincentive to slash plastic bag use in Ireland.

Now Australia's politicians, environmentalists and retailers are trying to come to some sort of agreement on how we should phase

Why are plastic bags an eco-no-no?

- Single-use plastic supermarket bags, like all single-use, disposable products, are a poor use of the materials and energy needed to make them.

- Plastic bags buried in landfill are basically inert (non-reactive and non-biodegradable). They will sit there for tens or even hundreds of years, wasting the material resources needed to make them. Putting it in perspective, though, they represent a tiny proportion of the total material sent to landfill, so we may be making a bigger deal of the problem than it deserves.

- Plastic bags disposed of with general rubbish are the most common item blown off landfill sites, accidentally becoming litter.

- Plastic bags are a litter problem that spoils the environment.

- Plastic bags floating in the ocean look like jellyfish, harming the marine mammals that mistakenly eat them. They can also strangle other aquatic animals.

- Some plastic bags are made from regular plastic, held together with a degradable binding plastic. Though they disintegrate fairly quickly so that you can't see the whole original bag, they leave a non-biodegradable plastic dust that contributes to and is ingested by animals.

out single-use plastic bags. Australians used an estimated six billion plastic bags in 2002, which dropped by 34 per cent to 3.92 billion in 2005. This was partly thanks to the development of the 'green bag'—a strong, convenient reusable bag—and driven perhaps by the threat of a levy. This showed that Australians are more than capable of changing their behaviour when given convenient alternatives and a disincentive (even if only a threat) to continuing with the old behaviour. But we're starting to go back to our bad bag habits: our plastic bag use for 2007 crept back up to 4.84 billion.

Some supermarkets offer degradable checkout bags. However, these are still a single-use, disposable product and still need resources to be produced. Plus, they cannot be recycled along with the non-degradable plastic bags as they contaminate the product. At the checkout, it is better to use reusable green bags than biodegradable single-use plastic bags.

Think about it

Old people know stuff! Some lived through wars and rationing, or were brought up on farms without easy access to department stores and their wide range of products, so they generally know how to live with less. Chances are your grandmother got along perfectly well without plastic bags. See what you can learn from our senior citizens.

Eco-action: bag the bag!

We can do without single-use plastic bags! Instead use green bags, calico bags, backpacks or other alternatives to take your shopping home. On the odd occasion you do get a plastic bag, remember to recycle it. Take your unwanted used plastic bags back to the supermarket as most supermarkets have special recycling bins for plastic bags.

Plastic bag facts

- In April 2003, Coles Bay in Tasmania became Australia's first plastic bag–free town.

- Plastic bags are made from high-density polyethylene (HDPE), a plastic polymer made from ethylene, which is derived from petroleum or natural gas.

- Just 8.7 checkout bags contain enough embodied petroleum energy to drive a car 1 kilometre.

- Currently, only about 3 per cent of plastic bags used in Australia are recycled.

Eco-byte

'Paper bags still use materials and still get thrown out, so fabric bags you can reuse are a good option.' **Meredith, 11**

Pollution

Pollution is something introduced into an environment that contaminates it and causes harm or injury to the life within it. We tend to think of pollution as harmful chemicals, but pollution can also be noise, light and heat pollution. Some people even think of introduced weed species as 'biological pollution'.

There are various types of pollution:

- **Soil contamination**

  Soil contamination is pollution of the land. It is caused by things such as the overuse of pesticides and other crop chemicals, leaking landfills, dumped industrial waste, chemical spills, leaking underground waste, or leaking chemical storage tanks or drums. Soil contamination can harm wildlife, make farming less productive and contaminate the food grown in the soil.

- **Radioactive contamination**

  A certain amount of radioactivity is part of nature, but humans are now producing radioactive materials and wastes in dangerous quantities. Exposure to unnaturally high levels of radioactivity can be deadly for people and the environment. Sources of radioactive contamination include the extraction and processing of nuclear fuels, waste from used nuclear fuels, waste from the use of radioactive materials in science and medicine, and fallout from nuclear explosions.

- **Noise pollution**

  Your parents might call your taste in music 'noise pollution', but it can be more serious than that, environmentally. Many animals rely heavily on their sense of hearing—their ears are like our eyes. The sound waves from navy sonar equipment and experiments have been known to cause bleeding around the ears of whales and other marine mammals, causing them to become disoriented and leading to them becoming beached.

Think about it

What do environmentalists, astronomers and migrating birds have in common? They all hate light pollution. Environmentalists don't like seeing energy wasted by outdoor lighting or night-time office lighting that isn't really needed; astronomers don't like the fact that light pollution makes the night skies harder to view; and migrating birds can get disoriented by bright lights on tall structures.

- **Light pollution**
  The changes in light from day to night are the clues by which animals can tell the time, so light pollution can confuse them. Migrating birds can also become disoriented by lights on tall buildings and other structures.
- **Thermal (heat) pollution**
  Thermal pollution is unnaturally high or low temperatures created in the environment, such as warm water released from power plants into colder waterways, or cold water from the bottom of a dam released into a river that is warmer downstream. Both can be harmful to aquatic life.

Air pollution (page 3) and water pollution (page 194) are vitally important environmental topics, so naturally they have their own sections in this book. Something important to note about air and water pollution is that they involve gases, liquids and dissolved pollutants. These are all fluid (able to flow freely), so they can move and spread beyond their source. In particular, greenhouse pollution adds to the global blanket of greenhouse gases, so pollution isn't just a local problem, its effects can be felt worldwide.

Eco-byte

'I like the environment because most of it is nature and I want to help the environment. If you pollute one place in the world, you're polluting the whole world.' **Ruby, 8**

Population

In 1965, the world's total human population was about 3.345 billion. It was the year that Soviet cosmonaut Aleksei Leonov took the first spacewalk, US combat troops joined the Vietnam War, and a young actress called Julie Andrews won a Best Actress Oscar for *Mary Poppins*. A little over thirty years later, the global population has doubled to nearly 6.7 billion.

United Nations population projections predict that the world population will grow to 9.2 billion by 2050, a huge number of people to feed, clothe, shelter and otherwise provide for. This represents a huge demand on the natural environment.

The rapid growth of the world's human population over the last hundred or so years has come at the expense of other species and the broader environment. Huge areas of land have been cleared to make room for cities and agriculture, causing decreases in the populations of other species.

Increase in global population

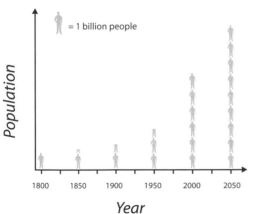

= 1 billion people

Population

Year

1800   1850   1900   1950   2000   2050

More bad news is that populations can only grow so much before they encounter the problems of overpopulation. For any ecosystem or particular environment, there is a certain number of a particular species (in this case humans) that this environment can support with its available water, habitat (shelter), food and other resources. This is called the environment's 'carrying capacity'. In Australia, there is a lot of argument over what the country's total population should be. Some people want higher birth rates and the immigration of more people from overseas so that the younger population can grow and provide the money, through taxes, needed to look after the country's growing retirement population. Others argue that Australia does not have the environmental carrying capacity to support many more humans, particularly with the stresses of drought, land degradation and water shortages.

But carrying capacity is only part of the equation. A given environment can support more people with a small ecological footprint than those whose high-maintenance lifestyle gives them a large ecological footprint. Because of this, moderate population growth in countries like Australia and the USA can have a higher environmental cost than high population growth in developing countries.

Did you know?
- Overall, 78 million people are currently added to the world each year.
- Eighty per cent of the world's population live in the less developed regions.
- A little over a half of the world's population now live in urban areas.

Recycling

Recycling takes waste and turns it into a useful material resource that can be made into new products. It's also one of the easiest ways to help the environment from the comfort of your own home (or school).

Recycling makes better use of our planet's material resources and gives old materials a new life, rather than condemning them to the dead end of landfill. Plus, making new products from recycled materials often uses a lot less energy and water. For example, it takes 75 per cent less energy to make steel from recycled food cans than from raw materials, so the overall environmental benefit is huge.

In Australia, New Zealand and many other countries, local councils often run recycling collection services. The councils, or the waste-management companies they employ to physically do the job, decide the range of materials that can be collected, the type of recycling bins used, and how often the collections will occur. Unfortunately, this means that recycling services can vary from one neighbourhood to another. So your cousin who lives on the other side of town may be able to recycle a different range of materials from those that you can recycle. This can lead to confusion over what can and can't be recycled, particularly in regional areas (outside major cities), where the range of materials recycled is often smaller. The easiest way to make sure that you're recycling all the material that you can is to call your local council and find out about their services.

Eco-action: get recycling!

In a nutshell, there are two easy ways to bring some environmental action to your home through recycling. First, make sure that you're recycling all that you can in your local area. Second, finish the recycling you started by buying back products made from recycled materials.

Don't put the wrong thing in the right bin!

A lot of things that are put into recycling bins shouldn't be there. They contribute to recycling contamination. This makes it harder to sort and recycle materials and can also pose a health risk for the guys on the garbage trucks who collect the materials or those who sort them at the recycling facilities. People (either irresponsible or just plain stupid!) have placed everything from live hand grenades and live puppies to used nappies and used syringes in recycling bins. If in doubt, leave it out.

Eco-byte

'My family and I recycle papers and cardboard, cans and cartons so they can be reused and don't go into landfill. All people could take the time and recycle paper products then we would do a lot to help the environment.' **Kate, 11**

Recycling: the ultimate guide

Here's a quick overview of the materials that are commonly recycled through local collections, the types that can be recycled, what they get turned into and some tips for recycling them. It's worth checking with your local council, because not all councils accept the same recyclables.

Material	Types commonly recycled	Recycling advice	What they're made into	Did you know?
Glass	Clear, brown and green bottles and jars	Don't put oven-proof glass, ceramics, wine and drinking glasses in your recycling bin as they can cause problems at recycling centres.	New glass bottles and jars, filtering material, sandblasting material and 'glasphalt' road-fill material	Recycling one glass bottle in the production of new glass containers saves enough energy to power a 100-watt light bulb for four hours.
Aluminium	Drink cans, foil trays and foil wrap	'Foil' potato chip bags should not be included in your recycling bin.	New aluminium cans	Recycling twenty aluminium cans uses the same amount of energy as is required to produce one new can from raw materials.
Steel	Steel food cans, pet food cans, aerosols, empty paint tins, coffee tins, bottle tops and jar lids	• Take the plastic lids off aerosols before recycling. • You can see if a can or jar lid is made from recyclable steel by checking with a fridge magnet: if it sticks, it's steel.	New cans, structural steel for buildings, car parts, bicycles, railway girders and a range of new steel products	Making steel from recycled cans uses 75% less energy than producing steel from raw materials.
Cartons	Milk cartons, juice cartons, aseptic 'brick' cartons	If your local collection doesn't accept milk cartons, reuse them by giving them to your school's art room.	Office paper, cardboard and fuel briquettes	Milk cartons have lost weight! The amount of material used to make the average milk carton has been reduced by more than 20% since 1970 through better design.

Material	Types commonly recycled	Recycling advice	What they're made into	Did you know?
Plastic	Soft-drink bottle plastic (PET or type '1'), milk bottle plastic (HDPE or type '2') and sometimes some opaque PVC bottle plastic (type '3'). A small number of councils recycle the full range of plastics (types 1–7). Note: many supermarkets also collect plastic supermarket bags.	• Leave the lids off plastic bottles. • Don't put plastic bags in your recycling bins. Only recycle them through the special recycling bins provided in some supermarkets and retail outlets.	New soft-drink bottles, fabric, garbage and compost bins, landscaping materials and plastic lumber products	Some kerbside recycling bins are made with up to 50% post-consumer plastic from recycled HDPE bottles.
Cardboard	Greeting cards, cereal boxes, larger cardboard boxes	Many programs don't want cardboard contaminated with food spills, such as pizza boxes. Check with your own local council.	New cardboard packaging, gift wrap and tissue products	Visy Recycling provided 400 000 pieces of recyclable furniture for the Sydney 2000 Olympic Games, including bookcases and desks made from recycled cardboard.
Paper	Newspapers, magazines, waste office paper, telephone directories	Leave out foil gift wrapping, waxed paper and tissues (particularly used ones—eeww!)	Cardboard, egg cartons, insulation materials, kitty litter and new newsprint	Making new newsprint from recycled fibres uses six times less energy than making it from virgin pulp. This means that the average Australian household that recycles old newspapers for a year can save enough electricity to power a three-bedroom house for five days.

Recycling: the products

So you've done the right thing with your rubbish and put materials out for recycling. But what happens to it after it disappears over the horizon on the back of a recycling truck?

Well, trucks collect recyclable materials from drop-off points and suburban kerbsides and take them to the nearest central facility for sorting. These sorting stations are called 'material recovery facilities', which are affectionately known as 'MRFs' (pronounced 'murfs') within the recycling industry.

At these facilities, the materials are separated and sorted into their own material types. The steel cans, glass, plastics and other materials then go their separate ways to manufacturing plants that will recycle them into new products.

Sometimes the recycling loop is quite simple. Old aluminium drink cans are made into new drink cans, saving 95 per cent of the energy that would be needed to make the cans from raw materials. Similarly, old glass jars and bottles are recycled into new glass products. Some glass also gets turned into road fill, filter materials and sandblasting material.

In Australia, soft-drink bottle plastic (polyethylene terephthalate or PET) is generally turned back into new soft-drink bottles or made into pellets and exported. In the USA and some other countries, soft-drink bottles can also be recycled into clothes! Recovered PET is melted, extruded into fibres by being fed through a device that looks like a showerhead, and woven into fabric for lingerie, clothing and blankets.

The surprising results of our recycling efforts

Paper Paper products that may contain recycled content include:

- newspapers
- cereal boxes
- writing paper
- fast food bags
- cardboard containers
- wrapping paper
- tissues and towels
- animal bedding
- mulch
- insulation.

Plastic Plastic products that may contain recycled content include:

- soft-drink bottles
- detergent bottles
- picnic tables
- office products
- bags
- bicycle racks
- carpeting
- highlighters
- markers
- benches
- T-shirts
- Polarfleece jackets
- compost bins and worm farms
- garbage bins
- decking and boardwalks
- landscaping materials.

Glass Products that can be made from recycled glass include:

- glass containers
- abrasives
- tiles
- insulation
- decorative tumbled-glass gravel
- filter material.

Steel Products that may contain recycled steel are:

- automobiles
- refrigerators
- bicycles
- nails
- steel cans.

Construction materials Construction materials that are made from recycled products include:

- concrete
- bricks
- drain pipes
- fence posts and fencing
- thermal insulation.

Rubber Products that are made from recycled rubber include:

- bulletin boards
- floor tiles and mats
- playground equipment
- traffic-calming devices, such as speed bumps.

Eco-bytes: what I do for the environment

Students from Baldivis Primary School have helped to grow the Baldivis Children's Forest and are learning to be Waste Wise Witches and Wizards. Here they tell us about their eco-activities. You might like to try them yourself!

'I help trees by planting new seedlings every year. I help the little trees grow by weeding the weeds that grow near them. Trees are important to combat the world's carbon emissions.'
Jazmin, 10

'I help the environment by using less plastic bags from the shops. Why is this? It is because plastic bags pollute the environment. I recycle plastic things because recycling helps the planet.' Draven, 10

'I recycle when I need to because I feel like the world needs cleaning up. If everyone helps clean their own environment the place will be a better place to live in.'
Shayna, 11

'I save water. I have a two-minute shower. I want everyone to do it. If they did we will have more water to share. Water is precious and we must look after it and use it wisely.' Nicole, 11

'In the Baldivis Children's Forest we have possum, bat boxes and cockatoo tubes. We study insects and macro-invertebrates which live in Outridge Swamp and at Folly Pool. We have a frog pond at school; we also have possum boxes near the frog pond. We also feed the possums at school. If every person cared for animals, we would protect the different species.'
Connor, 11

'I clean up the environment by picking up rubbish. Everyone should help to clean up the environment then the world would be a healthier, happier place!'
Shahnee, 11

'I turn off lights when I am not needing them. This saves energy and helps the planet. Everyone can do simple things, which all together add up to a great effort for the planet.' Dylan, 10

'At the Baldivis Children's forest we care for bushland, plant trees every year, learn about indigenous culture and measure the age of trees. This year we told others about our Baldivis Children's Forest. We performed a power point in play form at Earth From Above and the WA Youth Environment Conference. We performed it to the school before we performed it to the public. Our school choir sang, which I'm involved in. I was dressed up as a possum in this performance. I believe that letting everyone know how and why to save the environment can help lots.' Tegan, 11

'I grow vegetables to save the planet. I put drippers on my fruit trees. The good thing about drippers is that they only use a little water but they keep the plants healthy. Everyone should use water carefully especially now it is warming up.' Ryan, 10

'This year we performed at Perth's 'Earth From Above Festival'. We told the public about our work in the Baldivis Children's Forest. I really enjoyed playing a kangaroo and acted out how the kangaroos suffered because of the development in our region. People should be told about the effects on animals when their habitat is lost.' Justin, 10

'The class and I have made a veggie patch and a tyre garden from recycled tyres; we even have a compost tumbler and a worm farm. At home I use recycled tin for the chook pen and always turn electrical appliances of at the wall. Please keep the planet clean! We can all do our part to save the environment.' Ben, 11

'We have two possums in the school; their names are Nancy and Baby Nancy . We built a possum box for them to sleep in. They live in the roof of the classrooms. We feed them food scraps and some times bananas and apples. Every student across Australia should help the animals that live around them.' Demi, 11

Eco-activity: reuse— DIY recycling

Here are some handy, crafty ideas for stuff you can make by reusing old or waste materials. Some of these activities use hammers, nails, Stanley knives and other tools that can hurt you if not used properly. Ask an adult to help you.

Make a tea light lantern

You will need

- *Empty food cans (condensed milk cans, with their straight sides, work best)*
- *Hammer and nail*
- *Water*
- *Wire*
- *A tea light candle*

How to

Fill the cans with water and put them in the freezer. Leave them overnight. Using a hammer and a large nail, punch holes in the sides of the ice-filled cans to make a pattern. (Make sure the cans are held securely when you are hammering so that you don't end up hammering your fingers!) The candlelight will shine through these holes. Punch in an additional two holes near the rim at opposite sides of the can. Allow the ice to melt until you can remove the block from the can (put it in the garden to water plants as it melts). Use wire to make a handle for the can lantern, threading it through the two holes near the can rim. Place a tea light candle inside the can.

Plant trees in milk cartons

You will need

- *An empty milk carton*
- *A seedling*
- *Potting mix*

How to

Open up the top of the milk carton and punch some drainage holes in the bottom. Put some potting mix in the bottom of the carton. Take the seedling and gently ease it out of its tube and tease its roots a little. Plant it into the carton with more potting mix. Plant the whole carton, into the garden and water the seedling. The carton will provide the seedling with some protection from the weather and pests while it's young. As it grows, the carton will gradually break down into the soil.

Make cutlery wind chimes

You will need

- *Assorted old cutlery, the fancier the better!*
- *Fishing line*
- *An old bangle*
- *Beads (optional)*

How to

Securely tie a length of fishing line to the end of the handle of a spoon, knife or fork. You can then thread beads onto the line if you wish. Tie the free end of the line to the bangle. Repeat this until you have several pieces of cutlery dangling from the bangle. Tie four more equal lengths of fishing line to the bangle and tie the free ends together so that you can suspend it evenly from a single point. Hang the wind chimes from a tree or somewhere where they will catch the breeze.

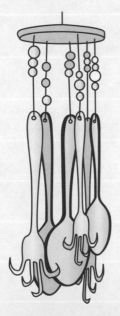

Make a poop scoop

You will need

- *An empty square plastic milk or juice bottle with an inbuilt handle*
- *Stanley knife*
- *Marker*

How to

Place the bottle on its side with the handle on top. With a marker, draw a diagonal guideline as shown. Using a Stanley knife, cut the bottom off the bottle along the guideline. The part with the handle forms the scoop. Keep the base so that you can scrape doggy-do into the scoop. You can then empty the scoop into a dog-poo-munching worm farm—see page 210 for details.

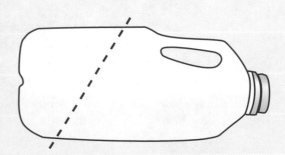

Rubbish by numbers

About **2.7 BILLION** newspapers are made and read in Australia each year. Of these, about **2.04 BILLION** copies (**75%**) are recycled, meaning that **592 600** tonnes of newsprint are recycled into new newsprint and other uses.

Australia generates waste at a rate of **2.25** kilograms per person per day.

Mobile phone handsets can be recycled to recover a range of materials, including plastics and some metals. Recycling around **50 000** mobile phones recovers **1.5** kilograms of gold.

In 2002, Australia's recycling rate for steel cans (such as food cans) was **43%**. Japan's was double that, at **86%**, while Portugal's was **28%**.

Developed countries represent **25%** of the global population but use **80%** of its resources and produce **75%** of its waste.

You can make **20** drink cans from recycled aluminium cans with the same amount of energy needed to make one drink can from virgin raw materials.

According to the Natural Resources Defense Council, the US airline industry throws away enough aluminium cans each year to build **58** Boeing 747 aeroplanes.

In 2007, Australians used **4.84 BILLION** plastic bags. If tied together end to end, that would be enough to circle the world more than **29** times.

15 000 steel cans are equivalent to around 1 tonne of steel. Every tonne of steel recycled saves **1131** kilograms of iron ore, **633** kilograms of coal and **54** kilograms of limestone.

The USA generates about **750** kilograms of municipal waste (which includes household waste and the rubbish collected in public places) per person per year. New Zealand produces **400** kilograms per person per year, and India produces **100** kilograms per person per year.

The average baby will have gone through about **6000–8000** nappies by the time he or she is toilet-trained.

Some of the planet's hardest workers are also its smallest. Actinobacteria are a class of bacteria. Among their number are many types of soil bacteria. These microscopic living things do the job of breaking down organic materials, like leaf litter and the remains of dead animals—nature's rubbish. This biodegradation is part of nature's recycling system of growth and decay. Dead stuff is recycled into nutrients in the soil, which then feeds plants and ultimately the animals that eat them. It's also part of how the carbon cycle keeps moving.

Online group profile: Actinobacteria

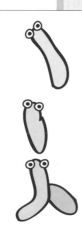

About us: To you huge humans, we're invisible, but you see the stuff we make. We are a hard-working bunch. We spend our days making humus, the organic part of the soil. Yes, we are a kind of bacteria, but we and our fellow microbes are misunderstood. While some members of our family (the pathogens) are enough to make you sick, most of us are really useful and important players in the natural environment. Even scientists find us useful—the *Streptomyces* members of our club are good at making antibiotic medicines. We also give soil its 'earthy' smell. So please try to understand us and value our contribution!

Friends: the other members of the decomposition gang—other microbes, fungi, worms and other creepy crawlies

Interests: Getting dirty and making humus—nice work if you can get it!

Favourite songs: 'From Little Things Big Things Grow' by Kevin Carmody and Paul Kelly, and 'We're All in this Together' from *High School Musical*

Favourite TV shows: *Backyard Science*, *Grossology*, *Growing Up Creepie*

Favourite food: anything slimy and putrid, washed down with compost tea, worm juice or rain water

Favourite movie: *A Bug's Life*

Role model: Oscar the Grouch—garbage: he just gets it!

Salinity

Salinity is not the condition that's making Great Aunt Betty a bit batty. That's called 'senility'. But salinity is still scary—it's a word that can get farmers shaking in their gumboots, due to the damage it does to farmland.

Salt is part of the natural environment. All water in nature contains small levels of dissolved salts, but sometimes there can be too much of a good thing. Salinity is a concentration of salt in the landscape that harms land and water resources. The higher than ideal salt concentrations can dehydrate, poison and even kill plants, animals and tiny soil organisms. The extra salt can come from the weathering and eroding of some kinds of rocks that contain salts or from salt deposits buried lower in the earth's crust, left behind by ancient seas. It can also be carried from the sea by strong winds. Some areas of Australia's natural landscape are so severely salinated that virtually nothing will grow—the ground is covered with a white crust of dry salt, occasionally interrupted by the pale trunks of dead gum trees. It's scenes like this that have led farmers to call salinity 'white death'.

Salinity is caused by a number of factors. One is the loss of vegetation that once soaked up rainwater. Another is irrigation—applying additional water to agricultural lands. The irrigation water and/or rainwater seep deeply into the soil, making the water table rise and bringing ancient salt deposits with it to the surface. There are two types of salinity: **dryland salinity** ('dryland' referring to land that isn't irrigated) and **irrigated land salinity**. With irrigated land salinity, the water used to irrigate lands can also contain dissolved salts, which add to the build-up of salt in the soil.

Australia already has around 2.5 million hectares of salinity-affected land, with much more at risk. The Australian government estimates that at the current rate of land salination, over 17 million hectares (42 million acres) of Australian land will be affected by 2050.

Salinity doesn't harm only living things. As well as farmland, river systems and natural vegetation, salinity can damage urban water supplies, building foundations, roads and other infrastructure. Salinity is an economic problem as well as an environmental problem, costing hundreds of millions of dollars each year in the loss of environmental assets, damage to urban infrastructure and through reduced agricultural production. It has been estimated that salinity in the Murray–Darling Basin costs A$304 million per year.

In Australia, there are many supporting government initiatives, agricultural trials and research programs coming into force that attempt to cope with and even reverse the effects of salinity. Farmers are experimenting with growing saltbush in salt-affected areas. As the name suggests, saltbush can tolerate high salt levels and help to regenerate the land. Sheep can be grazed on the saltbush, allowing farmers to earn a living from this land. Other things that can be done to help control and combat salinity are tree-planting and changing the drainage of the land.

Did you know … ?

- The remote thorny lignum, a shrub native to Western Australia, is critically endangered, largely due to its sensitivity to salt and to Western Australia's growing salinity problem.
- The main salt that causes salinity in soil is sodium chloride— the same stuff that you sprinkle on your fish and chips.
- Water dissolves salt and transports it. Up to 20 000 kilometres of streams could be significantly salt-affected by 2050.
- Saline groundwater can be twice as salty as seawater.
- Salinity affects about 5 per cent of Australia's cultivated land.
- Also currently at risk from salinity damage are: about 20 000 kilometres of major roads (Sydney to Perth five times!), about 1600 kilometres of railways, about 630 000 hectares of remnant natural vegetation and associated ecosystems, the infrastructure and community assets of sixty-eight towns, and eighty important wetlands.

Shopping

Do you want a new CD? A Nintendo DS game? New jeans? What's not to like about shopping? Everyone likes new stuff. 'Consumer' is the name given to a person who buys a product. 'Consumerism' is the idea that buying lots of stuff is a good thing. But in this environmentally stressed age, it's time for us to be green consumers who consider the planet when making our shopping choices.

For better or worse?

So what should you buy? The truth is that everything we buy affects the planet, but some choices are better than others. When you make greener shopping choices, you can ultimately save energy, save material resources, conserve water and prevent waste.

Green shopping tips

- **Get smart**
  Ask yourself if you really need something before you buy it. Or are you just falling for the advertising?
- **See if there's an alternative to buying** (a legal alternative—stealing is not environmentally friendly!)
  Some things can be borrowed or rented instead of bought. For example, borrow ski gear if you're going on a one-off ski trip, or rent a DVD instead of buying it. Some PlayStation and Nintendo games can be hired as well.

- **Buy second-hand**
  Second-hand goods can be cool, different and cheap! Or you can swap unwanted things among your friends.
- **Get the e-copy, not the hard copy**
  Send e-cards for birthdays and Christmas, instead of cards made from trees. Music, TV shows, movies and some books are also available as digital downloads instead of hard copies.
- **Reuse rather than dispose**
  Get products, like refillable water bottles and rechargeable batteries, that you can get good use from, instead of stuff that gets used once before hitting the rubbish bin.
- **Buy durable products**
  Instead of wasteful products with a short life span, buy better quality products that are durable.
- **Check out the packaging**
  Get products without unnecessary packaging. For those that must be packaged, choose those with packaging that can be reused or recycled.
- **Buy recycled**
  When you do need to buy paper and tissue products, like note pads and exercise books, buy those made from recycled materials.

The best labels

The best and greenest labels aren't necessarily the designer ones. Look for the following things on labels when shopping:

- **certified organic**: this means the product is made from some or all organically grown ingredients

- **carbon neutral**: this means that the greenhouse emissions made through the manufacture of the product have been 'offset' or removed by initiatives like tree-planting

- **not tested on animals**: as the name suggests, this means that the product hasn't been tested on animals

- **recyclable**: this means that the product (or its packaging) is made from materials that are generally recyclable.

Give green gifts

Sometimes you're shopping for others, not for yourself. Here are some green gift ideas for friends and family:

- Buy a living green gift, such as an indoor air-cleaning pot plant.
- If you're buying a battery-operated gift and have the budget, also get rechargeable batteries and a recharger to go with it.
- Give a recycled pet by going to the pound. However, make sure that the pet will be wanted first.
- Wrap presents in the cartoon pages from newspapers, or choose gift-wrapping paper and cards that are made from recycled materials.
- Wrap presents in a scarf, bandana or tea towel and make the wrapping a gift in itself.

Who's got the power?

Marketing and advertising industry experts are boldly reporting that 'tweens' and teens are the most powerful consumer group since the postwar baby boomers, and that Generation Y are big spenders. I bet you didn't know you were that powerful! The reason you are powerful is because they want your pocket money, and they know you don't have bills, car costs and home loans to pay off. So everywhere you look, magazines, television and billboards will be telling you to buy, buy, buy!

But you don't have to, if you don't want to. Get wise to marketing and decide whose pocket you want your pocket money to stay in!

Use pester power for good!

Another trick advertisers use is to encourage you and your friends to nag your parents to buy something for you. They call this 'pester power'. But you can use your annoying nagging to save the planet instead! Pester power your parents into recycling more, using less electricity, making the home greener or getting a more fuel-efficient car. After all, it's your future.

Soil

Soil is precious stuff! We know that plants are the basis of the food chain, but where do they get their food from? Soil. Early explorers knew that good soil was the key to starting a colony in far-away lands. In fact, many countries owe their food, prosperity and wellbeing to the quality of the soil.

Soil itself is renewable. In nature, soil is removed by wind and flowing water and replaced by soil formation. Soil formation is a complicated recipe, with mineral ingredients coming from the breakdown and weathering of rock, and organic components (called *humus*) provided by the breakdown of plant and animal matter. Many people think that it's just ground-up rock, but soil is an ecosystem teaming with life. Earthworms, insects and a variety of bacteria help to break down the organic matter, keeping the soil healthy and fertile.

This soil is the basis for plant life, and plants are the 'primary producers' in nature. As well as being the basis of the food chain, plants also provide timber, fibre and other useful materials. All these things stem from productive soil. But soil itself has to be looked after and kept healthy. Poor land management can lead to the loss of topsoil—the highest and most productive layer of earth—and desertification.

Threats to soil and soil quality

- Erosion
- Pollution
- Salinity
- Nutrient depletion

Sustainable soil, Amazonian style

The ancient Amazonian people are believed to have smouldered biomass (plant and animal wastes) to get rid of rubbish and improve their soil. The result is fine, rich, dark, loamy earth called *terra preta* ('black land'), which lives on today. *Terra preta* is the reason the Amazon rainforest thrives.

Agricultural scientists are experimenting with this idea, roasting biomass (such as garden waste and even chook poo) into 'biochar' through low-temperature pyrolysis (heating without oxygen). The process both enriches the soil and uses it as a place to store carbon that might otherwise contribute to the greenhouse effect. Now that's what I call barbecued chicken nuggets!

Living soil

Did you know that just 1 gram of fertile agricultural soil contains around:

- 30 000 single-celled animals
- 50 000 algae
- 400 000 fungi
- 2.5 billion bacteria
- an odd assortment of worms and insects.

Transport

Transportation gives us the freedom to get from one place to another. While our own two legs can do this at about 6 kilometres per hour, bikes, cars, buses and boats can get us further and faster. Plus transportation brings the things we want and need to us. Shipping means that we can buy goods made overseas in our local shops, with Swiss chocolate sold in Sydney and perfume from Paris sold in Perth. In this modern age, we're living in a 'global village'.

The trouble with transport is that most modes of transport need energy, and those that get their energy by burning fuels produce air-polluting exhaust. Some exhaust gases are greenhouse gases, contributing to the problem of climate change. In fact, our various forms of transport are responsible for about a seventh of all human-made greenhouse emissions. Some exhaust gases are also noxious gases that lead to smog and an unhealthy living environment for city dwellers. Most cars and planes run on fossil fuels, such as petrol, diesel (made from petroleum) and liquid petroleum gas (LPG). These have environmental impacts in their extraction and are not renewable in the long term.

Which way to go is worst?

To put it simply, transport and its impact on the environment is partly about weight. It takes energy to move weight; the heavier the load (or vehicle) the more fuel needed to move it. This is exaggerated for air travel, where the ground can't support any of the weight of the plane and its cargo and passengers, so more energy is needed to work against gravity and lift it into the air.

A huge four-wheel drive generally uses more than twice the amount of petrol per kilometre than a smaller car, and both use more than a motorbike. A bus uses more fuel per kilometre, but it carries more people, so a bus can replace thirty-odd cars, meaning less fuel use and less exhaust per person.

Private cars are becoming more and more popular as developing countries become richer and people adopt busier lifestyles. Cars, vans and four-wheel drives—also called 'recreational vehicles' (or 'RVs') or 'sport utility vehicles' (or 'SUVs')—together now are the biggest greenhouse-emitting types of transport.

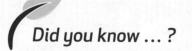

Did you know ... ?

- A single flight from Sydney to Melbourne produces about 250 kilograms of carbon dioxide per person, but it can vary depending on the size of the specific plane and how full the flight is.
- Planes use less fuel while cruising than during take-off and landing, so even short flights have a significant impact.

Greener getting around

So we know we need to cut our greenhouse gas emissions and our reliance on oil, but we still want to get around. What next? Sustainable transport is getting a lot of attention. There are a number of different approaches that are being considered and given a road test.

- Better urban planning (the designing of cities and suburbs) means that people don't have to go as far to get to work, shops, schools and other places.
- Better public transport, including more buses and trains, can allow people to go places with less greenhouse emissions. Many governments are making commitments to improve public transport as part of their plans to fight climate change.
- Many car manufacturers are making an effort to make their cars more efficient.
- Electric vehicles, such as electric cars and buses, are being developed.
- Hybrid cars, with both a petrol engine and a battery-powered electric motor, are now available (and Leonardo DiCaprio drives one).
- New lighter materials are being tested for use in aeroplanes.

Greenhouse Grand Prix

Which is the leanest, greenest car? If you challenge a late-model four-wheel drive, a mid-sized sedan and a petrol–electric hybrid to 20 000 kilometres of driving, the hybrid produces the least greenhouse emissions and the four-wheel drive produces the most.

Vehicle type	Tonnes of carbon dioxide produced over 20 000 kilometres
Hybrid	produces 2 tonnes CO_2
Petrol sedan	produces 4 tonnes CO_2
Four-wheel drive	produces 6 tonnes CO_2

Eco-action: going greener

See if you can walk, cycle or rollerblade to school, to friends' houses or to the shops, instead of asking an adult to drive you. Or see if you can organise a car pool with friends' families, sharing lifts to school.

Transport through the ages

~5000 BCE	The earliest vehicle known, the sledge, zips around the snowfields.
~4000 BCE	The oldest evidence of roads date back to this period.
~3500 BCE	The wheel is invented in Mesopotamia and used on animal-pulled carts.
~1000 BCE	Road rules are used in parts of China by this time.
~1500	Horsedrawn coaches or wagons are used to carry people.
1662	The first public transport service, a horsedrawn bus service, starts in Paris.
~1700	The first road tolls—money charged to pay for the repair of roads—are introduced.
~1700	By this time a coach could travel at speeds of around 8 kilometres per hour.
1781 from	British engineer James Watt makes an engine that uses steam boiling water to turn a wheel around.
1836	Horsedrawn coach speeds reach 14.5 kilometres per hour.
1847	The first electric car is invented by Moses Farmer in the USA.
1896	The first car with a modern design and petrol engine is invented.
1900	Horsedrawn coaches reach speeds of 18 kilometres per hour, but cars overtake them at 48 kilometres per hour.
~1930 AD	The first heavy traffic roads or 'autobahns' are built in Germany.

Transport by numbers

Every litre of petrol burnt in a car results in over **2.8** kilograms of greenhouse gas emissions.

About **8 MILLION** cars were made in 1950. By 2005, worldwide passenger vehicle production had increased to **45.9 MILLION** passenger cars and **18.5 MILLION** light trucks. Not to be beaten, global bicycle production grew from **11 MILLION** in 1950 to **105 MILLION** in 2004 and **130 MILLION** in 2007.

Each kilometre of car travel avoided saves up to half a kilogram of greenhouse gas and 20 cents in operating costs, depending on the type of car.

Roads, driveways, parking stations and other car-related infrastructure take up at least a third of the average city's land space, according to the Worldwatch Institute. That's a lot of real estate!

A person who drives for 2 hours to and from work every day over 40 years will have spent **2.3** years sitting in traffic.

Australian Bureau of Statistics figures for the year ending 31 October 2004 state that Australia's **10.7 MILLION** registered passenger vehicles collectively travelled **148 BILLION** kilometres, our **392 600** motorcycles travelled **1.5 BILLION** kilometres and just under **62 000** buses travelled **2 BILLION** kilometres.

Electric scooters can reach speeds of up to **50** kilometres per hour and can travel **50-65** kilometres before they need recharging.

In 2005, the number of passengers travelling on scheduled airlines in a single year passed **2 BILLION** for the first time. They collectively flew a record distance of **3.7 TRILLION** passenger-kilometres— equivalent to 4.8 million people flying to the moon and back in one year.

About **16 000** commercial aircraft currently pump out **600 MILLION** tonnes of carbon dioxide every year and consume some **190 BILLION** litres of jet fuel.

One aeroplane crossing the Atlantic can use **60 000** litres of fuel— as much as the average driver uses in **50** years.

Tree-planting

Hundreds of tree-planting initiatives have started up around the world to fix some of the problems caused by land-clearing. And you can join the global re-leaf effort.

How tree-planting helps the environment

Many tree-planting projects aim to regenerate and restore areas of native vegetation. They do so by planting a wide 'biodiverse' variety of seedlings that are native to the region. Ecosystems aren't just trees and animals, so grass and shrub seedlings are planted as well as trees.

- Regenerating native bushland and vegetation supports local wildlife by providing food and habitat. This may help save some species from extinction.
- Tree-planting can help combat salinity, which poisons farmland and natural ecosystems.
- Tree-planting in flood-prone areas can help protect the soil from erosion. Plant root systems hold down the soil. This cuts down the amount of dirt and debris swept away by floodwaters, which can cause further damage downstream.
- Tree-planting can also help lock carbon out of the atmosphere and help combat climate change.

Eco-activity: get down and dirty

The easiest place to plant a tree is in your own backyard. That way, you can watch it grow. Get a pot plant or seedling, put on some old clothes and gardening gloves, and follow this guide to planting a tree.

1 *Choose a location. Consider how big the plant will get and make sure it will have enough room and won't get caught in overhead powerlines.*

2 *Dig a hole twice as wide as the seedling pot. Lightly water the hole.*

3 *Squeeze in the sides of the pot to loosen the soil. Remove the plant gently from its container.*

4 *Place the plant in the hole. Make sure its root system will be lower than the surface of the ground and that it will stand upright and straight.*

5 *Gently put soil around the plant.*

7 *Press the soil down firmly to remove air pockets. Leave a slight dip in the soil around the plant so that water will collect there.*

8 *Cover the soil with mulch to reduce water loss and protect the roots.*

9 *Water the plant.*

Trees by numbers

Since European settlement, Australia's forest cover has been reduced from **69 MILLION** hectares to **41 MILLION** hectares.

Trees first appeared on earth about **400 MILLION** years ago. Dinosaurs came much later.

California redwood trees can live for up to **2200** years, can grow up to **115.5** metres in height and **8** metres in diameter at breast height. They're considered the tallest tree species, though there's some argument about this (there may be mountain ash trees in Tasmania to challenge for the title of 'tallest').

The dwarf willow, a species of creeping willow, is thought of as the world's smallest tree, growing to heights of only **1–6** centimetres.

The Wollemi pine is a 'living fossil' with a heritage of over **100 MILLION** years. There are only about **40** trees in the wild.

About **25–30 MILLION** natural Christmas trees are sold in the USA each year. The US Agricultural Census reported that for the year 2002 there were **21 904** Christmas tree farms with **180 900** hectares planted with Christmas trees in the USA alone.

A Bristlecone pine named 'Methuselah' is the oldest known tree. Methuselah is about **4800** years old and is estimated to have germinated in 2832 BCE, making it older than the Pyramids at Giza in Egypt. But a Norway spruce has been found in Sweden with an older root system. With this species, the part of the tree above the ground lives for about **600** years, but a new tree can shoot from the same root stock. This root stock has been radiocarbon-dated at **9550** years old.

The tallest known tree was possibly an Australian eucalyptus at Watts River, Victoria. In 1872, it was said to measure **435** feet (**133** metres), but it may have been over **500** feet (**152** metres) at some point in its life.

As for the fattest tree, in the late eighteenth century there was a European Chestnut known as the Tree of the Hundred Horses on Mount Etna in Italy. It had a waist measurement (circumference) of **190** feet (**58** metres). It has since separated into three parts.

Waste

Not many people wake up in the morning and set about deliberately trashing or poisoning the earth. We're not exactly burying used nuclear fuel rods under our oak or gum trees. However, humans in well-off countries produce a huge amount of waste. Part of this is the waste we see, the things we put into our own rubbish bin that are taken away to landfill by the local garbage-collection service. The other part, which we don't see, is the waste that's generated by the industries whose products we buy or whose services we use.

What is waste: trash or treasure?

Waste is simply unwanted or unusable by-products–the extra stuff produced by human activities for which we don't have further use. Humans are the only species that produces wastes that other species can't make use of. Elephants produce waste in the form of dung, which is a feast for dung beetles and fertiliser for the soil. When a sea creature gets rid of its shell, a hermit crab moves in or a small octopus uses it as a temporary protective refuge. Some businesses are getting their inspiration from nature and finding ways to make use of their waste. One Australian chicken company, for example, had the waste problem of chicken feet. Then they discovered that 'chicken's feet' are a traditional yum cha dish and are now exporting chicken feet to China.

Eco-byte

'Think about what happens to your waste and where it goes. If it doesn't go in the right place it might cause problems for the environment.' Ashley, 13

What's in our waste: a garbage bin autopsy

A while ago, a study was done of the contents of the rubbish bins of homes around Australia. It found that the average household throws away over 15 kilograms of rubbish per week. Good waste management means trying to produce less waste in total, recycling and reusing what you can and throwing what's left over in the right bin. The diagram overleaf shows the things they found in our bins, how much of each type they found, and how these waste items might otherwise be dealt with.

Think about it
Nature wastes nothing!

What's in our bins?

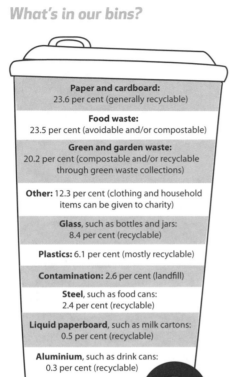

Paper and cardboard:
23.6 per cent (generally recyclable)

Food waste:
23.5 per cent (avoidable and/or compostable)

Green and garden waste:
20.2 per cent (compostable and/or recyclable through green waste collections)

Other: 12.3 per cent (clothing and household items can be given to charity)

Glass, such as bottles and jars:
8.4 per cent (recyclable)

Plastics: 6.1 per cent (mostly recyclable)

Contamination: 2.6 per cent (landfill)

Steel, such as food cans:
2.4 per cent (recyclable)

Liquid paperboard, such as milk cartons:
0.5 per cent (recyclable)

Aluminium, such as drink cans:
0.3 per cent (recyclable)

Hazardous: 0.2 per cent (special collections).

Source: Based on information from the Beverage Industry Environment Council

The waste hierarchy: 'reduce, reuse, recycle'

Everyone, from teachers to environment groups, and from celebrities to Bob the Builder, is saying 'Reduce, reuse, recycle'. But not many people know where this saying comes from. It's actually a short version of something called the 'waste hierarchy', a list of ways to minimise or manage waste in order of priority from the greenest or most desirable option to the least.

What's hot

What's not

Prevention is better than cure—this applies well to waste. Avoid producing waste in the first place!

Reduce the amount of waste you do produce. For example, if the shampoo you use comes in a larger size, buy that instead of smaller bottles. Buying things that won't go off in bulk reduces the amount of packaging needed per unit of product. This approach is often called 'waste minimisation'.

Reuse is the repeated use of a product in its current state, with little or no processing. Reuse your waste items wherever you can, instead of throwing them away. Reuse computer CDs as coasters or hang them in trees to scare away pest birds; reuse biscuit tins to store stationery; buy second-hand goods. You get the drift. The reuse of products and materials gives us better use of the resources needed to make them.

In the case of **recycling**, waste materials are collected, sorted, cleaned and converted into raw materials that are then made into new goods. When you put recyclable materials in your recycling bin, you're making these materials available for this purpose. Remember that, while recycling waste is good for the environment, avoiding producing waste in the first place is generally better.

Energy recovery is using the waste materials as a fuel to produce energy.

Disposal in landfill is the least desired waste management option—the last resort.

Learn more

What happens to the rubbish in my rubbish bin? See landfill on page 124 to find out.

What happens to the stuff I put out for recycling? See recycling: the products on page 156 to find out.

Hazardous waste

So far, we've mainly talked about waste and how it relates to using our planet's precious resources wisely. But there's also a nasty side to some kinds of waste. Hazardous wastes are those that can pollute or harm the environment or that pose a threat to our health. It is important that these wastes are managed by experts in ways that minimise their risks.

A waste is said to be hazardous if it is one or more of the following:

- **toxic**—harmful or fatal when touched or accidentally eaten. For example, some batteries contain the toxic heavy metal cadmium
- **flammable** or **ingitable**—creates fire under certain conditions
- **corrosive**—contains acids or bases that can corrode metal
- **reactive**—is chemically unstable under 'normal' conditions, will react easily and can cause explosions, toxic fumes, or vapours when mixed with water.

Household waste items that might be hazardous include the following:

- fluorescent light bulbs (they contain small amounts of mercury)
- solvents, paints and varnish
- used motor oil or car antifreeze
- pesticides
- weedkiller and other garden chemicals
- old mercury-containing thermometers
- old electronic equipment.

If you're throwing out any of these items, check that it's okay with an adult and suggest that they might like to get expert advice if they're unsure.

Water

There are nearly 1.4 billion cubic kilometres (1 cubic kilometre equals 1 billion litres) of water in the world, so you may be wondering why there's so much fuss about conserving water and keeping it clean.

We should all know the importance of water. We drink it, clean with it and bathe in it. Water is also great fun—hence the invention of surfboards, Super Soaker water guns and water slides. We ourselves are made up of 65 per cent water. All living things need it. It grows our food and is part of our weather. Water is especially important to people like surfer Layne Beachley, swimmer Michael Phelps or skaters Jayne Torvill and Christopher Dean. Without water, or ice in Torvill and Dean's case, they might all be playing lawn bowls on synthetic grass!

The trouble with water is that even though three-quarters of the planet's surface is covered with the stuff, over 97 per cent is undrinkable salt water. A further 2 per cent is fresh water trapped in icecaps and glaciers. More fresh water is below the earth's surface as groundwater and soil moisture, or in the air as clouds and water vapour. What remains as accessible fresh water in lakes, reservoirs, rivers, inland seas and other waterways is a tiny 0.02 per cent of all the earth's water.

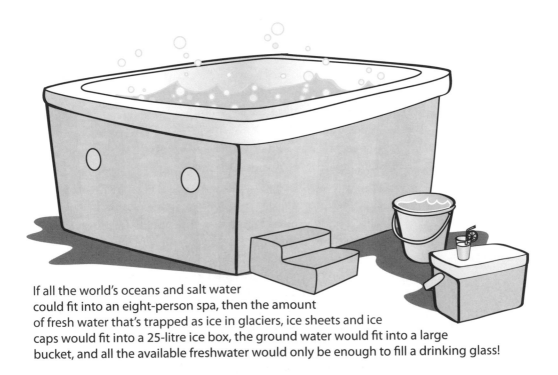

If all the world's oceans and salt water could fit into an eight-person spa, then the amount of fresh water that's trapped as ice in glaciers, ice sheets and ice caps would fit into a 25-litre ice box, the ground water would fit into a large bucket, and all the available freshwater would only be enough to fill a drinking glass!

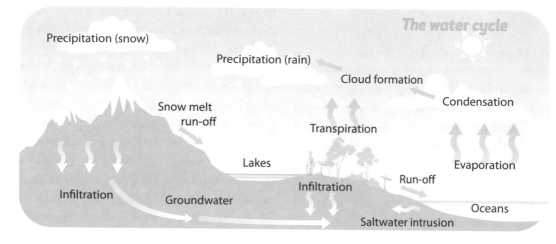

The water cycle

Precipitation (snow)

Precipitation (rain)

Cloud formation

Condensation

Snow melt run-off

Transpiration

Evaporation

Lakes

Infiltration

Run-off

Infiltration

Groundwater

Oceans

Saltwater intrusion

How water gets around: the water cycle

Water is the ultimate multipurpose recyclable material in nature. The earth always has the same total amount of water, but it moves through the environment in its various forms. In fact, a dinosaur may have drunk a molecule of water that is now part of the saliva dribbling out of your pet dog's mouth!

At any given moment, some of the earth's water is on the surface, in lakes, oceans and even puddles. Some of this liquid water evaporates (changes from liquid to gas), moving into the atmosphere as invisible water vapour. Water vapour also comes from evaporation from living things, such as the

transpiration of water from plants. Cooled water vapour condenses (changes from gas to liquid) to form tiny liquid water droplets suspended in the air, which we see as clouds. If it's cold enough, they freeze. When the tiny water droplets within the clouds join together to form larger, heavier droplets, they fall to the earth as rain, snow, hail and sleet—the different types of precipitation. Some of this precipitation falls back into the ocean or runs off the surface of the ground into lakes, other fresh water bodies, waterways or the sea. Some filters into the ground, becoming soil moisture or groundwater. Plants also take up water from the soil. Groundwater can eventually seep into wetlands, streams or the ocean. The cycle keeps repeating.

Did you know ... ?

- Our bodies are around 65 per cent water. Blood is 82 per cent water and the lungs are 90 per cent water.
- If you lose 1–2 per cent of your body's water, you may start to feel the symptoms of dehydration. Lose over 10 per cent and you'll probably die.
- Water is the only substance on earth found naturally in all three states: solid, liquid and gas.

What's up with water?

All life relies on water. Land-dwelling plants and animals drink water to remain healthy; aquatic (living in water) plants and animals call it home. Water-related environmental issues fall into three categories: those related to supply, quality and habitat.

Reliable water supplies

Humans have many uses for water. Aside from drinking it and using it in homes, it's also used to produce food, electricity and products, and to wash things or get rid of waste. Agriculture is the world's largest user of water, using 70 per cent of the total water withdrawn from the environment. Twenty per cent is used in industry. Together with the 10 per cent we use in our homes, these requirements create a demand for fresh water that will keep increasing as the world's population increases. These are the averages. However, it's also important to remember that in cities, where agriculture is nonexistent, households are one of the largest users of water. In some countries, crops fail and people get sick and die because there is not enough fresh water available locally.

Quality

All living things, including humans, plants, animals, crops and livestock, need water to survive—and not just any old water. Water has the ability to dissolve many chemicals or to carry fine particles or microbes. Humans need safe, disease-free, fresh water, while marine plants and animals need salty water. Water is also fun and a part of recreational activities, such as swimming and water sports, or riverside picnic areas. This water needs to be safe and healthy to play in! Human activities can pollute water environments and our supplies of fresh water or interfere with nature's own methods of cleaning or purifying it. For example, a huge rainstorm can wash rubbish and chemicals off streets and suburbs into waterways, rivers and the sea. We're chopping down the trees whose root systems help to filter the water. We're using rivers and waterways as convenient places to wash away liquid waste. These things contribute to water pollution, lowering its quality and its ability to do the things we and other species need it to do.

Habitat

Water isn't just something to drink or use; for fish, turtles, dolphins and seaweed, it's home. Aquatic plants and animals need healthy rivers, waterways, wetlands, bays and oceans in which they can comfortably live. Things such as litter, pollution, human overuse of water, and physical changes to water habitats can cause problems for the species that live there. For example, some fish species migrate at certain times in their lives, travelling a few metres up stream or, in some cases, thousands of kilometres across oceans. Dams can block this migration, so many dams incorporate 'fish ladders', which allow fish a way through.

Water: environmental flows

Earth is sometimes called the 'Blue Planet' because the water on the surface (largely oceans) makes it look blue when viewed from space. When scientists look for the potential for life forms on other planets, the first thing they look for is water because it's necessary for life as we know it.

The amount and quality of water in an ecosystem in many ways determines what that ecosystem is like: its characteristics, the plant and animal species that live there and how they work together. Humans in many parts of the world are using more than their fair share of the earth's fresh water. There is also the pressure of climate change, which is shifting and changing rainfall patterns. The world is facing a water crisis in which we need to find a balance between water for people and water for nature.

Environmental flows:
water for nature

When people donate blood to be given as transfusions to people in hospital, only 500 millilitres or so are taken, despite the average adult having several litres of blood. Why? Because donors still need much of their own blood to remain healthy themselves.

Water is the lifeblood of the land. Humans need water, so we withdraw it from the environment (our water donor), sometimes forgetting that the environment needs it too. There is a limit to the amount of water that can be safely extracted from nature before some of nature's systems and processes start to collapse. 'Environmental flow' is the amount of water needed in a river, wetland, coastal zone or other watercourse to maintain a normal, healthy, natural ecosystem, along with its benefits to people. This can change seasonally. For example, it is normal and healthy for some river systems to dry out periodically. Maintaining environmental flows or returning them to dying river systems, such as Australia's Murray–Darling system, can improve the health of the river system, flush out impurities, keep threatened species alive, reduce the effects of pollution and help the businesses that rely on the river system, such as fisheries.

Eco-action: save water!

Think about environmental flows when you're brushing your teeth or having a shower. Every bucket of water you save is one less that has to be withdrawn from the environment.

Think about it
Water is the ultimate recyclable material.

Changing flows

The human race has had a love–hate relationship with the planet's sometimes unpredictable watercourses and seas, relying on them for enriched soil, irrigation, hydroelectricity and transportation, while sometimes having to deal with the problems of flooding. Humans may find drought and floods and even the change of seasons inconvenient, but these sometimes dramatic cycles of scarcity and plenty can be part of how nature renews itself.

Changes to the flows and distribution of water supplies might be good for us in the short term but bad for the natural environment (and therefore us) in the long term. If our planet's water resources are poorly managed, land and river systems become degraded, vegetation dies, animals loose habitat, and a wide variety of species loose the conditions they need to breed. The costs are passed on to humans, through the loss of productive farming land to irrigation salinity (where irrigation causes the soil to become too salty to grow healthy crops), poorer water quality for drinking and irrigation, less electricity produced by hydroelectricity plants and in many other ways.

Human activities that change water flows include:

- the building of dams, weirs and river locks
- the diversion of rivers and withdrawal of water from lakes and groundwater to irrigate crops
- the construction of canals to connect watercourses for the purpose of shipping, such as the Panama and Suez canals
- the building of hydroelectric dams
- the introduction of pollution and weeds, which can clog up water courses.

Did you know … ?

Thanks to climate change and the over-withdrawal of water, cartographers (people who make maps) have had to redraw parts of some maps. Lake Chad in Africa is now 95 per cent smaller than it was in 1963 and the Aral Sea in central Asia has shrunk in size by three quarters over 40 years.

Groundbreaking groundwater use

In many cities, people are walking on water—well, sort of. Soil and porous rock can hold a lot of groundwater. Together, they support the weight of the buildings, roads and cities built on the surface. In some cities, groundwater is pumped from the ground to provide water for the city. If the city has too much concrete and roof cover and not enough garden and park space, rainwater doesn't get a chance to seep back into the ground to recharge the groundwater. As a result, the fine structure of the earth can collapse under the weight of the structures built on it. This damages the roads, pipes and buildings in the area. Bangkok and Mexico City are suffering from land subsidence due to the over-pumping of groundwater.

Think about it

When you hear about dams blocking fish migration or flooding surrounding regions, it's easy to think that they might not be such a good idea. But it's important to remember that dams are a key part of secure water supplies for many cities. Sydney is one example: there are 21 storage dams managed by the Sydney Catchment Management Authority, which together hold more than 2.5 million megalitres of water.

The highs and lows of Aswan High Dam

An example of the worst effects of changing water flow patterns is the effects of the Aswan High Dam on the Nile River in Egypt. The Nile River is often called the 'life source' of Egypt. It supports this otherwise dry country's agriculture and provides water for the people. Around 95 per cent of Egypt's people live within 20 kilometres of the Nile.

The Aswan High Dam was built to capture floodwater and release it during times of drought. It was also built to provide power, generating more than 10 billion kilowatt hours of electricity every year. Before the dam was built, the Nile's floodplain, Egypt's narrow strip of fertile land, was flooded once a year. Floodwaters would drop nutrient-rich silt on the plains around the river, fertilising the dry desert land.

The dam has blocked the flow of silt, which sits wasted on the bottom of Lake Nasser. Farmers now have to buy artificial fertiliser. Since the dam was completed in 1970, the fertility of Egypt's agricultural land has steadily declined, with many areas now suffering from soil degradation and salinity. The fishing industry downstream from the dam has also been badly affected. Although fishing boats can move around the river more easily now that the water flow has been tamed, they are catching less fish. The nutrient-rich floodwaters used to produce blooms of phytoplankton at the Nile Delta, which provided food for the fish. Now that there's less fish food, there are less fish. The Delta itself is also eroding at an alarming rate.

Canada: 1386 m^3

USA: 1599 m^3

Brazil: 318 m^3

 = Approximately 100 cubic
metres (100 000 litres)
per person per year.

Source: Pacific Institute, <www.worldwater.org>.

Around the world: water withdrawals

When you take money out of the bank, your action is called a 'withdrawal'. Similarly, when water is taken out of a water source for use by humans, it's called a 'water withdrawal'. The following map shows, for a few different countries, how much water is taken per person from the environment for use in homes, agriculture, factories and to serve other human needs.

United Kingdom: 197 m^3

China: 415 m^3

Egypt: 918 m^3

Australia: 1194 m^3

Mozambique: 33 m^3

New Zealand: 521 m^3

Water conservation and management

Good water management means that many water needs are met with minimal harm to the environment. Food can be grown, businesses can be successful, people and their communities can thrive, all the time maintaining a balance with the natural environment. Bad water management means water wasted, water polluted and some water needs not met. So whose job is it to manage our water? Everybody's!

Water management is a team sport. Like in a football game, there are many players playing different roles:

- **Scientists** study water supplies, natural water bodies and water environments, how we use water and how we can use it more sustainably. They seek out and provide the rest of society with the knowledge needed to make good choices concerning water. For example, some agricultural scientists are breeding grain crop varieties that need less water, while others may be researching methods of purifying dirty water.
- **Governments** make laws that govern the way we use water. For example, they set limits on the amount and type of fish that can be caught and make it illegal to dump poisonous chemicals in rivers. They use water in public places, such as public swimming pools or to water sports fields. Governments also spend money collected as taxes or rates on water infrastructure, the large-scale systems and projects that provide us with fresh water and take away waste water, such as urban sewage systems. Governments also issue licences to farmers, allowing them to withdraw certain amounts of water from the environment to use on the land.
- **Water authorities** manage our tap water supplies and the treatment of waste water on behalf of the government. In some countries they are part of government; in others they may be private companies.
- **Farmers** use water to produce our food and fibre for clothing. They set up irrigation systems to deliver water where it's needed. Good farming practices avoid wasting water.
- **Fishers** interact with water environments when they harvest fish from the water.
- **Factories** use water in their processes and to clean equipment. Ideally, they can do this in a way that avoids both wasting water and polluting it.
- **Residents** use water in their homes to drink, cook, clean, wash themselves, water plants, flush the toilet and occasionally squirt at each other! We have a job to do: save water and look after it.

Eco-byte

'I think if everybody works together they can succeed at anything.' **Wasim, 12**

Water by numbers

In the cities of many developed countries, drinking-quality water is used to flush toilets and to water gardens. Only around **1%** is used for actual drinking.

About **20%** of the world's population does not have access to safe drinking water.

According to the United Nations, the growing population, pollution and global warming will combine to cut the average person's water supply by a third in the next **20** years.

Older-style toilets use around **18** litres of water per flush. The latest ultra-low-flush toilets can use as little as **4.5** litres for a full flush and **3** litres for a 'half' flush.

Spending **3** minutes less each day under the average shower will save **13 140** litres of water in a year.

Each day the sun evaporates **1 000 000 000 000** (a trillion) US tons of water (**907 184 740 000** metric tonnes).

Lake Baikal in Siberia, Russia, is the largest freshwater lake on earth. It contains **23 000** cubic kilometers of water—about **20%** of the world's total surface fresh water.

The world's wettest place is Tutunendo, Colombia, with an average rainfall of **11 770** millimetres per year.

It takes **7007** litres of water to refine one barrel of crude oil.

A cow can drink up to **90** litres of water per day while only producing **12** litres of milk.

China has **20%** of the world's population but only **7%** of the world's fresh water. In contrast, the USA has **4.5%** of the population and **8%** of the fresh water.

Water in the home: where we use it

Despite living in the driest inhabited continent, the average Australian family uses hundreds of litres of water each day. This can vary a lot, depending on the size of the family's garden and the plants used, how many people live together and the climate in the area where they live. Water is a precious resource that we have to conserve.

With recent drought and water restrictions, we've become more aware of how much water we use and the need to use less. There are many things that you can do to save water. The bonus is that saving water will save your family money, especially if you reduce your use of hot water and therefore the use of the energy needed to heat it. Start by thinking about where you use water in the home.

Eau, so expensive!

Water is relatively cheap in Australia, the USA and the United Kingdom. However, in countries where safe drinking water is in short supply, it's a precious and expensive resource.

- In parts of Sudan, up to half of the average household income is spent on water.

- In Bogota, Colombia, pirates steal water by drilling into water mains.

Water use in the home

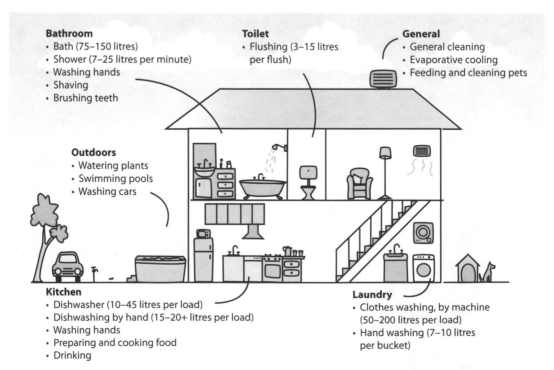

Bathroom
- Bath (75–150 litres)
- Shower (7–25 litres per minute)
- Washing hands
- Shaving
- Brushing teeth

Toilet
- Flushing (3–15 litres per flush)

General
- General cleaning
- Evaporative cooling
- Feeding and cleaning pets

Outdoors
- Watering plants
- Swimming pools
- Washing cars

Kitchen
- Dishwasher (10–45 litres per load)
- Dishwashing by hand (15–20+ litres per load)
- Washing hands
- Preparing and cooking food
- Drinking

Laundry
- Clothes washing, by machine (50–200 litres per load)
- Hand washing (7–10 litres per bucket)

How low can you go?
The five R's of saving water

There are five basic ways that households can cut their use of water from urban water mains:

1. **Reduce** your water consumption by changing your water use habits. For example, don't leave the tap running while brushing your teeth.
2. **Report and repair**: report any leaking taps, burst water mains or faulty plumbing devices to your parents or teachers so that they can get them fixed. A small drip can waste 75 litres a day.
3. **Retrofit** your home with more efficient water using fixtures, such as dual-flush toilets. Ask your parents to think about these changes.
4. **Rainwater** can be collected and used instead of tap water in some instances.
5. **Recycle** your grey water, following your local EPA guidelines or regulations.

Think about it

If you like singing in the shower, limit it to just one song, not a whole concert!

Eco-action: what *you* can do to save water

- Don't leave the tap running while brushing your teeth. Instead, use a cup of water to rinse your mouth, toothbrush and the sink.

- Don't spend too long in the shower. Four minutes is plenty of time. A shower timer can help you keep track of time.

- When you come back from the beach, rub sand off your feet with a towel instead of washing it off.

- Don't have more than one shower per day.

- Keep a bowl in the sink to catch water from rinsing fruit or washing your hands. Tip this 'grey water' on the garden.

- You know the toilet drill: 'If it's yellow, let it mellow. If it's brown, flush it down.'

- When you want warm water, you have to wait for the cold water that's sitting in the pipes to come through first. Catch the cold water in a bucket and keep it for washing your hands later or use it to water pot plants.

- With older style single-flush toilets, you can reduce the amount of water used per flush by putting a sand-filled plastic bottle (with the lid screwed tightly on) inside the toilet cistern (the top bit). The bottle takes up space, reducing the volume of water needed to refill the cistern.

- Instead of washing dishes, lick them clean ... just kidding!

Eco-activity: do your own household water audit

According to the United Nations Educational, Scientific and Cultural Organization (UNESCO), each person needs 20–50 litres of water free from harmful contaminants each and every day to ensure their basic needs are met. How much do you use? How much does your household use? How does this compare with the UNESCO figure? Could you use less?

Use some simple maths and the water use estimates in the guide below to fill out the table on the facing page. Adding together the numbers in the total column will give you an estimate of your average daily household water use. Think about things you and your family could do to save water, and fill out the final column to see how much you could make a difference.

Guide

Shower	• A water efficient showerhead uses around 9 litres per minute.
	• Older style showerheads can use about 20 litres per minute.
	• Test your showerhead's flow rate by running the shower into a bucket for 30 seconds (timed with a stopwatch). Measure the amount of water in the bucket and double it to get the flow rate per minute.
Toilet	• A dual-flush toilet uses about 4 litres for a 'half' flush and 6 litres for a full flush.
	• An older style single-flush toilet uses about 11 litres per flush.
Bath	• A bath uses 75–150 litres, depending on how full it is.
Dishwashing	• For hand washing dishes, each filled sink uses 15 litres of water.
	• Modern dishwashers use 15 litres for a quick cycle and about 20 litres for a normal cycle. You can check this in the dishwasher's manual if your parents have kept it.
Laundry	• A front-loading washing machine uses about 50–80 litres per cycle.
	• A top-loading washing machine uses 120–150 litres.
	• A twin-tub washing machine uses 70 litres.
Washing hands	• It takes about 5 litres to wash your hands.
Cleaning teeth	• You will use about a quarter of a litre to brush your teeth if you use a cup.
	• It will take 5 litres, though, with the tap running.
Watering garden	• If you water your garden with a hose, you will use about 10 litres per minute.
General use	• Allow 10 litres per person per day for general water uses such as cooking, drinking and cleaning.

Household water use table

Activity	Number of people in household		Number of uses per person per day		Amount of water per use (litres)		Total (litres)	Estimate how much you could save (litres)
Example: **Shower**	4	x	1	x	6 minutes @ 12 litres per minute = 72	=	288	144 by everyone having 3-minute showers
Shower		x		x		=		
Toilet		x		x		=		
Bath		x		x		=		
Dishwashing		x		x		=		
Laundry		x		x		=		
Washing hands		x		x		=		
Cleaning teeth		x		x		=		
Watering garden		x		x		=		
General use		x		x		=		
					TOTAL	=		

Water in the home: where we get it from

Tap water

We turn the tap on. Water comes out. We pull out the plug. Water disappears. It's easy to take water and sewerage systems for granted when you live in the city. Have you ever stopped to think about where it comes from and how it gets to suburban taps?

Very few people realise the colossal effort and investment that goes into making sure that we get enough tap water and that it's drinkable, that our waste water is safely treated, and that the stormwater run-off from our roofs and streets is manageable when it rains. In Australia, the state of Victoria alone has more than A$12 billion worth of water system–related assets, such as dams, pipes and treatment plants. Water is transported through tunnels and pipes from reservoirs, via regional storage tanks to homes. It is moved by pump, sometimes with the help of gravity. Along the way, it may be filtered, chlorinated and put through a series of tests. Some cities have fluoride added to the water supply to help look after our teeth. The flow and water pressure are maintained by pressure control valves on the mains. It takes considerable resources and money to make sure that the water that flows through our taps is fit for human consumption. In fact, most Australians use drinking water to wash their bodies, houses and clothes, water the garden and flush the toilet.

Our reservoirs and water storages are refilled by rainfall and melted snow. When this can't keep up with the rate at which we use water, our cities' water storages drop. As dam and water-storage levels get very low, there is less water to dilute dissolved salts. Closer to the bottom of the water body, the water also gets muddier. The result is deteriorating water quality. In some severely drought-stricken areas, the tap water is like smelly mud. In extreme cases, water storages can run out and residents have to have fresh water brought in by trucks, costing a lot more money. So it's important that we use tap water wisely, especially when water storage levels are low.

Rainwater and grey water

Tap water from urban water mains isn't the only option for our household water needs. We can also use collected rainwater and grey water (the water from showers, baths and washing machines, for example). Very few of the things we use water for in the home require it to be of a quality fit for human consumption. Some household water demands, such as watering the garden, or washing windows and cars, or toilet flushing, can be safely met using 'lower grade' water. If we use recycled grey water or collected rainwater for these jobs, we can slash the amount of water we take from our drinking water supplies.

Note that collected rainwater is not always safe to drink. Rain isn't the only thing that falls on your roof, after all; there's probably possum and bird poop, too! Plus, some of the materials used to make and paint roofs, water pipes, gutters and the storage tanks themselves can leach certain chemicals into the water, making it unsafe to drink. This water is still safe for use in garden watering or, with the right plumbing, toilet flushing and clothes washing. Never drink water from a rainwater tank unless you've checked with an adult, preferably one who is a health freak!

Eco-lingo

grey water   This is the waste water from the bathroom, laundry and kitchen.

black water or **brown water**   These are names for the waste water from the toilet.

Tanks a lot!

In Adelaide, South Australia, rainwater tanks are old news. Here the drinking water supply is largely drawn from the Murray River, downstream from the agricultural regions of the Murray–Darling system in the eastern states. South Australia cops the brunt of the irrigation problems of the eastern states through this water. Although it is safe and 'drinkable', it is quite hard water. Adelaide's residents find that they need more shampoo to work up a soapy lather in the shower; kettles get a crusty lining from the minerals that get boiled out of the hard water, and the water itself doesn't taste very good. Many houses in Adelaide use rainwater tanks to provide additional water supplies and a more palatable alternative to the water from taps.

Did you know ... ?   The ancient Romans were masters at rainwater collection and distribution. They built aqueducts to supply water to the Empire's cities. The remains of these aqueducts, some of which still function, can be found in many of the lands that were once under Roman rule, including the United Kingdom, Spain, Germany, Israel and Turkey.

Sources of water pollution

Mining also pollutes waterways. Rainwater run-off from open-pit mining and other excavation washes soil and debris into waterways. Hard-rock mining can pollute water and soil with heavy metals such as cadmium, lead and arsenic. Cyanide used in the process of extracting gold ore can also poison waterways and groundwater.

Land-clearing is removing the vegetation that holds down soil. The exposed earth is eroded and washed into nearby creeks and rivers. Worse still, clearing vegetation removes plants, which filter other debris and pollutants out of the water. Plants are our natural water purifiers.

Agricultural run-off from over-irrigation and rainfall brings pesticides, natural and synthetic fertilisers and soil into waterways. Some pesticides are poisonous chemicals that don't break down and, instead, build up in the food chain. Fertilisers in waterways cause algae to thrive, starving other aquatic life of oxygen. The loss of topsoil from farms makes the land less fertile and causes rivers to become clogged with silt.

Industrial factories may release waste water and other pollutants, such as solvents and chlorine bleaches, into waterways.

Water pollution

You may have noticed that water quality and pollution have been mentioned a few times while we've been looking at water. The world's freshwater supplies and the wellbeing of aquatic life are under threat from water pollution from a variety of sources. Water pollution is reducing the amount of drinking-quality water available and allowing harmful chemicals and pollutants to enter the food chain.

Animal farms, particularly large-scale hog farms, produce huge amounts of manure-filled liquid waste. Even in countries where the law requires this waste to be treated, periods of high rainfall can cause the systems to overflow, releasing untreated animal faecal matter into waterways.

Unlined solid waste landfill tips expose a range of products and chemicals to rainfall. The flow of water through the rubbish sees heavy metals and other hazardous chemicals leach into groundwater. Buried industrial waste similarly sees pollutants leach into the water table.

Air pollution mixes with rain clouds to produce acid rain. Acid rain pollutes otherwise pristine lakes, particularly in North America.

Thermal pollution is caused by hot water released from power stations. The water may be clean, but the heat can harm temperature-sensitive marine life.

Urban stormwater run-off from our city streets washes leaked motor oil, litter, household chemicals and a hoard of other pollutants into creeks, rivers and the sea. Road salt is another source of water pollution in cold climates, where salt is sprinkled on icy roads to help melt the ice.

Effluent and untreated sewage are polluting inland waterways around the world. Outflow pipes also dump these wastes at sea. Even treated sewage has chemical residues, such as phosphates, from cleaning agents and other household products. These chemicals harm aquatic life.

Oil spills from oil tankers and pipelines wreak havoc on the marine environment.

Dumped waste, both legal and illegal, is polluting our oceans. These chemicals and heavy metals (including mercury) enter the marine food chain, where they can accumulate. They end up in human diets, particularly in nations such as Japan, where fish and other seafood are often on the menu.

Eco-activity: distil water

It's a sunny day and you're feeling thirsty. Try this eco-activity to get yourself a mouthful of clean drinking water from salty or muddy water.

You will need

- 2 cups (500 millilitres) of salty or muddy water (or clean water with a teaspoon of salt or even coffee added to it)
- A large bowl
- A glass that is a little shorter than the bowl
- Cling wrap
- A large marble or smooth stone

How to

1 Put the salty or muddy water in the bowl.

2 Place the glass in the middle of the bowl, making sure none of the 'dirty' water gets inside it.

3 Cover the bowl with cling wrap so that it sticks to the entire rim of the bowl. This will keep warm air inside the bowl.

4 Place the marble, stone or other weight in the centre of the cling wrap so that it dips to its lowest point over the glass.

5 Put the bowl where it will get direct sunlight, but where it is unlikely to get knocked.

6 Leave it until a reasonable amount of clear water has appeared in the glass. This may take a few hours on a hot sunny day or a few days in winter months.

What's happening?

The heat from the sun evaporates the water, leaving the impurities behind. The water vapour produced condenses onto the plastic film, trickling down it before dripping into the glass.

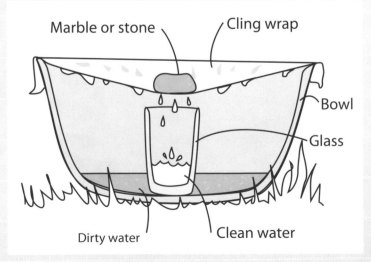

Marble or stone — Cling wrap — Bowl — Glass — Clean water — Dirty water

Eco-action: check for leaks

Sneaky leaky toilets

Drips and leaks waste hundreds of litres of water per day. Dripping taps are hard to miss; the drips are visible and the sound of a dripping tap can keep you awake when you're having trouble sleeping. If you spot one, let an adult know so that they can arrange to have it fixed. Toilet cisterns, on the other hand, can get a sneaky leak in which a slow but constant dribble of water runs from the cistern down the back of the toilet bowl without making a splash or noise.

If you suspect that your cistern is leaking, you can check by putting some food colouring into the cistern water. If you see the colour coming through into the bowl when the toilet hasn't been flushed, then you'll know it's leaking.

Check the meter

If your house has its own water meter, you can use this to check for leaks. When water is being used, the dials on the metre slowly turn. Write down the water meter reading when you leave to go to school on a day when no one will be in the house while you're away. Take a second reading as soon as you get home again and before you or anyone else uses any water. If there are no leaks, the two readings should be the same.

Drip, drip, drip

Imagine a leaky tap, slowly dripping at around one drip per second. It doesn't seem like much, does it? However, all those drips add up to about half a litre per hour. The longer you leave a leak unfixed, the more water you will waste.

Leave it dripping for a year and you will waste enough water to:

- fill 28 000 glasses
- wash twenty-eight loads of clothes
- provide fifty-six showers
- flush up to 700 toilets, or
- clean your teeth 14 000 times.

Water: sewage treatment

After we've used it, waste water flows down the plughole, toilet water is flushed away and rainwater runs down pipes and along gutters into stormwater drains. What happens next is a bit of mystery to most people.

Down the plughole and flushed away

In Australian cities there are generally two separate systems that take the water we don't want away from our homes. Everything that is flushed down the toilet or that flows down the bathroom, kitchen and laundry plugholes is referred to as 'sewage'. It can spread diseases if not managed properly. Before urban sewerage systems were built in developed countries, it was up to individuals to deal with their waste water. In Melbourne in the nineteenth century, there were open sewer drains along the streets. It wasn't pretty or hygienic—in fact Melbourne earned the nickname 'Smellbourne'. Governments set up centralised water management systems in heavily populated areas largely to control waterborne diseases such as typhoid, cholera and dysentery.

Isolated homes in 'non-sewered' areas rely on septic tank systems to treat their sewage. In sewered urban areas, the 'sewerage system' takes waste water away from homes through pipes to a treatment plant. Here it is treated to a level deemed safe enough for it to be released back into the environment. Sewage treatment plants use filtering systems to remove rubbish like cotton buds or tampon wrappers and bacteria, chlorine and sunlight to break down the solid stuff in the sewage and to disinfect the water. The treated sewage is called 'effluent'.

Some sewerage systems have coastal outflows that rely on the sea to water down the treated sewage. In some countries, raw sewage is released into the sea. Even worse, many developing countries have open sewers in populated areas or discharge raw sewage directly into waterways that people use for bathing. These countries see many millions of people die from waterborne diseases.

Down the drain

The stormwater system provides the second path by which uncaptured water leaves our homes, other buildings and streets. Rain that falls onto rooftops flows into pipes that feed into stormwater drains. These drains also collect the unabsorbed water that flows along the ground, off paved areas and roadways, into roadside gutters. The drains carry this water to nearby creeks and rivers or, if nearby, the sea. In coastal cities, the stormwater eventually ends up in the ocean, with litter picked up along the way washed onto the beaches.

This water is largely untreated, except for litter-trap cages in some drains. As it washes through suburbia, stormwater collects rubbish, cigarette butts, dog poo, grass clippings, leaves, leaked motor oil and petrol, garden chemicals, waste water from painting and car washing, and debris from building and renovation sites. A lot of this rubbish ends up harming wildlife and polluting our waterways and beaches. For example, it's estimated that up to 95 per cent of the litter on Melbourne's beaches comes from suburban streets.

Stormwater and sewage management in a typical city

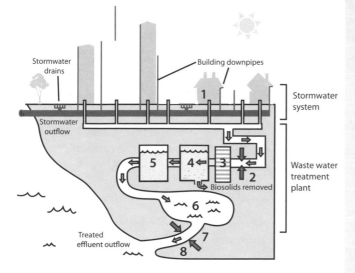

Stormwater

Water runs off rooftops, streets and the ground into stormwater drains, which empty into nearby creeks, rivers and beaches.

Sewage

1 Sewerage pipes from homes empty into main sewer and are transported to treatment plants.

2 At the plant, sewage may get a blast of oxygen to suppress odours or a blast of chlorine (a disinfectant).

3 Screens and skimmers remove large objects and some solid material.

4 Sewage is allowed to settle in a holding tank for a few hours. The sediment forms sludge (also known as 'biosolids'), which is removed. Scum is also removed from the surface.

5 In another holding tank, 'good' bacteria (not the disease-causing varieties) feed on and break down any remaining material in the waste water.

6 The water then passes through ponds, where sunlight helps to disinfect the water.

7 The water is given a final zap of disinfecting chlorine.

8 Water is released into the environment.

Eco-action: to flush or not to flush?

In *Finding Nemo*, a dead pet fish is flushed down the toilet. But should a toilet be used as a rubbish bin?

Don't flush the following items:

- *tampons, pads or other feminine hygiene products*

- *cotton buds or cotton wool balls*

- *uneaten food*

- *apple cores or fruit peel (compost it instead)*

- *bandages, bandaids or swabs.*

Water supplies

Ideally, there would be enough fresh water readily available in places where it is needed. But the earth's 1.4 billion-odd litres of water aren't evenly spread. Deserts are places where it rarely rains, with the odd oasis fed by a spring or by groundwater that is close to the surface. In contrast, the Himalayan town Cherrapunji is one of the world's wettest places, with rainfall averaging 11 430 millimetres per year. It also rains over the ocean. Hurricanes, cyclones and monsoons can bring too much rain. Droughts occur when there's not enough.

Human settlements have sprung up over thousands of years in areas with reasonable food and water sources. Over time, these settlements, towns and cities have grown, sometimes to populations larger than local water supplies can support. In these situations, governments and water authorities have to think about ways to secure freshwater supplies and alternative freshwater sources. Let's take a look at the different options and their good and bad points.

Pumping groundwater

In areas where groundwater is drinkable and reasonably close to the surface, bores (deep holes) can be drilled into the ground to access that water. Some of this groundwater is in aquifers, layers of permeable rock or sand through which water can flow. Aquifers are like huge underground rocky or sandy sponges. Though they may be recharged in areas that get good rainfall, they can extend underground into areas that don't get rain.

Pros

- There is about fifty times more groundwater than surface fresh water.
- Groundwater may be one of the few options in areas that don't get rain or that don't have waterways flowing through them.
- Water bores and wells can be relatively inexpensive.
- They take up little space.

Did you know?
In Gaza, Egypt, the quality of water drawn from wells is declining due to saltwater seepage.

Cons

- It's hard to estimate the amount of water that can be pumped sustainably.
- Removing too much groundwater can cause the land above it to sink, damaging the structures built on it.
- Removing too much groundwater in coastal areas may lead to 'saltwater intrusion', where sea water flows inland into freshwater aquifers.
- Groundwater may be polluted in areas where waste has been buried or near industrial areas.
- There's a risk of groundwater use being poorly managed as groundwater is out of sight.

Desalination

Desalination turns salt water into fresh water, either by **distillation** or **reverse osmosis**. Distillation produces fresh water from condensed steam, while reverse osmosis forces water through a membrane that blocks salt and other impurities. Desalination is already in use in countries such as Saudi Arabia, Israel, Australia and Hong Kong.

Pros

- We've got huge oceans full of seawater!
- Desalination can provide a virtually limitless supply of fresh water that is independent of rainfall. Rainwater tanks and dams, in contrast, don't get filled much during a drought.
- Desalination plants don't take up more land than a large factory or warehouse.

Cons

- Desalination plants cost billions of dollars to build.
- Desalination uses huge amounts of energy, which makes it very expensive on an ongoing basis.
- If the energy needed comes from burning fossil fuels, then desalination can make a huge contribution to the greenhouse effect.
- Desalination plants pump hyper-saline (extremely salty, more so than sea water) water back into the sea. This may be harmful to marine life.

Did you know? In the opinion of Australia's celebrity science guru Dr Karl Kruszelnicki, desalination is the process of turning saline water into fresh water by throwing heaps of money at it!

Better distribution

Fresh water is distributed to homes, factories and farms through pipes and along irrigation channels, but some of it is lost along the way. There are proposals to fix old or damaged leaking pipes or to cover irrigation channels, which are exposed to the air and sun, to reduce evaporation.

Pros

- Thousands of megalitres of water are lost due to leaks and evaporation, so there is the potential to save a lot of water.

Cons

- Fixing pipes and covering channels are expensive.

Did you know? Australia has about 175 000 kilometres of water mains.

Cloud seeding

In cloud seeding, water-carrying clouds that otherwise won't produce rain are coaxed into producing rain. When such clouds pass over catchment areas, a plane flies over the cloud, dropping silver iodide crystals into it. Raindrops form around these crystals as they fall, hopefully triggering some rainfall over the catchment. Special cannons can also be used to seed clouds from ground level, firing silver iodide-filled rockets into the atmosphere.

 Pros

- Cloud seeding is cheaper than some other water alternatives.

- Cloud seeding can be used to produce rain to remove some pollution from the air.

 Cons

- Cloud seeding relies on having clouds to cloud seed. Rain-bearing clouds are rare during a drought.

Did you know?

- Cloud seeding is sometimes carried out in the USA and Canada to produce snow over ski resorts.
- In the lead-up to the 2008 Olympics, the Chinese government announced cloud seeding plans to produce rain shortly before the Games to help clear the polluted air and to lessen the chance of rain during the opening ceremony.

Recycled water

Since many homes use drinking water to have showers and flush toilets, it's not surprising that some people want to get that water back! Waste water from sewage systems or collected stormwater is thoroughly treated and sanitised. It can then be used in agriculture, to water sports fields or to top up drinking-water reservoirs.

 Pros

- Recycling plants are cheaper than new dams and desalination plants.

Did you know?

- London's water recycling plants pump recycled water back into the Thames River, the city's water supply. Londoners often say that their drinking water has been through several kidneys.

- Recycled water is used in snow-making machines in some of Australia's alpine resorts. So you can ski on wee—and I *don't* mean 'yellow snow'!

 Cons

- Recycled water has an image problem or an 'ick' factor. Although many scientists and experts agree that recycled water has minimal risks, many members of the community are put off by the thought of the water's history.

- Water recycling plants are generally larger and need more land than desalination plants.

- Water recycling plants produce less water than desalination plants. They are limited by the amount of waste water that is produced and collected.

New dams

Dams can be built to halt the flow of water in rivers, collecting the fresh water in one place.

Pros	Cons
• Dams can be used to produce hydroelectricity.	• Dams are useless when there's no rain or snow to produce flows into the feed river.
• Dams allow human control over the flow of the river downstream from the dam. This can prevent flooding.	• Dams flood huge areas of land around the dam. While this can be planned for, it forces people and animals to move.
	• Dams can damage river ecosystems and block the migration of fish.

Did you know?

The Three Gorges Dam across the Yangtze River in China is the world's largest hydroelectricity power station. It has flooded hundreds of square kilometres of land, submerging many archaeological and cultural sites and requiring the relocation of over 1.2 million people who lived in the area.

Piping water over long distances

Giant pipes or aqueducts can carry water from areas with large reserves to regions lacking enough water. This method of ensuring freshwater supplies dates back to the Roman Empire.

Pros	Cons
• Bringing in water from areas of plenty can ensure a future for settlements that have run out of local water.	• There is a risk of removing too much water from the region supplying it.
	• Water can carry non-native aquatic species into the region.
	• Pipelines are large, complex and expensive structures that take a long time to build.

Did you know?

Some of Los Angeles' drinking water comes from the Colorado River on the other side of the Santa Ana Mountains. The water travels through nearly 400 kilometres of pipeline, known as the Colorado River Aqueduct.

Water: virtual water

When you have a piece of chocolate, you're actually consuming water. No, you're not drinking a glass of it, but by eating chocolate you're putting to use the water that was needed to make that chocolate. The milk in milk chocolate came from a cow. That cow drank water and ate feed that needed water to grow. The cocoa came from a cacao tree, which also needed water to grow. The ingredients were put together in a factory, which used water in its processes and cleaning. And I'm sure the Oompa Loompas have bathrooms and a water cooler in Willy Wonka's factory. All of this adds up to something called **virtual water**.

Virtual water, also known as 'embodied water', is defined as the amount of water needed to produce a particular product. This might be natural rainfall, soil moisture absorbed from the ground by plants, irrigation water applied to crops, processing water and so on.

People need to start thinking about virtual water. Water is precious, so everything that we eat or that we buy or that is made is precious. We don't need to go on a hunger strike, but we can avoid wasting food or buying stuff that we won't use. This will help us avoid wasting the water that was required to produce it. We can also avoid buying a lot of the things that have a high water cost or high 'virtual water content'.

Average water costs

💧 = 50 litres of virtual water

A glass of beer (250 ml):
75 litres

A glass of milk (200 ml):
200 litres

A cup of espresso coffee (125 ml):
140 litres

A cup of tea (250 ml):
35 litres

A slice of bread:
40 litres

An apple:
70 litres

A glass of apple juice (200 ml):
190 litres

2 potatoes (200 g):
50 litres

A bag of potato crisps (200 g):
185 litres

An egg (40 g):
135 litres

A tomato:
13 litres

A sheet of A4 paper:
10 litres

A beef burger (150 g):
2400 litres

A cotton T-shirt (medium size, 500 g):
4100 litres

a pair of leather shoes:
8000 litres

Source: AK Chapagain & AY Hoekstra, *Water footprints of nations*, volume 1, Value of Water Research Report Series No. 16, UNESCO-IHE, Delft, the Netherlands, 2004, <www.waterfootprint.org>.

Eco-bytes: an environmental issue that concerns me is ...

Students from Williamstown High School share their thoughts on a range of environmental hot topics.

'In my opinion an important eco issue is that the amount of cars on the road is insane. It is a hard thing to fix but a way of fixing that is getting Electric Cars. This way the amount of pollution going in to our air is lowered.' Anon.

'I'm concerned about littering. I think that people should stop littering and care for the environment. It's harming the animals and it's making our area dirty. Let's make the environment clean and make our future better.'
Lisa, 12

'An eco issue I'm concerned about is the melting of the glaciers, because eventually they will all melt and lots of the lower regions will be plummeted underwater from the melting of the glaciers.' Kit, 12

'An eco issue I'm concerned about is that we are wasting a lot of water and we're using a lot of trees for paper.' Vanessa, 13

'I'm concerned, not about an environmental issue, but the way one is being dealt with. Global warming is putting many species into the endangered category, but only the cute ones are being cared for, like dolphins, whales and Giant Pandas. You see a lot of t-shirts saying "save the Pandas" or "no whaling", but there aren't many around saying "save the scorpions" or "help our lobsters". We need all our animals for our many eco systems and food chains to work effectively.'
Jasmin, 13

'My top eco issue is cars and petrol. We should invent environmental cars and not pay for petrol. We need to save the environment and the animals. YAY!!!'
Krystal, 13

'An eco issue that I am concerned about is that we are wasting too much electricity. When we use a lot of electricity we are damaging our world.' Eva, 13

'We've come a long way from not caring about the environment to all of us putting in our own efforts for the planet. It's great publicity for caring for the environment when top designers put out clothes with logos on them telling people to help the earth survive, and when they design bags that say "I'm not a Plastic Bag!" on them, but apart from raising awareness, it's not really doing anything. It's not taking action.' Ellie, 12

'An eco issue I'm concerned about is ... CHOCOLATE!!! The more money my parents spend on petrol and fresh produce the less money they have to buy me chocolate. This is a very, VERY bad problem. I LOVE chocolate!' Megan, 12

'In my opinion, food shortages and rising price highs for petrol and even the everyday banana is a big eco issue. It might not be a massive deal to the Prime Minister or Pink but to the everyday family it can be worrying to walk up to the cash register and stand anxiously waiting for the final price. I think this is a worrying problem and needs to be fixed. You can link this problem to Warming and Natural Disasters, but human footprints have left a big mark on the world and it needs to be improved.' Sam, 11

'An eco issue I'm concerned about is land development. I hate it that cute little animals are becoming homeless and don't have any place to go. Why can't humans treat other beings the way they want to be treated? Anyway, if animals go extinct, we go extinct! Save the animals, they are cute!' Julia, 12

'The drought within last year and this year is pretty bad for Melbourne. If we had no water left we wouldn't be able to survive without drinking or taking a shower. If we didn't have water we wouldn't be able to make yummy food and that's pretty bad because then there wouldn't be any food left.' Renee, 12

Worms and worm farming

Earthworms are fantastic things for the earth. They do a great job of aerating and enriching the soil, which is good for the plants that grow there. Worms can munch through huge amounts of organic waste and, like composting, are great helpers in reducing the amount of household waste we send to landfill.

Soil and organic matter go in one end of the worm, and worm castings (a polite name for worm poo) pass out the other end. Worm castings are a good natural fertiliser and soil conditioner. Plus, as soil passes through the worm, it undergoes changes that make the minerals in the soil available for plants and more easily taken up into their tissues. The castings contain five times the nitrate, seven times the available phosphorus, eleven times the potassium, three times the exchangeable magnesium, and one and a half times the calcium that occurs in the top 15 centimetres of uneaten soil. That's why avid gardeners get so excited about worms.

However, worms don't need a garden to chomp through food scraps. They can be kept in a worm farm—a food scrap garbage-disposal unit of sorts. Worm farms do not even require a yard to be kept in; they can be kept in a garage or laundry or on an apartment balcony. In fact, worms can't survive cold temperatures, so worm farms are best kept indoors in very cold climates, at least for the winter months. They're a great way to compost kitchen scraps, and 1 kilogram of worms can eat and recycle 1 kilogram of food every day.

Worm farms are made up of a series of layers with holes in their bases, stacked one on top of the other, allowing a comfortable amount of room for the worms in between. Food scraps are put into the upper layer. Worms wriggle up through the holes into this layer to eat the food, leaving their castings in lower layers. Liquid worm wee trickles down to collect in the bottom, which doesn't have holes.

Eco-lingo

vermicomposting
Composting using a worm farm is also known as 'vermicomposting'.

Worm farms, like compost bins, are available from hardware and garden stores. Live worms are sold separately. Alternatively, you can make your own worm farm (see the next eco-activity). Believe it or not, worm farming can become a hobby.

Worm trivia

- There are many different types of worms. Reds, tigers and African night crawlers are just a few.
- Each worm will consume its own weight in organic waste every day.
- Compost worms are hermaphrodites; each worm is both male and female. Mature worms can fertilise or be fertilised.
- Each egg capsule contains between one and twenty young (four on average), and these young worms hatch in about twenty-one days.

- Worms take about 60–90 days to mature. Given the right conditions, the number of worms in your farm can double every two months.
- Worms regulate their own population.
- Worm castings hold up to nine times their weight in water, and their Ph level is neutral, so they will help in releasing the maximum available nutrients and minerals into the soil. This helps to make the water-soluble nutrients in worm castings accessible for plants and their root systems.
- Worm castings contain many times the available potassium, nitrogen and phosphorus of average garden soil.
- Worm castings contain other micro-organisms that will enhance plant growth and will not harm even the most delicate plants. There is never any chance of over-fertilising or burning your plants.

Worms like to eat	Worms don't like
• Most fruit and vegetable scraps	• Onion
• Soaked and shredded pizza boxes, cardboard, paper and newspaper	• Citrus fruit
• Leaves	• Doing their homework (just checking to see if you're paying attention!)
• Dirt	• Raw potato
• Hair	• Anything you shouldn't put into a compost bin (such as meat and dairy)
• Eggshells	
• Cooked potato	

Eco-activity: make a worm farm

1 Making the layers

The layers are three stackable crates, which can be made of plastic, some kinds of wood or any other lightweight, waterproof material. You could ask your local greengrocer for three polystyrene foam fruit boxes. The bottom floor has to be solid (free from holes) so that the collected liquid doesn't leak. Ideally, the bottom floor should have a tap near the base so that the liquid can be drained. Make holes in the bottoms of the other crates or boxes.

2 Putting the layers together

Put a brick or rock into the bottom layer. Any worms that fall into the liquid can use this rock to climb back up to the upper layers, instead of drowning in the liquid. Put on the second layer, which should be perforated (have holes in it), and line it with a layer of shredded newspaper and a few handfuls of soil. This newspaper and soil provide bedding for the worms. Moisten the newspaper and soil with water, and add some worms and a small amount of food scraps. Worms don't have teeth, so make sure food scraps are finely chopped to speed up the breaking-down process.

Worms don't like light, so cover the bin with some hessian or newspaper or a lid. Allow the farm to settle in for a fortnight or so before adding some more food scraps. Over the next few weeks, the worms will multiply, continue eating the scraps and produce castings. Make sure the worms have enough to eat, but don't overfeed them. Uneaten food will just rot and cause the worm farm to smell. Worms like moisture, so make sure that the worm farm doesn't dry out. After the initial moisture, the worm farm shouldn't need additional water, provided it's kept in a cool, dark place. If it does dry out a little, spray it lightly with a mist of water.

3 Adding a layer

Once the worm layer is half-full of worms and castings, remove the covering and place the second perforated bin on top. Put fresh bedding and food scraps into this new layer and again cover it with hessian, newspaper or a lid as before. In a week or so the worms will have moved up into the new bin, leaving behind castings in the lower level.

4 Harvesting the castings

Once worms have moved into the top of the three layers, the castings can be removed from the middle layer. This tray can later be recycled as a fresh new top layer. Spread the castings on your garden or use in potting mixes. At any time, the liquid can be drawn off from the bottom layer. Use the liquid diluted with some water as liquid fertiliser for pot plants.

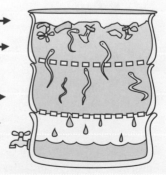

Lid, newspaper or hessian cover ➡

Holey bin number 2: worms enter through holes in the floor ➡

Holey bin number 1: scraps have been converted into worm castings ➡

Lower bin collects excess liquid ➡

Tap ➡

Zoos

Zoological gardens, called 'zoos' for short, have come a long way since the days of cages with cold, hard concrete floors. Once places that kept animals captive just for the amusement of people, zoos are now often educational, research and veterinarian facilities as well as tourist attractions. Many zoos are also ripping up the concrete and replacing it with carefully planned gardens that recreate the natural habitat of the animal on display, making it a little more like home and less like captivity. Aquariums are basically zoos for water-dwelling species.

A brief history of zoos

Over thousands of years of human history, many households have considered a collection of domestic animals necessary for milk, eggs, wool and meat. But a few hundred years ago in Europe, aristocrats and royalty began keeping private collections of animals, called menageries, purely for their novelty value. These menageries, such as King Louis XIV of France's menagerie at the Palace of Versailles, were a luxury, not a necessity. Over time, some private menageries were opened for public viewing, becoming public institutions that anyone could visit. The modern recreational zoo was born.

Modern zoos

These days, the world's 10 000 or more zoos do more than entertain. Many zoos recognise their potential to promote ecology and nature conservation by celebrating biodiversity and educating visitors on the needs and habitats of animals and their inherent value. Some zoos also play active roles in conserving and breeding endangered species. Zoos can also be involved in scientific research into the various species to which they play host. The Zoological Society of London, for example, includes the public London Zoo and the Institute of Zoology, its research division.

Types of zoo

- **City zoos** are probably the type you've visited on school excursions, if you live in the city. Examples include San Diego Zoo in California and Taronga Park Zoo in Sydney. These are the classic storybook zoos you see represented in popular culture. Such zoos tend to have limited space and often focus on species that are popular or have curiosity value.
- **Open-range zoos** are built where they can have more space. They have fewer species than city zoos, but give a lot more space per enclosure, which makes them better suited to large mammals that like to roam about through large ranges. The Werribee Open Range Zoo, outside Melbourne in Victoria, is an example that has focused on re-creating savannah-like habitat that suits its resident rhinoceroses, zebra herds, giraffes, lions and cheetahs. Visitors can take safari bus tours to see the animals.
- **Safari parks** are similar to open-range zoos. They are typically commercial (money-making) tourist attractions and

often allow people to drive their own vehicles on designated roads or tracks around the park to view the wildlife.

- **Animal sanctuaries** are set up primarily for the care and protection of animals, particularly vulnerable species. They may act as rehabilitation centres for injured or mistreated animals. Visitor access at such zoos is restricted.

- **Petting zoos**, or children's farms, are intended to bring people and animals into direct contact. Visitors can pat or feed some of the animals. These zoos mainly have domesticated animals, such as ducks and sheep, which are reasonably comfortable around people. Petting zoos may be mobile, rather than having a single location to which visitors come.

Zoo fundraising

Aside from entry charges, zoos can have other novel ways of raising money to support their work.

- Many zoos have animal 'adoption' programs, where people can sponsor particular animals.

- Friends of the Zoos' 'Corks for the Elephants' campaign collects corks from the public. They sell collected corks to a cork recycler, with the proceeds funding the 'Trail of the Elephants' exhibit at Melbourne Zoo.

- Zoos Victoria sells a compost product called 'Zoo Gro' to raise funds. Zoo Gro is made from elephant, giraffe and kangaroo manure, bedding material from gorilla and orang-utan enclosures, and plant waste from the zoos' landscaping activities. It sounds gross, but your garden will love it!

Zoo debate

Some people love zoos, while others think zoos are morally wrong. What do you think?

For zoos	Against zoos
• Zoos can be important in environmental education and research.	• Zoos can use and abuse animals to make money for people.
• Breeding programs in zoos can help save endangered species.	• Animal rights campaigners question whether or not animals should be used as a form of entertainment.
• Zoos can encourage people to care for and respect nature.	• Zoos keep animals under the control of humans, which goes against the idea of animal rights.
• Zoos can provide a home for animals that have lost their habitat or that have been rescued from ill treatment.	• Poorly run zoos keep animals in poor conditions.

Eco-websites

Environmental sites for kids

Planet Patrol
www.planetpatrol.info
Eco stuff written for kids by kids

Ollie Saves the Planet
www.olliesworld.com/planet
Join Ollie to learn how to help save the planet

National Geographic Kids
www.kids.nationalgeographic.com
Games, activities, information, stories, pictures
and more

Planet Slayer
www.abc.net.au/science/planetslayer
Meet Greena and find out about all things
Greenhouse (by ABC science guru Bernie Hobbs)

Hippo Works
www.hippoworks.com
Cartoons and fun stuff to help you learn about
the planet and its animals

The Sustainables
www.dse.vic.gov.au/thesustainables
Meet an ordinary cartoon eco-superhero
household

Mongabay.com
kids.mongabay.com
Tropical rainforest information for kids

KidsGeo.com
www.kidsgeo.com
Geology and geography info and activities for kids

Weedbusters
www.weedbusters.info/kidscorner.htm
Info about weeds and what to do about them

ibuydifferent.org
www.ibuydifferent.org
Shows the eco-cost of stuff, and that you don't
have to have all the latest stuff to be cool

Australian Sustainable Schools Initiative
www.environment.gov.au/education/aussi
Encouraging schools to take a whole-system and
whole-school approach to sustainability

The CERES Sustainability Hub
sustainability.ceres.org.au
Resources from the CERES Community
Environment Park

UNESCO
www.unesco.org/education/tlsf/index.htm
Resources for teaching and learning for a
sustainable future

Stephanie Alexander Kitchen Garden Foundation
www.kitchengardenfoundation.org.au
A program that gets schools growing and cooking
their own food

Seed Hunter
www.seedhunter.com
Find out how biodiversity may provide climate-
proof food

UNEP Tunza
www.unep.org/tunza/
Provides young people with information and tools
on how to 'treat Mother Earth with care'

Our Cool School
www.ourcoolschool.org
Teaching resources from the people behind
coolmelbourne.org

Discovery Education
school.discoveryeducation.com
Classroom resources from the Discovery Channel

Green groups

Australian Conservation Foundation
www.acfonline.org.au
Campaigns for conservation for a healthy
environment and a more sustainable Australia

Clean Up Australia
www.cleanup.org.au
Get involved in Clean Up Australia Day

Clean Up the World
www.cleanuptheworld.org
Clean Up Australia Day goes global

Fauna & Flora International
www.fauna-flora.org
Works to conserve threatened species and
ecosystems worldwide

Friends of the Earth
www.foe.org.au
Targets climate injustice, nuclear energy,
nanotechnology and dangerous chemicals, and
campaigns for sustainable food and indigenous
rights

Greenpeace
www.greenpeace.org.au
Activism that provides a voice for the earth

Keep Australia Beautiful
www.kab.org.au
Fosters community conservation efforts and gives
awards: Tidy Towns, Clean Beaches and
Sustainable Communities

Planet Ark
www.planetark.org
Get involved in National Tree Day and National
Recycling Week, read online environmental news
and more

Sustainable Gardening Australia
www.sgaonline.org.au
Find out how to help the planet by gardening in
the greenest possible way

The Wilderness Society
www.wilderness.org.au
Aims to protect and conserve Australia's forests
and natural environment

Trees for Life
www.treesforlife.org.au
A volunteer organisation dedicated to revegetating
the landscape and protecting its remnant
vegetation

WWF
www.wwf.org.au
Aims to conserve Australia's plants and animals,
and to pave a path to a sustainable future for
humans

Government sites

**Australian Government Department
of Climate Change**
www.climatechange.gov.au
Information about climate change and what the
federal government is doing to address it

**Australian Government Department of the
Environment, Water, Heritage and the Arts**
www.environment.gov.au
Information about biodiversity, pollution and
other issues, and what the federal government is
doing about them

ResourceSmart
www.resourcesmart.vic.gov.au
Information from Sustainability Victoria on how
to be resource smart (Victoria)

You have the power. Save energy
www.saveenergy.vic.gov.au
Energy-saving advice and information (Victoria)

Warm (Aurora Energy)
www.warm.com.au
Advice on adopting a lifestyle that's comfortable
but energy efficient (Tasmania)

Living Smart
www.dpi.wa.gov.au/livingsmart
Tips for greener living for households (Western
Australia)

GreenPower
www.greenpower.gov.au
Government-backed renewable energy

Sustainability Education Learning Centre
www.environment.sa.gov.au/education
Information and resources for educators from the
South Australian Department of Environment and
Climate Change

Schools noticeboard

Students from three Australian schools provided the 'eco-byte' quotes throughout this book. These three schools have something in common: an interest in protecting and preserving the planet. Yet they are all different. Here is a quick look at each school and its unique approach to going green at school.

Altona North Primary School

'Consider others' is the motto of Altona North Primary School, and its broad sustainability program is a natural extension of this. The school is an accredited waste-wise and sustainable school. One particularly fun part of the program is the school's worm factories—a series of worm farms recycle food and vegetable scraps from classrooms, the staffroom and canteen. This resourceful school has developed a saleable product from the liquid worm castings produced. It is bottled in recycled bottles, sealed with corks and sold as 'Wormitage Estate' plant fertiliser to nurseries throughout Melbourne. Funds from its sale are used to support and develop the school's environmental program and the establishment of the school's Environmental Education Centre, which now houses all parts of the program and is a resource learning centre for students and teachers.

The environment was also the inspiration for Altona North Primary's entry in the 2007 Wakakirri National Story Festival Story-Dance Competition. Their entry, 'Our Only Home', told the story of how pollution is harming our planet, warned that quick fixes provide only temporary solutions, and showed how a simple action can give us hope for a better future. As well as winning first place in the National Story-Dance final (primary), the school was awarded the prestigious Wakakirri Prize for the Environment.
www.altonanorthps.vic.edu.au

Natalie Bassingthwaighte gives Altona North students a hand on Planet Ark Schools Tree Day.

Baldivis Primary School

Baldivis Primary School is a bush school on the edge of suburbia with a proud tradition of serving its unique rural community. In recent years, the school has led the community in valuing its local environment through the establishment of nature trails, a frog pond, a tuart tree walk in nearby Settlers Hills and, perhaps most famously, the Baldivis Children's Forest.

The Baldivis Children's Forest lies about fifty kilometres south of Perth, Western Australia. It includes remnant tuart woodlands and a portion of the Outridge Swamp, which is a conservation category wetland. In 2000, the local school children became concerned about the clearing of bushland in the Baldivis district for housing. They chose this nearly 20-hectare site for tree-planting and conservation activities. With the help of local partners and the community, they have rehabilitated the tuart woodlands and wetlands with locally sourced plant species, with more than 20 000 seedlings planted to 2008. The forest now provides food and shelter for local wildlife, including the western grey kangaroo, southern brown bandicoot and twenty-five different species of reptile. The forest also hosts year-round Nyoongar cultural workshops and school activity days to teach environmental conservation, science, the arts and Aboriginal culture. The school's efforts have won an impressive collection of environmental and reconciliation awards.

www.baldivis-childrens-forest.com.au
www.baldivisps.det.wa.edu.au

Lessons in Nyoongar culture.

Williamstown High School

The Middle Years campus of Williamstown High School is a shining example of the ultimate in green education. For starters, the school has made good use of its seaside location, which borders the Jawbone Marine Sanctuary, and now has an in-house Marine Education Centre. The centre is used by the school and a number of other nearby schools,

together known as the '4 Schools 1 Planet' cluster.

When the time came for the campus's derelict buildings to be replaced, the school pushed for new buildings to be designed and built according to environmentally sustainable guidelines. The result is a school that's more sustainable, liveable and workable. All buildings at the campus are naturally ventilated and designed to purge hot air efficiently in the summer months. The site features recycled brick-veneer walls, high-performance single glazing, hollow core concrete plank construction, rainwater collection that is used for toilet flushing and irrigation, solar hot water, recycling of existing materials and low-energy light fittings. An integrated energy-monitoring system has been installed, displaying water, gas and electricity consumption on screens around the school. Students are able to compare their usage on a daily basis.

The school's environmental features are integrated into the students' learning. For example, the school's environment club recently worked on a signage project to produce an educational tour that explains the school's water conservation systems, such as rainwater tanks.

www.willihigh.vic.edu.au
www.4schools1planet.vic.edu.au

Green stuff for parents: a note from the author

Train up a child in the way he should go: and when he is old, he will not depart from it. PROVERBS 22:6

Parents (and other adult role models) can play a crucial role in shaping the values, habits and expectations of the children they influence. I can trace my own interest in the environment back to my mother. She taught me that nature is beautiful and fun to explore, that litter goes in the rubbish bin, to be kind to animals and respect their needs, and to not waste anything. She also taught me to make my own fun rather than relying on gadgets, new toys and material goods.

Now I am a mother, I want to teach my children the same things: that the world is an interesting place, that the best things in life aren't 'things' and that for every right there is also a responsibility. I want to foster in them both a care and an affection for our planet, recognising that the environment is cause for concern and a source of excitement and inspiration.

I encourage all parents to foster their children's care and affection for our planet, both to enrich their lives now and to set them on a path towards becoming responsible adults. Here are a few tips and ideas you might like to try.

Grow some food

With our increasingly urbanised population, many children don't know where their food comes from. Involve your children in growing some food at home so that they can learn and appreciate how the environment provides us with food, how plants need water and how food production takes time and effort. Fruit trees, a vegetable patch or even just a couple of potted herb plants on a windowsill can serve the purpose.

Have some good green fun

Once upon a time, a father took his four-year-old son on a camping trip, beginning his son's lifelong love of nature. Sixty-five-odd years later, that little boy is now world-renowned environmentalist David Suzuki. As David Suzuki's father recognised, it's important to give our children positive associations with the planet. We're all more motivated by fun and encouragement than by guilt, so give your child (and yourself) the gift of good times spent in the natural environment. Make them aware of the affects humans have had on the environment without wallowing in guilt. Involve your children with the natural environment and teach them our connection with it. Kids love a birthday party, so celebrate World Environment Day (5 June) each year with your children and their friends by organising a litter clean-up day at a local park followed by a barbecue, or go on a fun nature hike or trip to the zoo.

Bring in the junior eco-police!

Deputise your kids as your home's water and energy monitors. When water, electricity and gas bills come in, they are compared with last year's bills for the same period. Any savings made are given to the children as extra pocket money and a reward for keeping their eyes on household consumption. For example, if the bill is $23.85 less than last year, that's $23.85 cash in the kids' piggy banks. You'll find your children are quick to switch off lights and turn taps off properly. You might even convince them to spend less time playing electronic games and watching TV.

Set an example

As with all aspects of parenting, practise what you preach. As your children grow, they learn from you what is normal and acceptable behaviour. If you can demonstrate respect for the environment, your children are likely to adopt your example in the years to come.

About the author

Photo by James Geer

Tanya Ha is an author, television presenter and environmental campaigner. A well-known figure in the Australian green movement, she is often described as the 'people's environmentalist'. Tanya is a firm believer that the environment is relevant and important to everyone, and that ordinary people can achieve great things when they're made to feel empowered, rather than guilty.

Tanya featured in the award-winning SBS television show *Eco House Challenge* as the show's resident eco-coach and is the host and main presenter of *Warm TV* (WIN Television). She spent seven years working for the green group Planet Ark and continues to support and assist the work of a range of other environmental organisations. She also serves on the boards of the state government authority Sustainability Victoria and the green group Keep Australia Beautiful.

Tanya's first book, the best-selling *Greeniology*, is now in its second edition and fifth printing, and has been published in Canada and translated into French, with a Chinese language edition in the works. Her second book, *The Australian Green Consumer Guide*, was published in late 2007 to rave reviews, followed by the 'Greeniology' series of pocket-sized guides. This is her third major book (or her eleventh if you count all the various editions and translations).

Together with her young-at-heart husband Andrew, Tanya has two children, who, along with their very cool but slightly crazy friends, have been the inspiration and helpers for this book. Archer is five and will eventually read this (once he learns to read). Jasmin is now thirteen, but was eleven when her mother started writing this book. Jasmin helps with the household recycling, and funnily enough, her favourite colour is green.

Acknowledgements

This book is not the result of my efforts alone, so I have several people to thank.

First, thank you to my family for their love, support and understanding (particularly during deadline times), particularly Andrew, Archer and especially Jasmin. Thanks also to Daryl, Jill and Auntie Wendy for the times you baby-sat or entertained my kids so I could concentrate on writing.

Thank you to the teachers and students from Altona North Primary School, Baldivis Primary School and Williamstown High School who contributed their thoughts, ideas, tips and 'eco-bytes' to the book. Thanks to the three extra ring-in eco-byte writers, too: Meredith, Ruby and Ashley.

A really big thank you to the junior foreword writers, Alastair, Freya and Imogen Wadlow (yes, and you too Erika), for both their feedback and their words. You're such an inspiration; you guys rock! Thanks to the VIP foreword writer, Rove McManus, for his words and support and also to his pals at Fauna & Flora International Australia. Thanks also to Dr Karl Kruszelnicki and Professor Tim Flannery for supporting the book. And to Rob Gell, who gets the glory for the green version of the Antaeus story.

A bunch of wonderful people read sections of this book and provided their expert feedback and I thank them heartily for this: Georgina Bailey, Daniela Santucci, Vicki Barmby, Colin Ashton-Graham, Jenny Pickles, Sara Phillips, Don Chambers and Kate Kearns and her colleagues at Melbourne Water.

Then there's the team at Melbourne University Publishing—an author provides the brain and the DNA of the book, but the publishing team provides its body and helps deliver it. So thank you very much for your work and support through some difficult times to Louise Adler, Foong Ling Kong, Eugenie Baulch, Terri King, Jacqui Gray (and Maria and Clare) and the rest of the team at MUP and their colleagues at Pan Macmillan. Thanks also to editor Lucy Davison, illustrator Elizabeth Botté and especially designer and dear friend Nicholas Mau.

Thanks also to my manager Phill McMartin and the team at Claxton Communications for looking after me

I'd also like to acknowledge the broader environmental science community, particularly my late brother-in-law Graham Treloar. I'm always mindful that the things I write about today were discovered or researched years ago by our clever and curious scientists and our society is indebted to them.

Finally, thank you readers for taking the time to find out some green stuff. I wish you well in your continuing green journey.

Index

Notes